Slapstick
& Sausages

Norman Robbins

Trapdoor Publications

First published 2002 by
Trapdoor Publishing
41 Post Hill
Tiverton
Devon
EX16 4NG

isbn: 0-9542987-1-3

SLAPSTICK & SAUSAGES

Printed and bound by
Lazarus Press
Unit 7 Caddsdown Business Park
Bideford
Devon
EX39 3DX

For Ailsa

Introduction

I saw my first pantomime over sixty years ago, but where I saw it remains a mystery. In addition to the Theatre Royal in my home town, there were seven others within a sixteen mile radius and dependant on which artiste and what the production was, my family would visit them all. I know the subject was "*Little Red Riding Hood*" (no political correctness in those days), but apart from a flying ballet sequence and the scene where the wolf chased "Grandma" round and round the cottage, remember very little about it. It was, however, enough to entice me into regular theatregoing and eventually make my stage debut as a child "super" in a touring play at our local theatre, featuring Tod Slaughter of "*Sweeny Todd*" and "*Maria Marten*" fame.

By the late 1940s I was well and truly hooked on any form of theatre. Pantomime, however, had a special appeal for me and every Christmastide I saw two or three at Leeds, one at our Local, and another in Wakefield or Doncaster, or, if visiting my Great-grandparents in the Midlands, Birmingham or Wolverhampton.

At sixteen, I had written my first pantomime for the local Church, and in the early 1960s had Church and Village Hall productions all over Britain, with occasional outlets in Canada and Australia. By this time I was a professional performer, having made my debut in pantomime (of course) and had begun to take an avid interest not only in the famous routines, which were never written down, but in the background of pantomime itself.

Where did it all begin, for instance? My years at Drama School had not even touched on pantomime, so on my journeys around the country I began haunting the second hand shops, eventually unearthing battered volumes that provided answers to many of the questions I'd often asked. Fellow performers such as Lauri Lupino Lane, Roy Hudd, Peter Butterworth, Jimmy Lee, and Claude Zola helped fill in gaps, but as several of the books contained conflicting information on dates, routines and performers, I decided to try and make sense of it all by going back to the very beginnings of theatre and jotting down things that could be verified.

The first thing I'd discovered was that British pantomime began in London and most of its history had its origins there. It was not, however, the full story. It had not sprung from the ground fully formed like Cadmus's warriors from the dragon's teeth; its evolution had been shaped by location, events, and a host of fascinating people, most of whom I'd never even heard of. The more I delved into it, the more complex it became and for the next forty years the evolution of pantomime became my great passion. An exciting find was the discovery in a charity shop of several original "books of words" which could be purchased at many pantomime producing theatres from the middle of the nineteenth century to around 1950.

By the 1970s, I was writing for publication, several of my scripts being published by Samuel French Ltd. with gratifying results. An unexpected spin-off was an invitation to teach drama at Iowa State University U.S.A. (a country with so little experience of pantomime that most Americans were unaware they had ever been performed there). Such was the interest from students and faculty alike when I mentioned the subject, I was asked by Professor Frank Brandt to direct a British pantomime for them. It broke every box-office record in the Fisher theatre's history and was re-staged on American television some time later, making it the first British pantomime ever to be seen on the small screen. This triggered off an explosion of pantomime productions across the country, including the first New York production since the start of the century.

On returning to England, I was constantly urged to write a book on the subject, so after forty years as a pantomime performer (nineteen of these as "Dame") I offer this volume.

Though not a history, (which would require several books to contain the information), just a broad outline of how British pantomime evolved, it is, I hope, accurately dated, with glimpses of the period, people, and events that shaped it, and gives the origins of many "traditional" gags and who devised them.

So welcome to my version of British Pantomime, with its comic routines, shameful spectacles, amusing anecdotes, dreadful accidents, silly songs, tongue-twisting titles, crass commercialism, and audience participation such as you've never imagined. In short, the fascinating world of Slapstick and Sausages.

*T*hat no-one ever attempted to kill Christopher Rich, one-time lawyer-turned-theatre manager and perhaps the greatest villain in theatrical history, is a complete mystery. For almost twenty years he cheated, stole from and blackmailed the unfortunate actors and dramatists who fell into his clutches, gleefully lining his pockets with their pitiful earnings and tossing them into the streets when their usefulness was past. Many a Wicked Squire has unknowingly been based on his character by pantomime writers, yet without this repulsive and miserly man's influence, it's possible that we'd never have had the pleasure of watching (or performing in) this peculiarly British form of family entertainment.

So what part did he play in the evolution of pantomime? He'd certainly never seen or heard of them, for he died in 1714, two years before the word first appeared on a theatre poster. To find the answer, we must ignore the greenery and flowers of the allegoric plant for a while and examine its roots, for the seed it grew from was planted over two thousand years ago in Ancient Greece.

Some five hundred years before the advent of Christianity, the city of Athens was the heart of civilisation. It was here both tragic and comic theatre sprang into being, the former inspired by the worship of Dionysus, the great God of wine and fertility, and the latter making light hearted fun of it.

In the early days, at Spring festivals, a white robed chorus of forty or fifty danced and chanted or sang a paean in praise of Dionysus and his rejuvenation of the earth, but later, as other heroic deities and subjects were introduced to these performances, the content became more dramatic. In addition to this, the first actor, Thespis of Attica, (6th century BC) made his appearance, thus allowing an informative prologue to be performed and provided opportunities to clarify questions asked if the chorus's recital of events became unclear to the audience. Not only an actor and playwright, he devised a kind of linen mask which enabled him to portray both male and female characters, so as women played no part in drama at that time, he must therefore be regarded as the first female impersonator, too. Today, however, he is mainly remembered for the synonym of *thespian*, as used to describe members of the acting profession.

The playwright Aeschylus (c525-456 BC) added a second actor to the drama, reduced the chorus to a dozen and introduced both the raised stage and striking costumes, whilst Sophocles (c496-406 BC) went one step further by tossing aside the stylized traditions of his day, introducing painted backdrops and adding a third actor to the proceedings. From this time on, the chorus became no more than interested observers of the action leaving actors, in their wooden or clay masks, the freedom to tell the story in a more realistic fashion. Centuries later, the situation was to repeat itself in plays, musicals and pantomimes.

Not everyone however, was impressed by Gods, mighty deeds, or dark tragedy. Even before the time of theatrical entertainments, humans had laughed at the downfall of their betters. There was something very satisfying in seeing a pompous character coming a cropper at the hands of a sly tormentor. Satire reared its head. Comic characters in every-day clothing but with padded bellies or behinds and usually flaunting red leather phalluses, took the emphasis away from things spiritual and directed it to more entertaining things such as libel, blasphemy, vulgarity and obscenity, though violence if any, as in all Greek drama, took place off-stage and audiences were simply informed of it by one of the performers.

The Roman drama showed no such reticence. Though many respected playwrights borrowed heavily from the Greek, wit and philosophy gradually took a back seat to bawdy clowning and crowd pleasing action in the vast theatres. On-stage violence became commonplace as audiences demanded "reality" in their entertainments. Actor troupes, once engaged by the playwright himself (who often took a leading role), were gathered together by a manager and usually consisted of slaves of both sexes who could be flogged or slaughtered with impunity. Few people chose to take up the mask of Thespis, and even those who became popular with the crowds seldom lived to a ripe old age.

Philemon, the most popular clown of his day, refused to sacrifice to the Roman gods following his conversion to Christianity. As the law stated clearly that sacrifices proved loyalty to the State and it was mainly Christian transgressors who suffered the penalty for spurning them, his audience roared with laughter, assuming their favourite was making fun of the new religion. Taken before the governor who pleaded with him to change his mind, Philemon remained adamant, and to the sorrow of the entire populace was put to death.

As savagery increased, the poet Catullus (d. 54 BC), eager to please the crowds, wrote a play concerning the crucifixion of a slave. In the interests of reality, the unfortunate actor selected for the role died in agony on a real cross. It was a great success. During the reign of Nero, (37-68AD), an actor by the name of Paris was slaughtered for giving a better performance than his Emperor (who fancied himself as a thespian), and just a few years later, in what may have been a revival of the popular Catullus production, the Emperor Dometian (51-96AD) arranged a display of newly crucified Christians to form an impressive back-drop to the proceedings. The glorious days of intelligent drama were vanishing. Rome was awash with blood and explicit sex. With the death of Seneca

(4BC-AD65), scripted plays to all intents and purposes ceased to exist and what did remain were merely improvised, popular low-life revels and *mimi*, the sole surviving reminder of Grecian dramatic art.

The *mimi* had arrived in Rome around the second century BC. Unlike the actors who preceded them, the *pantomimus*, as the solo performers were known, performed silently and without masks, using dancing and body movements to suggest the events described by a backing chorus, which was usually an adaptation of a Greek religious play or a tragedy. For Roman audiences, the content of these entertainments gradually changed, forsaking gods and goddesses, and extracting bawdy humour from everyday life. The drunken husband, scolding wife, cheating fishmonger and passionate young lovers were easily recognisable as contemporaries of the watcher, and were keenly appreciated, but as women were allowed to join the *mimi* troupes under Roman law, it soon became "necessary" for performers to appear totally naked, if only to convince audiences they were not watching an all male production. Eliogabalus (?204-222AD) obviously needed more persuasion, for he demanded scenes of actual sexual intercourse before giving his approval to Royal performances. Lewd songs and dances were added, the whole concept disgusting and horrifying the rapidly increasing Christian sect, though it did not prevent the beautiful Theodora (508-548AD), a *pantomimus* famed for her obscene dances, from charming the Byzantine Emperor, Justinian (483-562AD) and becoming his Empress around the year 523AD. On the contrary, she remained well-loved by the populace, earning a reputation for intelligence, wit and great courage, and built the first home in Europe for disgraced women. Almost five hundred years earlier, the Roman Emperor, Tiberius (BC42-37AD), had passed a law forbidding Roman citizens to walk or converse with actors in the streets. It took Justinian no time at all to repeal it.

The excesses of Roman theatre were ended swiftly when the Christians came to power (c324). Clergy and followers alike were forbidden to attend theatrical performances, actors and entertainers denied permission to be baptized, marry a Christian or even convert to the religion unless they publicly renounced the stage, and the hated "temples of iniquity" were razed to the ground. From the sixth century, and for almost a thousand years, theatres and their playwrights vanished from Europe.

Public entertainment, however, did not entirely cease to exist. Driven from the city, the performers wandered far from Rome, exercising their skills in any open space to which an audience could be attracted. Even the invading barbarians, who were notoriously prudish, allowed them a certain freedom providing they did not offend sensibilities. To the anger and bitterness of religious leaders, many found employment at Royal Courts, particularly the clowns, jugglers and *mimi* (now known as *histriones*, a title covering, dancers, and musicians) who did not need language. In the seventh century, Isidore of Seville wrote scathingly:

> "Histriones are those who, dressing as women, presented the doings of common women....mimi they are called in Greek because they are imitators of human life."

whilst the English scholar, Alcuin (735-804 AD), who had taken up residence at the court of Charlemagne before becoming the Abbot of Tours told the Bishop of Lindisfarne:

> "It is better to feed paupers at your table than actors"

Throughout the writings of the Dark and Middle ages, there are references to *histriones*, *ministri* (Balladsingers) and *jongleurs* (Merrymen), so it's patently clear that despite the efforts of the Christian Fathers, the ancient roots of drama did not wither away completely but simply bided time until a second flowering. Ironically, it was the Church itself that began the recovery.

The Betrayal, Crucifixion and Resurrection of Christ was the heart of its faith, and a means of presenting it to the laity in the strongest possible way was very important. Many were unable to read or write, and the majority knew no Latin, the Church's chosen language. The answer was simple, though it was not until the tenth century that anyone put it into practice.

From a three-lined exchange at an Easter Mass in a Swiss monastery between an Angel (represented by half of the choir) and the two Marys (the other half) who discovered it by the empty tomb, religious drama was reborn. Spreading rapidly through Europe, this very simple "play" began to grow. Soon the two Marys (now played by members of the clergy) were paying a visit to a spice merchant before going to the tomb. Cue for a little comedy business. The Disciples, Peter and John, were added to the storyline. Amazement at the shroud, etc. Further scenes and characters were introduced as the authorities realised they had at last found a solution to their problem.

Within a relatively short time, the Birth of Christ appeared as a playlet at Christmastide Masses, complete with angels, shepherds and wise men, though the later addition of King Herod and his fury at the child's escape created another problem. Could such an evil character be played by a member of the clergy, and should indeed, such evil be portrayed inside a church? The answer was found. Herod became a figure of fun and a layman was engaged to perform the role. It must have caused great embarrassment to the clergy of Padua, when in their version of the play, the chosen Herod got so carried away with his characterization that he actually hit the Bishop with an inflated pig-bladder.

If the language was unfamiliar to the devoted, however, the stories it told were blindingly apparent. Before long the largest churches were proving too small to accommodate the crowds who came to watch and worship, and the only solution the authorities could think of was to move the liturgical dramas outside, so removing them from the actual services. Performances could be given on the steps of the church and congregations would watch from its churchyard. It was at this point that ecclesiastical leaders realised that the plays were becoming more popular than desired, and a flurry of criticisms, edicts and complaints were passed down from on high culminating in the clergy being forbidden to take part in any production outside the church walls. Without hesitation, Town Guilds stepped in to continue the tradition.

In 1262, Pope Urban IV decreed a new Feast, that of Corpus Christi, and raised it to the same status as Easter and Christmas. As this was in Summer, huge open air celebrations took place, when religious and Town Guild leaders came together for worship, the processions winding through the streets behind the consecrated Host for a final service in front of the church or cathedral. Each Guild represented its own trade, carried its own banner, and displayed their devotion with elaborate pageants of Biblical events on richly decorated carts, either horsedrawn or pulled by craftsmen. At first, mainly tableaux, these were rapidly re-shaped with dialogue and music, and evolved into what became known as Miracle or Mystery plays.

The almost immediate benefit was the change from Latin to the language of the countries (including Britain) presenting the plays, which in turn led to greater audiences, increasingly spectacular productions, larger casts, more scenes, and new stories drawn from both Old and New Testament. By the end of the century, churchyards were unable to contain the teeming crowds, carts and musicians, so the players, who were all Guild tradesmen, were moved to the marketplaces where special areas, known as *mansions* were set out, each one containing boxes or platforms in close proximity, where the "scenes" could be played out before promenading spectators. At the rear of the *mansion* were usually the platforms designated for Heaven and Hell: the former on the left, and the latter right. It is from here, some hundreds of years later, that pantomime took the tradition of Fairy always entering stage right, and Demon stage left.

The English, for some reason, preferred to stage *their* productions on large carts, (sometimes as many as thirty), stopping every few yards to repeat the dialogue so that audiences could see, hear and wonder. It was inevitable that the strolling players would take their chance. Jugglers, dancers, fire-eaters and clowns all found a niche in the productions. Noah's wife, a loud mouthed and bossy figure of fun was played by a man, and the crafty Sheepstealer made his first appearance, much to the delight of audiences who had been deprived of bawdy comedy for all too long. Even the devil and his helpers became an unlikely source of amusement. Performers were whipped if they forgot their lines, so perhaps the introduction of payment for services rendered took the productions to a more polished level. At Hull, it is recorded that Thomas Sawyr was paid ten pence (4p) "for playing God". Elsewhere, both Devil and Judas were paid 1s.6d. (7p) and Herod as much as 3s.4d (16p). Obviously crime paid better.

In the fifteenth century, a third form of drama had evolved; the Morality play. Whereas the Miracle plays had huge casts and elaborate settings, it was impossible to move them to rural villages whose inhabitants were unable to travel far and so missed out on the great Spectacles. The Morality plays required little scenery and props. A few self employed players and a cart could provide these hamlets with entertainment providing the local Justice of the Peace would issue them with a licence to perform on the village green. Others found employment in the great houses. Drama was on the move. No longer reliant on Biblical events, the actors portrayed characters closer to the people.

"*Everyman*", perhaps the best known of all Morality plays, shows how the hero (representing humanity) is abandoned by his so called friends Fellowship, Kindred and Goods, etc., when Death summons him. Fortunately, Good Deeds decides to lend a hand and the rest of the play concerns Everyman's eventual fate.

The Renaissance began with a vengeance. In Italy, religious drama was opposed by the new thinking of modernists. The plays of Terence (c190-159 BC) and Plautus (c252-184BC) were re-discovered and performed. Old plays were re-written and populated with different characters, and entirely original plays made a welcome appearance. The new movement swept across Europe and the Church reeled. In 1548, religious drama was banned in Paris because of degrading innovations. In England, the Wakefield mystery cycle was suppressed in 1576. "New" was the buzz-word of the sixteenth century, and as if in answer, Opera, shortly to become the highlight of court festivities, took its first faltering steps.

With beautiful costumes, spectacular scenery and special effects, it rapidly spread throughout the whole of Europe. As the seventeenth century began, mechanical devices enabled characters to float on clouds, gallop across the skies on winged horses, or appear and vanish apparently at will. Great palaces could be replaced by mountains or raging seas at a moment's notice. It was an age of theatrical miracles, and all due to the skills of scenic designers and painters. It can be no surprise that Opera soon left the Royal Courts and moved into theatres especially built to display their wonders to a wider public. In or around the year 1615, Inigo Jones the great architect and painter at the Stuart court visited Italy and realizing the potential of these amazing spectacles, returned to London to create his famous Masques, using the techniques he had recently observed.

Opera, however, was not the only new entertainment to emerge at the end of the sixteenth century, and its competitor was vastly different. It was known as the Commedia dell' Arte.

A creation of itinerant acting troupes who based their "plays" and characters on outlines of Greek and Roman comedies passed down through the ages, the Commedia dell' Art was entertainment for the uneducated masses.   Noble thoughts and valiant deeds were not the centre of these productions. Here was a world of buffoonery, its only purpose to make audiences laugh. There was no written script, each storyline being outlined by a *concertatore*, or manager, and each performer playing one role only, perhaps till the day he died. The words they spoke were all their own invention, as was the comic business they added. Should they wish to leave the troupe and join another, everything went with them and slotted perfectly into place with the new company. It is hardly surprising that the technical skills of these players were extraordinarily high.

Using stock characters derived from the old Roman mimes, a troupe could expect to feature Pantalone, a richly dressed Venetian merchant, avaricious, cuckolded and a figure of fun; Dottore, his friend, a doctor or philosopher, full of pedantic wisdom and the butt of jokes for rascally servants or criminals who constantly beset him; Arlecchino and Brighella, two *zanni*, or comic characters who create most of the laughs at others' expense; the former dressed in a shabby, loose, many-patched costume and wielding a wooden short-sword, and the latter a Ferrarese pimp who carried a sharp dagger; Capitano, boastful and swaggering but who runs for his life whenever danger threatens; ugly Pulcinella with his hooked nose, bad

17

temper and hump; a pretty young girl (Flaminia or Isabella); a handsome youth (Orazio or Ottavio); maidservants (Ricciolina, Nina, Olivetta and Columbina); manservants (Scapino and Mezzatino); and a dancer who took no role in the plays but entertained the audience during scene changes. Many other characters were introduced as the popularity of the shows increased, though these were only used as storylines required. As in antiquity, masks were worn by all (with the notable exception of Columbina). Not the full-face clay ones as before, but soft leather or fabric half-masks that were highly stylized and left the mouth area completely free. It has been suggested that Michaelangelo designed the mask for the character of Arlecchino, but sadly there appears to be no actual proof of this.

A typical production of the early days would have shown old Pantalone determined to marry his pretty daughter, Flaminia, to Capitano, who has boasted of his riches or position. She, however, is in love with Orazio who enlists the aid of crafty Arlecchino who, helped by the other servants, frustrates Pantalone's scheme with tricks, misdirection and physical obstructions, thus allowing the lovers to elope.

This simple plot remained almost unchanged for a hundred years or so, but the costume of Arlecchino underwent a transformation in the late sixteenth century, when Joseph Dominique Biancolelli (d.1688) improved the patches by shaping them into brightly coloured, diamond shaped pieces and slightly lengthened the wooden sword.

By the seventeenth century, the Commedia was a familiar sight at English and French feast days and fayres, though in both countries, changes were made. In France, many of the characters were discarded for the sake of simplicity and others were re-named. Out went Pulcinella, nose, hump and temper, (though he lingered on in England for some time before being reborn as Mr. Punch of Punch and Judy fame). The colourless young lovers vanished, their places being taken by a more dashing and less comical Arlecchino and Columbina (who also assumed the dancing role), and we also said good-bye to most of the servants. As compensation, in came a new character to fill the comic servant role vacated by Arlecchino. He was, of course, The Clown.

At this point, a brief history of the Clown must be inserted, for today we think of them almost exclusively as Circus performers with painted faces, baggy, ridiculous costumes and a propensity for hurling buckets of water or paste in all directions. They also prat-fall, get blown up, knocked down, run over, hand out balloons and toss popcorn and sweets to the audience. In short, almost everybody loves them. They are giant dolls come to life in order to make us laugh.

In Greek and Roman days, little of the above would apply. Their clowns, as we have noted, wore masks and padded clothing, but the comedy was usually cruel and in the later days, extremely savage. More than one Christian died at the hands of a clown. The word itself is of German origin, meaning countryman or peasant, and first became used in the sixteenth century, being aimed at someone ill-bred or doltish like the buffoons of the miracle and mystery plays. Clowns of this period were maskless, wore cap and bells and parti-coloured tunics and tights, or long robes with hoods sporting asses ears, and carried folly-sticks or inflated pig bladders with which they jokingly beat people.

Court Jesters were also regarded as clowns, but did not depend on comical costumes for effect. Many were as richly dressed by their Masters as the courtiers themselves, and relied on their wit to gain laughs. Some were acrobatic, some deformed, and others were singers of bawdy songs. More than one was actively feared by everyone but his ruler.

Archy Armstrong for instance, a one-time sheepstealer, was Jester to the Stuart Kings, James I and Charles I and amused not only their Royal Majesties by causing quarrels among the courtiers, but amassed himself a fortune by collecting bribes from sycophants who hoped to gain his backing when pleading their causes before the Sovereign. In contrast, Jeffery Hudson, the last Court Jester in England, was much loved. Only 18 inches high, he was placed in the service of Charles I and Queen Henrietta Maria, after the Duke of Buckingham presented him to them, concealed in a pie.

19

The Hopi Indians of North America also had clowns; Choqapolo, the Mud Thrower, Kokopelli, the hump-backed flute player and Kwikwilyaka, the Mocking Kachina who imitated everyone are just a few; while in Ancient China there are many stories of influential Clowns who did good deeds by lightening the hearts of their masters.

We have it on record that around 214 BC, in order to save money, the Emperor of China ordered his Mint not to make any coin smaller than a 10 yen piece; a whole day's pay for a peasant. Although this caused considerable dismay, no-one dare protest. Two of his clowns devised a plan. One pretended to be a shopkeeper selling drinks costing 1 yen, the other a customer wishing to quench his thirst. As he now had nothing smaller than 10 yen coins, the clown reasoned it would be only fair to give the customer ten drinks. With difficulty, the "customer" drank them all. "It's good we aren't made to use 100 yen coins" he groaned afterwards "or I'd have burst". The Emperor laughed, but the next day ordered the 1 yen coins to be made again.

The French Clown who became part of the Commedia dell' Arte was Gros-Guillaume (Fat William) a character with huge padded stomach, short trousers and a beard, the creation of sixteenth century actor, Robert Guerin. Guerin was a baker by trade, and performed in low farces. One evening, after a hard day's work and running late for the performance, he arrived on stage, face still covered in flour. The audience was highly amused and white-face clowns were born, though it was not until the nineteenth century that noses were painted red to suggest drunkenness, and *augustes* added colour to highlight cheeks and exaggerate eyebrows. The English version of Clown appears to be a combination of Gros-Guillaume and the early character of Vice as portrayed in the mystery plays.

It was not only with characters that changes took place. The English public, never too fond of the Commedia troupes because women took part in them, also found problems pronouncing their names. To simplify matters, *Arlecchino* and *Columbina* became Harlequin and Columbine, *Pantalone*, Pantaloon, and *Capitano*, Captain or Dandy. *Gros-Guillaume* was Pierrot (not the gentle, love-lorn Pierrot of France, but stout, white faced and comical) while Scaramouche alone retained his name. Another problem for the English was the language. Visiting troupes were hard to understand. Wit in Italian or French meant little or nothing to the lower classes. Visual foolery, dancing and song were much easier to follow, and taking the hint, dialogue was reduced to a minimum whilst comic routines were expanded upon. In its new form, the Commedia troupes found greater favour, but certainly not the success they enjoyed in their homeland.

On the other hand, legitimate drama was thriving. England's first public theatre had been opened in 1576 by James Burbage (c1530-97) much to the displeasure of the authorities who protested that its existence would keep apprentices away from work, provide opportunities for immorality and increase the danger of infection during plague years. Their arguments fell on deaf ears. Elizabeth I was an enthusiastic patron of theatre. Several plays were performed each winter at Court, and she attended many others during her travels around the country. A painting of an open air production at Kenilworth Castle in 1575, by Marcus Gheraerts the Elder, even shows the Queen and her court watching what is probably one of the first Commedia dell' Arte troupes to visit England.

Burbage had begun his acting career when plays were still performed in inn-yards. With the aid of his wealthy father-in-law, his theatre was built near London's Shoreditch, well out of the City bounds in order to avoid interference by London's self-important magistrates, and was simply called The Theatre. It had backstage changing facilities for the actors, a partly covered roof to provide dry seats for its wealthier patrons, and stood for twenty years before being demolished. Its timbers though were later used by his son, Richard Burbage, to build the famous Globe theatre which is forever linked with the name of actor and playwright William Shakespeare.

From 1576, English playwrights came into their own. George Chapman (c1560-1634), Christopher Marlow (1564-1593), Ben Johnson (1572-1637), William Shakespeare (1564-1616), John Fletcher (1579-1625) and Thomas

Middleton (1580-1627), are just a few of the great names who contributed to this Golden Age of theatre. At the same time, Masques, with all their mechanical and scenic wonders, were being performed at Court, and Commedia dell' Arte troupes were slowly gaining popularity, their characters being introduced even into legitimate drama.

In 1607, a play written by John Day was presented at the Curtain Theatre, in which Will Kemp, (Shakespeare's original Dogberry) is telling the character, Sir Anthony Shirley, about a play produced in London at the Swan Theatre in 1602. A Harlequin is then introduced by Sir Anthony, who asks him to imitate the events recited by Kemp. Shakespeare himself must have seen many of the Commedia in action for his reference to "lean and slippered Pantaloon" in "As you like it" proves they were now a fairly commonplace addition to theatrical entertainment.

Despite disapproval by the Puritan movement who had already managed to supress the Wakefield mystery cycle, the great flood of drama swept on, and the building of new theatres continued. The Red Bull in Clerkenwell, The Cockpit in Drury Lane, and The Salisbury Court in Fleet Street are perhaps the best examples. It was, however, two other theatres that inadvertently triggered off the events which led to the birth of British pantomime.

William Davenant (1606-68), reputedly the illegitimate son of William Shakespeare (by the landlady of the Crown Inn, Oxford), was educated at Lincoln College, Oxford, became page to Frances, first Duchess of Richmond, and on the death of Ben Johnson, was appointed Poet Laureate to the Court of Charles I. On the 26th March 1639, having found some success as a playwright, he obtained from the King a Royal Patent, or Licence, to build a theatre in Fleet Street. Before work could start however, Civil War broke out. Every theatre in the country was closed and from 1642, theatrical performances were forbidden by Oliver Cromwell's parliament. The Golden Age abruptly ended.

Davenant, having fought as a Royalist soldier, had been knighted, but after the execution of Charles I and his own imprisonment in the Tower of London, he joined the Court of the exiled Charles II in Paris and re-established himself in Royal favour. When Cromwell died and Charles II returned to England in May 1660, Davenant came with him, still holding his precious Patent.

One of his great friends at Court was Thomas Killigrew (1612-83), Master of the King's Revels, and also a popular playwright. The two men were eagerly looking forward to the resumption of theatrical life, but were shocked to discover that three acting companies were already flourishing in London under the auspices of Sir Henry Herbert who had been the previous Master of the King's Revels, and now charged the three playhouses £4 per week each, plus other fees, to remain open. On July 9th, Killigrew obtained a warrant from the King to open his own theatre, but realizing that Herbert was likely to cause trouble, both Davenant and Killigrew asked the Merry Monarch for a monopoly charter which would effectively prevent any other theatre from presenting the spoken word. This was granted and in August 1660, they were given complete control over all London theatres.

Herbert protested loudly, claiming he held his position of Master of the King's Revels by virtue of a charter dating from King Henry VIII's reign, and having never been dismissed, insisted upon his rights. Charles pointedly ignored him, and Davenant and Killigrew took over the management of the Cockpit theatre, signed up the best players, and most importantly, since to that time all female parts in British theatrical productions had been played by boy actors, engaged the first woman to appear in legitimate theatre, Margaret Hughes.

By 1661, Davenant had moved to a theatre in Lincoln's Inn Fields with his actors, The Duke's Men, and Killigrew's company, The King's Company of Players, performed in a converted tennis court until May 1663, when his new building, The Theatre Royal, Drury Lane finally opened.

For the next few years, despite the Plague and Great Fire, the two Royal Theatres fought each other for supremacy, whilst the disgruntled managers of the remaining theatres could present nothing but light entertainment and opera. One word spoken on stage could cost them a heavy fine, imprisonment, or both. Only outside of London could actors ply their trade, and even then, a costly local licence was needed. Davenant died in 1668 but his sons Charles and Alexander, together with actor Thomas Betterton (c1635-1710), continued the battle.

To Killigrew's dismay, in 1672 the Theatre Royal burned to the ground and the new Davenant/Betterton theatre in Dorset Gardens which had opened the year before, became the talk of London with its spectacular productions and fine acting. Employing Sir Christopher Wren as his architect, Killigrew at once began rebuilding and temporarily moved his company to the vacant Lincoln's Inn Field Theatre with borrowed scenery and costumes. It was not a success. By the time the Theatre Royal opened again in 1674, he was hopelessly in debt for though he still held the patent, he had mortgaged it to finance the rebuilding. Audiences proved indifferent and the new theatre struggled to survive.

It was during this difficult period for Killigrew that Edward Ravenscroft's play "*Scaramouch a Philosopher, Harlequin a Schoolboy, Bravo, Merchant and Magician*" was performed there in 1677, and from this production came the oldest of our pantomime "set pieces"- the Schoolroom Scene".

In the third act, Harlequin and his classmates are being instructed in English by a stern schoolmistress. Every time he makes a mistake or gives a silly answer, Harlequin is beaten with a slap-stick to the delight of the others. The scene ends as, pursued by his laughing and jeering classmates and the irate schoolmistress, he makes his escape with his head jammed in the back of a chair. Over three hundred years later, the schoolroom scene is still bringing the place down at Christmas.

The despondent Killigrew at last retired, handing his precious patent to his two sons, Charles and Henry; but the constant warring of the unreliable brothers, the retirement or death of many of their best players, and audiences so small that sometimes money was refunded and performances had to be cancelled, finally forced the theatre into closure. In desperation, the actors and shareholders appealed to Betterton and the Davenants for a merger. After some discussion, this was agreed, and when the Theatre Royal re-opened in November 1682, Betterton was the leading man, stage director and theatre manager too. Under his artistic guidance, the theatre prospered while the theatre in Dorset Gardens began its long downhill slide, unable to present anything but musical entertainments or mimes.

Both Patents were now at Drury Lane, as were Britain's most talented performers. It should have been the start of another Golden Age but the Davenants were not the men their father was. The plays they bought for the theatre became increasingly salacious as writers like Aphra Behn (1640-89), the remarkable woman author of "Lucky Chance", "The Rover" and "The Emperor of the Moon", and William Wycherley (1640-1716) peppered their scripts with sexually explicit dialogue that appealed greatly to the newly liberated audiences.

Protests were made by the remaining Puritans who were not without influential friends, and dramatists took side in the political uproars that affected both inside and outside the beleaguered theatre. It all became too much for Charles and in a weak moment he offered his part of the Davenant patent for sale. Like an evil genie released from a bottle, Christopher Rich materialized at his side.

Quite how Christopher Rich came to involve himself in the troubles at Drury Lane has never been explained, for he neither knew nor cared anything about theatre. His calling was the Law, and his well earned reputation was one of venal double-dealing. It is possible, however, that this could provide a solution, for Charles Davenant had also been a lawyer before his father's death forced him into taking over the Dorset Gardens theatre and could well have been acquainted with the notorious Rich. Whatever the answer, in 1688, for the sum of £80, Rich acquired part of the Davenant Patent and so became a shareholder. Within three years he was in total control of the theatre, having also bought Alexander Davenant's share and used his legal knowledge to outflank all competitors.

Despite the fact that Betterton was the greatest actor in England and the House was often sold out, according to Rich's creative book-keeping, profits began to fall. His actors frequently received less than their agreed pay, though all were promised faithfully that "when the money came in" they'd be fully reimbursed. Needless to say, it rarely did so, and if a settling up could not be avoided, he always managed to find a deduction or two in order to keep the status quo. The theatre was full of odd passageways and rooms, and builders or carpenters could be plainly heard working in them at all hours of the day. If the actors or shareholders (who never received a penny for over twelve years) asked what was happening, Rich would groan about the ruinous cost of repairs and alterations that were eating away at theatre profits, though oddly enough, no-one ever saw any improvement. In the meantime, experienced and higher salaried actors were given less to do, and as they were paid according to the amount of performances they gave, their earnings took a nose-dive while their usual roles were being performed by hopeful young thespians engaged for the sum of 15 shillings (75p) a week plus theatre training. It was not until pay-day these innocents discovered that 10 shillings (50p) of it had been stopped for the non-existent training. As one wrote later:

> "He was as sly a tyrant as ever was set at the head of a theatre; for he gave more liberty and fewer days pay than any of his predecessors; he would laugh with them over a bottle, and bite them in their bargains. He kept them poor that they might not rebel, and sometimes merry that they might not think of it. All their articles of agreement had a clause in them that he could creep out at"

Plays were frequently replaced by entertainments featuring ladder-dancers, rope-walkers, animal acts and jugglers, and as most of these worked for almost nothing to appear on the stage of the Theatre Royal, it meant extra cash diverted into Rich's bottomless pockets. His effort to get a fully grown elephant into the theatre was only prevented when his tame builder told him that to make an entrance for it may endanger the structure of the whole building.

Other managements protested bitterly. Not only had the Theatre Royal forced them into presenting nothing but music and variety, it was now taking the bread out of their mouths by stealing their entertainers. Rich ignored them. Their loss was his gain and he had a new scheme for making money. He persuaded his newly hired performers to sign profit-sharing agreements with him, making quite sure that the small print also required them to share responsibility for any of the

losses. It was a simple enough matter to produce a "paper" loss after each show, for no one was ever allowed to see the actual books. The unworldly performers simply had to take his word for it.

Despite Betterton's protests, Rich's cheese-paring tactics continued, though on one occasion the tables were turned on him when an inexperienced young player he had hired messed up one of the great actor's scenes. On leaving the stage, Betterton demanded the offender be stopped five shillings from his pay. When told that the actor worked for nothing but experience, Betterton, fully aware of Rich's tricks, told the paymaster to give the man ten shillings a week, and stop five of them as punishment. The young actor, Colley Cibber, went on to become not only a popular playwright, but eventual manager of the Theatre Royal.

Enough was enough, however, and greatly angered by the conflict inside the theatre, Betterton had a bitter quarrel with Rich and decided to leave. Unfortunately before he could plan his future, disaster struck. As the war between England and France continued, he invested heavily in an East Indies venture with his friend Sir Francis Watson, and was devastated when their ship was captured in the Channel by the French, losing him some £8,000 and leaving him penniless. Rich, ever sympathetic, responded by cutting his wages, claiming poor audience attendances, but Betterton's supporters rallied around him, putting up subscriptions to re-fit the old theatre at Lincoln's Inn Fields, whilst he appealed to the Lord Chamberlain for a patent.

On March 25th, 1695, King William granted this, and also allowed him to present anything that took his fancy. To Rich's fury, Betterton and many of the best actors at Drury Lane departed, and making matters worse, William Congreve (1670-1729) the greatest comic playwright of the day promised to write Betterton a new play every year, health permitting. "*Love for Love*" was advertised to open on April 30th, but the cunning Rich swiftly advertised the revival of a popular play by Aphra Benn, hoping to steal Betterton's thunder. On the opening night, the Theatre Royal was packed to the rafters and Rich rubbed his hands with delight. The second night, his theatre was deserted. His actors could not compare with those of his rival.

Across the Channel, theatrical storm clouds were gathering. For some time, the *forains*, or itinerant entertainers of the street fairs had been a thorn in the side of the influential Comedie Francaise. Not only did the French public seem to prefer their comical antics, but they dared to make fun of the snobbish Establishment theatre and its performers. Taking a leaf from the English, the management of the Comedie Francaise had petitioned King Louis XIV for a Silencing Order on them which was swiftly granted.

The *forains*, easily a match for their pompous persecutors, responded by singing their lines and thus avoiding the ban on spoken words, but when this was stopped by the authorities the actors continued to perform in silence and carried outsized scrolls printed with essential dialogue so audiences could follow the plot without problem; an idea eagerly adopted in England. When both countries prohibited this too, from above their stages they lowered large cards on which the necessary information was written and it is to this device that the Song Sheet feature of today's pantomimes owes its origin.

We cannot know for certain, but this last attempt to circumvent the law may have been the straw that broke the camel's back, for in 1697, the *forains* were evicted from Paris. Though many continued to roam the countryside, despite the war others made their way to England and eventually arrived in London.

For Rich it was a godsend. The Commedia dell'arte troupes were desperate for work, and he invited them to perform at Drury Lane, paying them far less than his own actors. "Italian Night Scenes" by which title their little comedies had become widely known, were becoming more popular at the great English fairs. As one disgruntled playwright complained in 1700:

> "Show but a mimic ape, or French buffoon,
> You to the other house in shoals are gone,
> And leave us here to tune our crowds alone.
> Must Shakespeare, Fletcher and laborious Ben
> Be left for Scaramouche and Harlequin?"

The answer was a decisive "yes", for the acrobatic, amusing Harlequin who had appeared on the legitimate stage since 1607, and the sinister Scaramouche were soon to be joined by their companions, Columbine, Pantaloon, and Pierrot the Clown.

The Royal Theatres were locked in battle again; Betterton with his plays, and Rich his mixture of plays, Italian Opera, variety and "Italian Night Scenes", each company sneering at the other in specially written prologues. In 1705, with the permission of Queen Anne, Sir John Vanbrugh (1644-1726) architect and playwright, opened his new playhouse, The Queen's Theatre, in the Haymarket and invited Betterton to join him there. As the seating capacity at his own theatre was so small it was difficult to make a profit, the actor agreed and giving up his Patent moved to the larger building as a salaried actor. Both move and theatre were a disaster.

The Haymarket at that time was a well known haunt of foot-pads, and audiences stayed away in droves. The disappoint-ed Vanbrugh attempted a merger with Rich, but was turned down. He then approached Owen Swiney, Rich's manager with an offer allowing him to rent the Queen's Theatre for £5 every acting night. Swiney, of course, went straight to Rich and they came to a verbal agreement. Swiney would accept the offer, take some of Drury Lane's actors with him and once things were settled, Rich would have control of both theatres. All went according to plan, but an unexpected command from the Lord Chamberlain put paid to it. The Queen's Theatre could only be used for the presentation of Opera and all the actors must return to Drury Lane. In spite of this setback, Rich was delighted. Once again he had the only theatre in London where the spoken word was allowed.

The next moneymaking scheme his eye alighted on was the Actor's Benefit nights. These had been established in the time of King James II, the first performer to be granted one being the famous actress Mrs. Barry. Players who supported the beneficiary gave their performances for nothing, the profit of the evening going to the beneficiary after agreed expenses had been taken by the management. It was a method whereby a respected player could receive a lump sum to help provide against sickness or go towards a retirement pension. Since 1695, Rich had used it as an alternative to paying proper salaries.

On March 4th, 1708, Anne Oldfield, the unrivalled actress of her day sued Christopher Rich for deducting £71 as expenses from her Benefit Play instead of the agreed amount of £40. Rich fought the case, but on April 30th the Lord Chamberlain ruled that the Drury Lane management could not deduct more than £40 for any Benefit performance. Rich's answer to this was to reduce the Benefit nights and increase the productions of variety, "Night Scenes" and Opera, so cutting his actors earning capacity even further.

At last they found courage to rebel and led by Colley Cibber, appealed to the Lord Chamberlain. On June 6th 1709, a Silencing Order was issued against the theatre, ordering its immediate closure and "those in possession of it to be expelled and dismissed therefrom." *The Tatler* of July 15 1709, gave notice that "A magnificent palace, with great variety of gardens, statues and waterworks," was to be bought cheaply at Drury Lane theatre, together with "A sea consisting of a dozen waves, showers of snow, a dozen and half of clouds, a rainbow, a new moon and a gilt coach with dragons, etc." By the time the outraged actors and creditors stormed the theatre to take possession and toss Rich into the street, the wily old scoundrel had vanished – together with most of the scenery and costumes.

It was not quite the end of him, though. On May 6th 1710, he was arrested in connection with suites brought against him by Vanbrugh and Robert Wilks (one of his old actors) and four years later, still clutching his Davenant Patent, made his way to the derelict Lincoln's Inn Field theatre, took a lease on the ground it stood on, and began to plan its re-building. He was never to see it completed. On November 4th, 1714, he died, leaving his two sons, John and Christopher Jnr. to "perfect and finish it".

John Rich (1692-1761) found his way into theatrical history for several reasons, though at the time of his father's death, he appeared an unlikely candidate for fame. Twenty two years old, uneducated because of his father's parsimony, his aspirations to be a tragic actor met with derision from his critics. Uncomfortable in Society and often inattentive to introductions, he had developed the habit of addressing all males as Mister. After irritating Samuel Foote, (1719-88), the renowned actor and dramatist by constantly calling him Mister, Foote snapped peevishly that if Rich wanted to speak to him, he should refer to him by name. Rich flushed and begged him not to be angry. "I sometimes forget my own name" he stammered. "That's extraordinary indeed" replied the caustic tongued Foote rudely "I knew you could not write your own name, but I did not suppose you could forget it."

In later years, Charles Dibdin (1745-1814) called Rich "perhaps the most ignorant of all human beings", though as Dibdin was only 16 years old when Rich died, should we really take his statement seriously? Tate Wilkinson (1739-1803) another detractor, talked of Rich's "natural stupidity", but as Rich had sacked Wilkinson for unprofessional behavior and the insult still rankled, it's more than possible that bias played a good part in his accusation. There are many references to Rich's ungrammatical and vulgar speech, but we are also told that after the beautiful actress Peg Woffington (c1714-60) approached him for work, he later said to Sir Joseph Reynolds

> "It was a fortunate thing for my wife that I was not of a susceptible temperament. Had it been otherwise, I should have found it difficult to retain my equanimity enough to arrange business negotiations with the amalgamated Calypso, Circe and Armida who dazzled my eyes. A more fascinating daughter of Eve never presented herself to a manager in search of rare commodities. She was as majestic as Juno, as lovely as Venus and as fresh and charming as Hebe"

Hardly a speech for a so-called illiterate, inarticulate man. On the contrary, he proved himself quite able to deflate Colly Cibber, the snobbish tragedian of Drury Lane theatre who was famed for the size of the monstrous wigs he invariably performed in. Hearing that Cibber had rejected an offered comedy play with the words "There's nothing in it to coerce *my* passions", Rich commented, "Mister. There's too much *horsehair* in *your* tragedy."

In December 1714, just one month after the death of Christopher Rich, the new Lincoln's Inn Fields theatre opened to an audience more curious about the rebuilt playhouse than the comedy they were about to see. The play was George Farquhar's *The Recruiting Officer*, and John Rich spoke the prologue himself. "You see an orphan of the British Stage", he began, going on to beg their sympathy for his father's recent death and ending with the plea "For the Father's sake, support the Son".

He could have saved his breath. Though the performance grossed £143 it was not the success he had hoped for. The Drury Lane theatre had re-opened some years ago to excellent business, and the actors employed there were far superior to his own. In addition, his players were older and more experienced than he was and treated him with contempt, considering him, according to Thomas Davis the biographer of David Garrick

> "...as one very unfit to give laws to them, and manage the business of a theatre."

As the years slipped away, Rich struggled to keep afloat with a mixture of poorly done plays, cheap variety acts and his father's profitable "Night Scenes". It soon became public knowledge that the most frequent attenders at the Lincoln's Inn Fields theatre were bailiffs and catchpoles waiting to arrest actors as they left the stage, whilst the building itself was on the verge of closure.

Drury Lane, however, continued to thrive. They too were presenting "Night Scenes" which followed the main play of the evening, but only because they knew Rich relied heavily on them for income, and had no intention of allowing him to steal away the audiences who were growing worryingly fond of them.

John Weaver of Shrewsbury, the Dancing Master at Drury Lane, is often credited as the actual originator of pantomime, for as he says in his book "The History of the Mimes and Pantomimes"

> The first Entertainment that appeared on the English stage where the representation and the story was carried on by dancing, action and motion only, was performed with grotesque

characters after the manner of the modern Italians, such as Harlequin, Scaramouche, etc., and was called *The Tavern Bilkers*, composed by Weaver and first performed at Drury Lane theatre, 1702.

Unfortunately, there is some doubt about this, as according to theatrical records, Weaver was part of Betterton's company at Lincoln's Inn Field in 1702. Perhaps memory was playing tricks for it was not until 1728 that his book was published and no record of the above production has ever been found. Weaver did, however, devise the "New dramatic entertainment of dancing, after the manner of the ancient pantomimes" called *The Loves of Mars and Venus*, on March 2nd, 1717. Though Harlequin and his companions played no part in this neo-ballet, it was the first time the word "pantomime" had appeared on a theatre poster, and the public were intrigued by it.

Of course, it was nothing like the pantomimes of today, and would not even be recognized as a pantomime of any kind. As Colly Cibber stated later, it was simply:

> "a series of connected presentation dances in character wherein the passions were so happily expressed and the whole story so intelligently told by a mute narration of gesture only, that even thinking spectators allowed it a pleasing and a rational entertainment"

Whatever its merits, it greatly appealed to the audience, and Weaver composed a second pantomime called *The Shipwreck; or Perseus and Andromeda* which opened on April 2nd, featuring Harlequin as Perseus and Columbine as Andromeda. It also included *Monster by Crocodile* and *Four Sailors and their wives by the Comedians*.

Purists protested that Harlequin and Co. were Italian, and had nothing to do with the *pantomimus* of Ancient Greece, but the public ignored them. They liked the sound of the word "Pantomime". It was easier to say than "Italian Night Scenes", and they wanted more.

Response to these pantomimes galvanized the desperate Rich into action and he quickly constructed one of his own for Lincoln's Inn Fields; *The Cheats; or the Tavern Bilkers*. With the Harlequin of the piece performing under the pseudonym of "Lun", it met with a good reception, and a second "Lun" pantomime *The Jealous Doctor; or The Intriguing Dame* followed on April 29th.

Exactly who Lun was is something of a mystery. Many pantomime historians have named Rich himself, but it seems highly improbable that the twenty five year old Rich, having failed as a serious actor, could transform himself into the mercurial character of Harlequin almost overnight, displaying, as he did, such expert knowledge of all the recent French developments in stage machinery and theatrical tricks, yet still find time to run his struggling theatre. It is more likely that the Lun of the above pieces was one of the French or Italian Harlequins and at a later date, Rich, hoping to cash in, assumed the name.

In spite of his revived fortunes, financial problems continued to beset the theatre and on September 18th 1717, Rich was forced to farm the management out to Christopher Bullock and Theophilus Keene, two of his own actors. For almost two years, the hapless pair struggled to attract audiences, but by 1720 the theatre was in badly in debt, the Company was dissolved, and all playing was suspended. Following a lawsuit, and losing some £2,000 in the transaction, Rich once again took possession of the theatre. His forced absence, however, had given him time to take stock, and the badly educated actor-manager was soon to show London he had at last found his true metier; that of Harlequin.

A failure as a tragedian he may have been. Handsome and a good singer, he most certainly wasn't, but without a doubt, as a dancer Rich was second to none. Not only that, *his* Harlequin was intriguingly different from those seen elsewhere in London. The Harlequins of the Commedia dell' Arte were low comedians who sang and danced. The Harlequins who appeared in English stage plays were given amusing lines to speak. In Rich's *pantomimes*, the low comedy was left to others. His Harlequin was romantic ... and totally silent. In addition, though his dancing and gestures were said to be "so brilliantly descriptive that speech was made superfluous", the most remarkable thing about the new Harlequin was his apparent ability to work miracles.

When the French Arlequins came to England towards the end of the seventeenth century, they had already transformed the traditional wooden swords they carried into slapsticks; thin, double-lathed batons which could be used either to beat other characters unmercifully, making a maximum amount of noise whilst causing the minimum amount of pain, or act as a signal for the off-stage workers to effect a scene change. In later years, they were a favourite prop for Schoolroom scenes and "slapstick comedy" took its name from the style of chaotic activity it inspired. A second French innovation was the magical wand of the Wizard or Enchantress of their pieces, often loaned to Arlequin by one of these characters in order to save himself from capture by his pursuers. In a moment of pure genius, Rich had combined the two ideas, and using his knowledge of Masque machinery, no doubt picked up from the French and Italian performers he was forced to employ to keep his theatre open, added a new dimension to the English Harlequinades.

As Thomas Davis was to write later:

> To retrieve the credit of his theatre, Rich created a species of dramatic composition unknown to this, and, I believe, to any other country, which he called Pantomime. It consisted of two parts, one serious, the other comic; by the help of gay scenes, finehabits, grand dances, appropriate music and other decorations, he exhibited a story from "Ovid's Metamorphosis" or some other fabulous history. Between the pauses of the acts he interwove a comic fable, consisting chiefly of the courtship of Harlequin and Columbine, with a variety of surprising adventures and tricks which were produced by the magic wand of Harlequin; such as the sudden transformation of palaces and temples to huts and cottages; of men and women into wheelbarrows and joint stools; of trees turned to houses; colonnades to beds of tulips, and mechanic's shops into serpents and ostriches... Excellent were his "statue scenes" and his "catching the butterfly", as also were his other dumb show performances.

On February 3rd, 1721, a party of drunken men arrived at the theatre to see a production of *Macbeth*, and during the performance, one of them, a member of the nobility, crossed the stage, pushing aside the two leading players, and began haranguing a friend who had found a place in the wings, a common enough occurrence in those days. Rich, annoyed at the interruption to the play, sharply informed the offender that because of his rudeness he would no longer be welcomed back-stage and received a savage blow to the face in reply. Rich struck back, swords were drawn in the boxes, and the drunken hooligans invaded the stage. The actors snatched up whatever weapons they could lay hands on and a free for all ensued before the rioters were thrown out. Once again, they stormed the theatre, tearing down the hangings and doing considerable damage before being arrested by a number of constables. The incident was recorded in the *Weekly Journal/Saturday's Post* of Feb. 11th, when the Grand Jury of Westminster found a Bill of Indictment against the rioters. So outraged was King George I, he ordered a Guard of Foot Soldiers, "A Serjeant and 12 men, every Night they play" to attend Lincoln's Inn Fields, the Theatre in Drury Lane, and the Opera House in the Hay-market "in regard that his Majesty and their Royal Highnesses do often Honour this latter Place with his Presence". For the next hundred years, the military were present at every performance.

On March 16th, a production of *King Lear* at Lincoln's Inn Fields was followed by *The Magician; or Harlequin a Director*, which poked satirical fun at the recent collapse of the South Sea Bubble the previous autumn, thus ending the craze for speculative dealing in South Sea and other companies stock which left hundreds of investors ruined. The Directors of the company, several of them politicians, were still being investigated, and a specially written song, referring to the Treasurer of the South Sea Company who had disguised himself and escaped to Calais to avoid arrest, delighted audiences who revelled at the Company's discomfiture.

As the battle between the Royal Theatres escalated, a production of *Blind Man's Buff* boasting eight Harlequins was staged at Drury Lane – only to be hissed off stage by an irate audience who plainly thought them no match for Rich, despite their comical antics and knockabout humour. Further success at the rival house pushed them into staging *Harlequin Dr Faustus* in November 1723, devised by John Thurmond, ex Dancing Master of Lincoln's Inn Field, who had left there in a huff after Rich engaged a German by the name of Swartz for his pantomimes. Not that Thurmond was anti-German. It was just that Swartz had a team of performing dogs that danced a *minuet*, (at a fee of £10 per night) and the audiences preferred them to him.

A description of Thurmond's new pantomime was published in a periodical paper of the day. "An account is very honestly published to save people the trouble of going to see it" wrote the critic, sourly.

> "A devil, riding on a fiery dragon, rides swiftly across the stage. Two country men and women enter to be told their fortunes, when Dr Faustus, (played by Harlequin) waves his wand, and four pictures turn out of the scenes opposite representing a judge and a soldier, a dressed lady, and a lady in a riding habit; The scene changes to the outside of a handsome house. Enter Punch, Scaramouch and Pierrot. They dance a short dance then knock at the door; a boy opens it and lets them in. The scene changes to the inside of the doctor's house and at the same instant a supper ready dressed rises up. The Doctor enters alone and dances a short dance; then enter the three students as before. The Doctor compliments 'em and invites them to drink wine with him; while they are drinking, the Doctor waves his wand and the table rises and forms a rich canopy under which the spirit of Helen of Troy sits. She rises, dances on entry, retires to the canopy, and sinks. The Doctor waves his wand, and asses ears appear at the side of their heads. The students seem surpriz'd; they perform a dance and exit. A usurer lending money to Dr. Faustus demands a limb as security and cuts off the Doctor's leg, several legs appear on the scene and the Doctor strikes a woman's leg with his wand, which immediately flies from the rest and fixes to the Doctor's stump, who dances with it ridiculously. During a quarrel between the salesman and his wife, The Doctor, Scaramouche, Punch and Pierrot rob a shop and fly away upon four spirits in the shapes of a cat, a hog, a goat and an owl. When caught, the Doctor flies up through the ceiling, whereupon the mob seem very much surprised and go away. The Doctor's companions take refuge in a barn. When the door is forced, they run upon the roof and jump into the chimney. The barn is set on fire. A tune of horror is played. The next scene opens disclosing the Doctor's study. He enters affrightened and the clock strikes one; the figures of Time and Death appear. Several devils enter and tear him in pieces, some sink, some fly out, each bearing a limb of him. The last, which is the grand scene, is the most magnificent that ever appeared on the English stage – all the gods and goddesses discovered with the apotheosis of Diana, ascending into the air expressing their joy for the enchanter's death."

Despite the oddity of story, Thurmond's pantomime was so successful that the First Night's performance raised £260. A remarkable sum for those times.

The Haymarket theatre, (not Vanburgh's Queen's Theatre, but a tiny privately owned playhouse opposite this, and built by a carpenter named John Potter in 1720) was quick off the mark with its own version of the Faust legend, but being without dialogue, escaped censure by the Lord Chamberlain's office.

Rich, noting the public's sudden interest in all things Faustian, not to mention the financial return it brought to Drury Lane, retaliated with *The Comical History of Dr Faustus*, and followed it rapidly with *The Necromancer; or Harlequin Dr Faustus* in December. It was packed with the most amazing transformations and tricks that had been seen to date and was his greatest success, continuing right through January and February with over sixty performances to its credit in 1724 alone. *The Daily Journal* of January 9th, stated:

> "The Concourse of People to see it was so exceeding great, that many hundreds were obliged to go back again, as not being able to gain admittance; the Entertainment was wonderfully satisfactory to the Audience, as exceeding all the Legerdemain that has hitherto been performed on the Stage".

Not that the production was without its problems. The complicated stage machinery that worked the miraculous transformations of Dr. Faustus proved highly dangerous to several unfortunate performers. One was flung headlong with such force that he shattered a plank on the stage with the impact and died. Another was maimed so dreadfully that he survived for less than a week, and a female performer broke her thigh.

The public demand for pantomime, and especially those of Rich, had now surpassed that of drama, and feathers were being ruffled. A satirical engraving by William Hogarth shows legitimate drama being driven from the theatre by pantomime and Italian opera. Beneath the print this verse appears:

> Could now dumb Faustus, to reform the age,
> Conjure up Shakespeare's or Ben Johnson's ghost,
> They' blush for shame, to see the English stage
> Debauch'd by Fool'ries at so great a cost.

Colly Cibber most heartily agreed. Left to him, there would be no pantomimes at Drury Lane. He had already re-written several of Shakespeare's plays, removing many of the boring speeches and substituting pretty dances and charming songs, but audiences chattered loudly throughout their presentation, quieting only to watch the hated after-pieces. Barton Booth, a great tragedian of the day, took a broader view.

> "Men of taste and judgement" he said "must necessarily form but a small proportion of the spectators at a theatre, and if a greater number of people were enticed to sit out a play because a Pantomime was attached to it, the Pantomime did good service to all concerned."

He went on to remind Cibber that Italian Opera had drawn the nobility and gentry away from the playhouses, as receipts proved, until pantomime came to the rescue "when pit and gallery were filled and the boxes too put on a nobler appearance". The peeved Cibber was forced to agree, but never got over his dislike of pantomimes, referring to them as "Monstrous medlies".

The next major pantomime at Drury Lane was based on the exploits of the criminal Jack Sheppard (1702-26) and one of his escapes from Newgate Jail – "With New Scenes Painted from the Real Places of Action". The Harlequin played Jack Sheppard. Over at Lincoln's Inn Fields, Rich pulled out all stops with *Harlequin a Sorcerer; or the Loves of Pluto and Proserpine* which opened on Jan. 21st, 1725, to a libretto by Lewis Theobald. It was a fantastic success and featured one of the "gags" that retains its popularity even today; the "slosh" scene where Harlequin disguised as an old washer-woman douses his pursuers with soap-suds and boiling water.

In browsing though the records of this production, perhaps the most amusing story concerns a dance routine. Says the writer:

> "A dance of infernals having to be exhibited, they were represented in dresses of black and red, with fiery eyes and snaky locks, and garnished with every pendage of horror. They were twelve in number. In the middle of their performance, while intent upon the figure in which they had been completely practiced, an actor of some humour who had been accommodated with a spare dress, appeared among them. He was, if possible,

40

more terrific than the rest and seemed to the beholders as designed by the conductor for the principal fiend. His fellow furies took alarm; they knew he did not belong to them and judged him to be an infernal in earnest. A general panic ensued and the whole group fled the stage in different ways; some to their dressing rooms and others through the streets to their own homes. The odd devil took himself invisibly away through fear of another kind. The confusion of the audience is scarcely to be described. They retired to their families informing them of this supposed appearance of the devil and every official assurance which could be made the following day did not entirely counter-act the idea."

A statement, given later by the irate Rich, revealed that "The contriver of the scheme had designed it only as an innocent affair to confuse the dancers, and had not considered the consequences."

Such was the success of *Harlequin a Sorcerer* that Rich and Theobold returned to the subject just two years later. It had music and songs by the composer Johann Ernst Galliard, and two of its most spectacular backdrops were painted by George Lambert, Rich's principal scene painter, who had travelled down to Middlesex to sketch the remarkable gardens of Thomas Chambers, a close friend of Rich's and at whose house he had gone to "project and perfect the whole plan." *The Rape of Proserpine; with the Birth and Adventures of Harlequin* opened in January, 1727, and was the rage of London. Taking place in Sicily, the palace and gardens of the goddess Ceres, and the Elysian Fields of Pluto's Underworld, it had eleven scenes, each breathtakingly executed, seven of them serious and the rest comical. As before, the comic interludes of Harlequin and Co were played between the serious scenes.

As the curtain rises, the goddess Ceres flies through the air in her dragon drawn chariot, floating on clouds. An earthquake destroys part of the palace, and Mount Etna can be seen erupting in the background. Pluto emerges from the ground in his great chariot, seizes Proserpine, the daughter of Ceres, and forces her inside it. It then sinks through the ground again. The distraught Ceres takes revenge by burning the corn crops of Sicily and the "classical part" moves on to its conclusion.

The Harlequinade provided Rich with one of his best pieces of mime. In a scene depicting the exterior of a farmhouse, a great dung-hill is prominently featured, on top of which is a large egg. As the sun's rays beat down upon it, it begins to grow in size, eventually cracking to allow Harlequin to hatch. As the Scottish historian, Jackson, reported:

> "This certainly was a masterpiece in dumb-show. From the first chipping of the egg, his receiving motion, his feeling the ground, his standing upright, to his quick Harlequin trip around the empty shell, through the whole progression, every limb had its tongue, and every motion a voice, which spoke with most miraculous organ, to the understandings and sensations of the observers."

Though hailed as a masterpiece by the public, it caused the vitriolic Alexander Pope (1688-1744), still smarting after a scathing criticism, (written by Theobald) of his recent edition of Shakespeare, to revenge himself in *Dunciad* (1728), his satire on scholarly dullness. Describing the Rich and Theobald interpretation of *Rape of Proserpine*, he famously declared it to be "Not touched by nature, and not reached by art."

A glance at a selection of verses from *Dunciad* concerning the production is well worth reading.

> All sudden, Gorgons hiss, and Dragons glare,
> And ten-horn'd fiends and Giants rush to war.
> Hell rises, Heav'n descends, and dance on Earth:
> Gods, imps and monsters, music, rage and mirth,
> A fire, a jigg, a battle and a ball,
> 'Till one wide conflagration swallows all.
>
> The forests dance, the rivers upwards rise,
> Whales sport in woods, and dolphins in the skies;
> And last, to give the whole creation grace,
> Lo! one vast Egg produces human race.
>
> Angel of Dulness, sent to scatter round
> Her magic charms o'er all unclassic ground:
> Immortal Rich! How calm he sits at ease
> 'Mid snows of paper, and fierce hail of pease;
>
> Dire is the conflict, dismal is the din,
> Here shouts all Drury, there all Lincoln's Inn;
> Contending theatres our empire raise,
> Alike their labours, and alike their praise.

With audiences now fighting for entry to his theatre, Rich could afford to smile at the carping of his critics. Besides, pantomime was not the only arrow in his theatrical quiver. He had recently accepted a script from a West Country playwright that held extraordinary promise.

Unlike anything seen before on an English stage, it was crammed with political satire, merry songs, and characters straight from a Hogarth etching. Most importantly, it had already been turned down by Drury Lane, and Rich was convinced it would make him a fortune and wipe the sneer from Colley Cibber's face. He was absolutely correct, for the show was England's first musical, *The Beggar's Opera*, and John Gay was its author.

3

*B*orn in Barnstaple, North Devon, the poet John Gay (1685-1723) was a friend of Alexander Pope, Jonathan Swift (1667-1745) and John Arbuthnot (1667-1735) the Scottish surgeon to Queen Anne, who created the national character of John Bull, a prosperous farmer, in 1712. Gay's earlier poetry had little to commend it and his friends in fashionable literary circles considered him merely a pleasant hanger-on. His first play, *The What D'ye Call It* in 1715, was a farcical comedy, but it was not until Swift suggested to him that "A Newgate pastoral might make an odd pretty sort of thing" he began writing his masterwork. As mentioned earlier, it was first offered to Drury Lane who turned it down. Undaunted, the amiable Gay took it to John Rich who at once saw its possibilities and produced it at Lincoln's Inn Field on January 29th, 1728 to a reception never before seen in a London theatre. The excited Gay wrote to Swift:

> "It is acted with such success that the playhouse hath been crowded every night; tonight is the fifteenth time of Acting, and 'tis thought it will run a fortnight longer. I make no interest either for approbation or money, nor hath any body been prest

to take tickets for my Benefit, notwith-standing which, I think I shall make an addition to my fortune of between *six and seven hundred pounds*. The outlandish (as they now call it) Opera hath been so thin of late I fear I shall have remonstrances drawn up against me by the Royal Academy of Musick"

He badly underestimated himself. It is often said; "*The Beggar's Opera* made Gay rich and Rich gay," and over two centuries later it is still being revived, delighting both managements and audiences with its satirical swipes at corrupt politicians represented as thieves, highwaymen and pimps. How little things have changed.

With money flowing into the coffers in undreamed of amounts, (£4,000 by March 20th) Rich began to think of building a new theatre with better facilities, and to this end on March 16th 1730, leased a plot of land in Bow Street from the Duke of Bedford, opening a Subscription which swiftly raised £6,000. In the meantime, Drury Lane had attempted to compete with *The Beggar's Opera* by presenting *The Village Opera*.

According to *The Flying Post; Or Weekly Medley*, the reception given to this production was:

"A Serenade of Cat Calls, Penny Trumpets, Clubs, Canes, hoarse Voices, whistling in Keys, Heels, Fists, and Vollies of whole Oranges". The actors continued but could not be heard. At the end "a new kind of Shower compos'd of Candles fell thick as Hail on the Stage. The whole concluded with breaking to Pieces several of the Sconces. In short, this exceeds anything that was ever done at the Ampitheatre or the Bear Garden"

Rich's new theatre took two years to build, and in that time he continued to do what he did best; present pantomimes. He had little time for Drama, perhaps because the classical actors had so often mocked him in the past, and even when the House was packed to the rafters, it is said that he used to peer through a peep-hole in the front cloth at the expectant audiences and growl "Ah, there you are, you fools, are you? Much good may it do you." If the story is true, it was perhaps said tongue in cheek, for he knew quite well that whatever the play that evening, his audiences were there for one thing only; the fabulous forty minute afterpieces known as Pantomime.

The move to the new theatre in Covent Garden, scheduled to open on Nov. 26th 1731, was delayed when a great part of the roof collapsed. According to *Reed's Weekly Journal*; Nov. 6th, 1731:

> "Last Tuesday, a great part of the roof of the new playhouse which is building near Covent Garden fell in, when several of the men that were at work had their limbs broken and one had his skull fractured and dy'd in about eight hours."

Rich was forced to re-open Lincoln's Inn Fields again until the damage could be made good, and in the meantime, the satirists sharpened their pens. Any successful person was a target for spiteful comment, and Rich was perhaps the most successful of all. Sneered one critic:

> "Thespis, the first of the dramatic race
> Stroll'd in a cart for gain, from place to place;
> His actors rude, his profits came but slow,
> The poet he and master of the show,
> To raise attention he employ'd his art
> To build another and more costly cart.
> New asses he procured to drag the load,
> And gain'd the shouts of boys upon the road.
> Awhile the gay machine attention drew,
> The people throng'd because the sight was new;
> Thither they hurried once and went no more,
> For all his actors they had seen before;
> And what it was they wished no more to see
> The application, Lun, is left to thee."

Nevertheless, on Dec 6th, 1732, The Covent Garden theatre opened with a production of Congreve's *The Way of the World*, then continued its season with *The Beggar's Opera* which ran for twenty nights (a very good run for those days), before transferring to Lincoln's Inn Fields with a new cast for a further run. There were also productions of Shakespeare's plays with "new and extremely well painted cloths" whilst Rich himself appeared as Harlequin in a spectacular revival of *The Cheats or The Tavern Bilkers*. By the end of the first season, which ended on June Ist, 1733, the new playhouse had been visited six times by King George II who loved pantomimes, and Rich had been congratulated on his "Excellent, excellent, Harlequin".

Though Rich was riding high, the rest of theatrical London was in turmoil. Despite objections, by 1735 a new theatre had been built in Goodman's Fields, one at Richmond and others in Hampstead and Southwark. Drury Lane was involved in a massive internal wrangle, and German born composer George Frederick Handel (1685-1759) who had been director of the Opera at the King's Theatre in the Haymarket from Dec. 1729 to June 1734, had quarrelled bitterly with its manager James Heidegger, reputedly the ugliest man in London, and terminated their partnership agreement. After an unsuccessful attempt to attract audiences to Lincoln's Inn Fields, he approached Rich with a proposal that he join him at Covent Garden with his Opera company. Rich at once agreed. It was good competition for Drury Lane, and he also benefited financially. On the evenings Handel occupied Covent Garden, Rich took his company of actors back to Lincoln's Inn Fields and played there.

In 1736, Henry Fielding, (1707-1754) took over the management of the tiny Haymarket theatre and like others before him, quickly found that London audiences were far more receptive to Rich's pantomimes than serious drama. He mounted a burlesque production called *Tumble-Down Dick; or Phaeton in the Suds* which he advertised as "A Dramatick Entertainment of Walking, in serious and Foolish Characters; Interlarded with Burlesque, Grotesque, Comick Interludes, call'd "Harlequin a Pick-Pocket", Being ('tis hoped) the last such entertainment that will ever be exhibited on any stage. Invented by the Ingenious Monsieur Sans Esprit. The Musick Composed by Harmonious Signor Warblerini. And the Scenes painted by the Prodigious Mynheer van Bottom-Flat". It was dedicated to Mr. John Lun, "Vulgarly called Esquire" and was played as a rehearsal for a pantomime to evade censure for infringing the Patents.

In one scene, set in the King's Coffee House, a song is sung in praise of gin. Harlequin is captured picking pockets and chained. The spirit of Gin emerges from a tub and holds out a baton, saying:

47

Take, Harlequin, this magic wand,
All things shall yield to thy command;
Whether you would appear incog.,
In shape of monkey, cat or dog;
Or else to show your wit, transform
Your mistress to a butter-churn;
Or else, what no magician can,
Into a wheelbarrow turn a man.

In another dig at Rich it poked fun at the scene in *The Rape of Proserpine* where Harlequin is hatched from an egg. After Jupiter blows out a candle (representing the sun) with a pair of bellows, he exclaims to Phaeton. "I would not have you think I want suns, for there were two very fine ones that shone together at Drury Lane play house." Phaeton replies, "You had better send for the sun from Covent Garden house, for there's a sun that hatches an egg there, and produces a Harlequin". Jupiter snorts. "Do you know what animal laid that egg?" he asks. When Phaeton replies in the negative he is told "Sir, the egg was laid by an Ass."

Fielding next turned his attention to corruption and wrote two savage and satirical attacks on the clergy, the Royal Family and Prime Minister Robert Walpole. *Pasquin* and *The Historical Register for the year 1736.* Though a source of great amusement for the public, there was an unexpected backlash. With frightening speed Walpole took action. On June 21st 1737, with an Act of Law, he closed down the Haymarket and Goodman's Fields theatres, and ordered the Lord Chamberlain's office to obtain copies of every dramatic piece prior to public presentation, and remove anything they found offensive before issuing a licence for its performance. In spite of vehement protests, and a near riot by a patriotic audience when French performers (who had been granted a licence at the Haymarket by the Lord Chamberlain) were pelted with dried peas that turned the stage into a skating rink, this ruling remained in force until 1968.

At Covent Garden, Rich continued with his varied productions, seemingly unconcerned by the troubles around him, though a small fire which broke out in the scene room in 1739 and alarmed the audience provided an amusing anecdote. Rich ordered Joe Hall, the original Lockit in *The Beggar's*

Opera to run onto the stage and explain what was happening backstage. This extraordinary speech was the result.

> "Ladies and gentlemen, for heaven's sake don't be frightened – don't stir-keep your seats – the fire is almost extinguished; but if it was not – we have a reservoir of one hundred hogshead of water over your heads that would drown you all in a few minutes"

He then quickly exited.

During his time at Covent Garden, Rich had presented few new pantomimes, preferring to re-vamp his old ones with even more spectacular costumes and scenery. Only the best was good enough, and British theatre owes a great deal to the artistic skills of the people he employed. In 1739, however, he presented *Orpheus and Eurydice*, spending over £2,000 to mount it, an unheard of figure in those days. In addition to the breathtaking decor and costumes, it boasted the most amazing piece of mechanism ever seen on the English stage – a glittering green and gold-scaled serpent of enormous size that "twisted and twirled and wriggled about, eyes shining brightly and making an awful but very natural hissing noise".

Constructed by Samuel Hoole, Rich's principal machinist, it cost more than £200 to make and was said to be so life-like as to "frighten half the ladies who see it". Not only did it attract the attention of the Royal family, it also drew what appeared to be the entire population of London. So overwhelming was the reaction, it affected poor Hoole's reason and he developed an obsession with creating more. With no outlet for them, and his refusal to make anything else, he swiftly ended up in court, "Ruined, Bankrupt and Undone".

An interesting addendum to *Orpheus* is that the Pantaloon who played opposite Rich's Harlequin was Guiseppi Grimaldi, (1713-1788) father of the great Clown who single handedly re-shaped the pantomimes of Regency times.

The complacency of Rich and Fleetwood, the latest manager of Drury Lane, was rudely shattered on October 19th, 1741. The theatre at Goodman's Field had re-opened; its manager, Henry Gifford, getting round the legal regulations by presenting concerts of music and slipping in a play between the items.

Admission was paid for the musical pieces, but the play was free of charge – in effect, a rehearsal for which no licence was needed. This device was used by almost all the "unauthorized" theatres. *Harlequin Student; or the Fall of Pantomime with the Restoration of the Drama* was the title of the musical part of the show, and *The Life and Death of King Richard the Third* the play. In the title role would be, "a young gentleman who never appeared on any stage".

The statement on the poster was not exactly true. Born in Lichfield, in 1716, the actor concerned had been attracted to the theatre at a very young age. On the death of his parents, he dissolved his partnership with his brother in the wine trade and in the Summer of 1741, using the pseudonym of Lyddal, joined Giffard's company of players in Ipswich, studying most of the Harlequinade parts, plus several Shakespearean roles. He was small of stature – only five feet four inches – but his natural delivery of lines together with "every gesture, facial expression and gleam in his eyes lending force to the dramatist's words" made him an instant success.

On his return to London, he eagerly approached the managements at Drury Lane and Covent Garden for engagements, only to be turned away. Undeterred, he crossed to Goodman's Fields and arranged with Gifford to make his debut there. It may only have been curiosity that filled the House that night, but by the end of the performance the name of David Garrick was on everyone's lips. As Thomas Davies was to write:

> "Mr. Garrick shone forth like a theatrical Newton he threw new light on elocution and action; he banished ranting, bombast and grimace; and restored nature, ease, simplicity and genuine humour"

Henry Gifford was not slow to realize he had a "star" on his hands. Over the next few weeks he mounted a series of plays that showed off Garrick's prowess. The *Daily Post* announced that his reception had been "The most extraordinary and great that was ever known on such an occasion" and the nobility responded by flocking to the unlicenced playhouse in droves. By May 1742, the Royal Theatres had become so alarmed at their loss of custom, they used all their influence to have Goodman's Fields shut down. Their aim fulfilled, the crafty

Fleetwood at once engaged Garrick for Drury Lane at a salary of six hundred guineas, where he met and plunged into a passionate *affair* with the infamous Peg Woffington.

This extraordinarily beautiful and talented Irish actress was almost as well known for her *affairs* as her acting, and her most famous role was a breeches one, that of Sir Harry Wildair in Farquar's *The Constant Couple.* It is recorded that one occasion, following a triumphant exit from the stage after appearing in this play, she exclaimed smugly: "I do believe half the gentlemen in the house believe me to be a man". To which James Quin, another famous actor who knew all about her private life retorted "Perhaps so, but the other half know otherwise"

Back at Covent Garden, Handel, who had been absent for some time, had taken out a further lease and on February 18th, 1743, presented his new oratorio *Sampson,* to be followed on March 23rd, by the first performance in England of *The Messiah.* It is said that the effect of the "Hallelujah Chorus" was so startling, the entire audience, including King George II, spontaneously rose to their feet and remained standing till the chorus ended, thus starting the tradition that continues today in many parts of the country.

By 1745, Fleetwood had run into financial trouble and was forced to sell out. His patent was bought by two financiers who appointed James Lacy, an actor and stage manager at Covent Garden, to act as manager for them. Garrick, who had been ill and out of London, returned to find the theatre in a bad way, so quickly accepted an offer from John Rich to appear at Covent Garden. On June 11th, 1746, Garrick made his first appearance there and remained until May 1747. It is possible he could have stayed longer but he disliked pantomime intensely and Rich, although he had produced very little new material was still drawing the crowds with them. A suggestion from Lacy that Garrick should buy a share of Drury Lane and become artistic director of the house was seized upon, and for the sum of £8,000 an agreement was signed on April 9th. Though Rich made a profit of £8,500 on the 1746-7 season, after Garrick's departure for Drury Lane, things took a turn for the worse.

Determined that under his management Drury Lane would thrive, Garrick gathered around him the finest actors and actresses in the country. Abolishing the tradition that certain parts belonged to certain actors by right of seniority and custom, he cast according to merit and unlike the actor managers of the past, was quite content to play minor roles if the leading ones did not suit him. Punctuality at rehearsals was enforced and those who were slipshod in learning lines – a common occurrence in those days – were suspended. Standards immediately rose, and once again the Drury Lane theatre was packed to the rafters.

It is often said that Garrick re-invented stage lighting, but the credit for this must really go to Philip James de Loutherbourg (c1735-1812) who arrived in England around 1770 and found employment at Drury Lane. A skilled scenic artist and possibly the first in Britain to paint backdrops with perspective, he also devised the method of painting scenes on gauze which appeared to vanish when illuminated from behind. Other de Loutherbourg innovations were the method of producing stage thunder by shaking a suspended sheet of copper; imitating the sound of waves with dried peas and shot in an oblong tray tilted from side to side, and producing visible rainfall from a perforated and seed-packed rotating cylinder fixed high above the stage. Many of these devices were still being used in the 1980s, and, I suspect, continue to play a part in amateur theatres around the world today.

Lighting, however, was de Loutherbourg's greatest innovation. By hanging coloured silks or stained glass in front of the stage lamps he was able to add interesting variations to the usual stark illumination of the time. He lit, not just from the floats at the front of the stage, but from the wings and overhead, even producing moonlight effects by suspending lamps behind the scenes. It may all appear very primitive, but in those early days of theatre the effects were startling and played an important part of Garrick's productions at Drury Lane.

Rich, though now too old for playing Harlequin, hit back with spectacular revivals of his old successes, but it was almost two years before the public grew tired of serious drama and began to drift away again.

In the meantime, Samuel Foote, the waspish frustrated actor and satirist had re-opened the Haymarket theatre with a series of scurrilous attacks on Garrick (who he despised), and Rich. Again, the patent law had been avoided by Foote's invitation to the public to take tea or chocolate with him at the theatre for a charge, and watch the "rehearsal of a play" for nothing if they so minded. Ironically it was one of Foote's darts at pantomime "miracles" that gave Rich his next success. In 1749, the following advertisement was published:

> At the New Theatre in the Haymarket, this present day, to be seen a person who performs the several most surprising things following, viz: First he takes a common walking cane from any of the spectators, and thereon he plays the music of every instrument now in use, and likewise sings to surprising perfection. Secondly, he presents you with a common wine bottle, which any of the spectators may first examine: this bottle is placed on a table in the middle of the stage, and he, (without any equivocation) goes into it, in the sight of all the spectators, and sings in it: during his stay in the bottle, any person may handle it, and see plainly that it does not exceed a common tavern bottle. Those on stage or in the boxes may come in masked habits (if agreeable to them) and the performer (if desired) will inform them who they are.
>
> Stage 7/6d. Boxes 5/-. Pit 3/- Gallery 2/-.
> "To begin half an hour after six o-clock"

On the night of Jan.16th, the theatre was besieged and even at the inflated prices asked, was full to the rafters. By seven o'clock, the audience were restless, and cat-calling. By half past, the theatre was in an uproar as the stage remained empty. At last Foote's prompter appeared and appealed for silence. The audience hushed at once, and were informed that owing to an indisposition, the Great Bottle Conjuror could not appear. Those who wished it could have their money refunded, but if they returned the following night, for double the ticket price, the Great Bottle Conjuror would squeeze himself into a pint bottle. The audience exploded with rage. Within minutes, curtains, scenery and hangings were torn down. Seats and boxes were kicked to pieces, carried outside and burnt, and everyone thoroughly enjoyed themselves.

Rich swiftly put together a new pantomime *The Royal Chase; or Harlequin Skeleton* and advertised:

> "Lately arrived from Italy, Sig. Capitello Jumpedo, a surprising dwarf, no taller than a common tavern tobacco pipe; who can perform many wonderful equilibres, on the slack or tight rope: Likewise he'll transform his body in above ten thousand different shapes and postures; and after he has diverted the spectators two hours and a half, he will open his mouth wide, and jump down his own throat"

The last mentioned remarkable effect was achieved by having a large Harlequin's head perched on top of a pedestal. Rich's Harlequin of the piece simply dived into the open mouth of this and vanished from view. The public were highly amused at his ingenuity, and once again, he was flavour of the month.

A revival of *Perseus and Andromeda* later in the season also filled the theatre, though the curtain had to be rung down at one performance when Perseus, who was strapped to a huge spinning wheel that soared above the clouds as he journeyed to save Andromeda, had a lucky escape after the wheel broke, causing him to fall several feet onto body of the great dragon and pulverize it.

In *Tom Jones*, published that same year, Fielding resumed his attacks on pantomime. The two parts, he said, should not be called the "serious" and the "comic", but the "dull" and the "duller", for the boring antics of Harlequin and Co. could only be made bearable by contrasting them with the even more boring gods and goddesses of the first part. The public smiled, but continued to clamour for more productions.

At Drury Lane, Garrick was suddenly alarmed when several of his best actors, tired of his autocratic ways, left his company and joined that of Covent Garden. Discovering that the rival theatre was to present *Romeo and Juliet*, he announced that Drury Lane would also present the play, and on the very same nights. Not only that; for the first time in his career, he would appear as Romeo. The word spread like wildfire and eager to pass judgement, theatregoers flocked to both houses. For eleven days the opposing players battled for supremacy, but playgoers visiting London complained bitterly that if they wanted to see anything, it could only be

Shakespeare. This caused a Mr. Hewitt to write the following epigram in the General Advertiser.

"Well, what's tonight?" says Angry Ned,
As up from bed he rouses.
"Romeo again!" and shakes his head,
"Ah! Pox on both your houses"

Taking the hint, Rich withdrew his production and Garrick followed suite the next day. Both theatres had lost money and were looking for something to restore confidence. Garrick struck first.

On Boxing Day, 1750, Drury Lane theatre presented *Queen Mab*, "an entertainment with Italian grotesque characters", written by Henry Woodward, who having worked for Rich in pantomime under the name of Lun Jnr., also appeared as the Harlequin of the piece. In a prologue spoken by Garrick, he said:

"Sacred to Shakespeare was this spot designed,
To pierce the heart, and humanise the mind,
But if an empty house, the actor's curse,
Shows us our Lears and Hamlets lose their force;
Unwillingly, we must change the noble scene,
And in our turn present you Harlequin.
Quit poets, and set carpenters to work,
Shew gaudy scenes, or mount the vaulting Turk.
For though we actors one and all agree
Boldly to struggle for our vanity,
If want comes on, importance must retreat;
Our first great ruling passion- is to eat"

Woodward, was no Rich – who in his heyday could "scratch his ear with his foot and rapidly execute two or three hundred steps in an advance of three yards" – but he was younger, slimmer, and well versed in all the tricks of his old master. In one routine where Harlequin had to dive through a series of walls and windows, a "double" was engaged to give the impression that Harlequin, after disappearing through a wall, could pop up out of the ground a split second later. The "double" would then exit through a window and the real Harlequin would appear unexpectedly somewhere else. One night by accident, both Harlequins rushed on stage together and collided, sending the audience into peals of laughter. A new comic routine was born, and two and a half centuries later, you can find the "gag" appearing not only on stage, but in films and television too.

The ageing Rich was stunned by the reception to *Queen Mab*. Whereas most plays ran for a week in those days, this went on for over a month. In a fit of pique, he decided not to present any pantomimes that year but began planning an ambitious revival of one of his greatest successes and on February 11th, 1752, *Harlequin Sorcerer* was presented. Tate Wilkinson, who as mentioned earlier was never on the best of terms with Rich, related:

> "There was never anything before like the rage of it. The doors had to be opened three hours before commencing to relieve the streets about Covent Garden of the crowd. It made Garrick and Old Drury tremble – for all they got was the discontented overflow of children and the grown-up masters and misses who failed to get in and see the pantomime"

The following year, Garrick presented pantomime again, *The Genii*, again written by Woodward, but the wily Rich revived *Harlequin Sorcerer* for a second year, adding new embellishments that dazzled and delighted packed houses. Even the spiteful Foote was impressed by the spectacle which included for the first time, a featured ballet performed in diaphanous drapes. Reported *The Adventurer*:

> "I gazed at the prodigies which were every moment produced before me with astonishment; I was bewildered in the intricacies of enchantment; I saw woods, rivers, and mountains, alternately appear and vanish; but I knew not to what cause or to what end. The entertainment was not adapted to my understanding, but to my senses; and my senses were indeed captivated with every object of delight; in particular, the dress of the women discovered beauties which I could not behold without confusion; the wanton caresses which they received and returned, the desire that languished in their eyes, the kiss snatched with eagerness, and the embrace prolonged with reciprocal delight, filled my breast with tumultuous wishes, which, though I feared to gratify, I did not wish to suppress. Besides all these incentives to dissolute pleasure, there was the dance, which indulged the spectators with a view of almost every charm that apparel was intended to conceal"

With a review like that, it's no wonder that audiences were largely male and Rich is said to have cleared £11,000 on the season.

In 1754, George Colman the elder, suggested in *The Connoisseur* that rather than persist in sinning by representing "Heathen gods and goddesses before Christian audiences", pantomime writers should take their subjects from Moral Ballads or Children's fairy stories:

> "Suppose they were to exhibit a Pantomime of the Children in the Wood;- 'twould be vastly pretty to see the paste-board robin redbreasts let down by wires upon the stage to cover the poor innocent babies with paper leaves ... I am sure that instead of ostriches, dogs, horses, lions, monkeys, etc., we should be full as well pleased to see The Wolf and the Little Red Riding Hood; and we should laugh vastly at the adventures of Puss in Boots. I need not point out the excellent Moral which would be inculcated by representations of this kind; and I am confident they would meet with the deserved applause of all the old women and children in both galleries"

Colman's advice went unheeded. Pantomime was doing very nicely in its present form and another fifty years were to pass before anything of the kind occurred. The irritated Garrick bitterly expressed his views on its supporters in one of his famous Prologues:

> "They in the Drama find no joys,
> But dote on Mimicry and Toys,
> Thus when a Dance is on my Bill,
> Nobility my Boxes fill;
> Or send three days before the time
> To crowd a new-made pantomime"

In truth, Pantomime was now so popular, a suggestion was made in *The World* that theatre managers should forget the Drama, and only stage pantomimes.

> "People of taste and fashion having given sufficient proof that they thought it the highest entertainment the stage was capable of"

Garrick was inclined to agree, and recalling the success of Rich's ballet sequence the previous year became convinced that Ballet was the new form that would set the world alight. Forsaking the detested pantomime, Garrick hired a Swiss ballet master to stage a gorgeous entertainment entitled *The Chinese Festival*, scouring Europe for the best dancers and billing them as all as French. Unfortunately, another war with France was announced shortly before the production took place, and on November 12th, 1755, despite the presence of King George, the theatre became a battleground and the dancers were pelted with rotten fruit and vegetables. The company struggled on, but every night was pandemonium and on the sixth night, swords were drawn in the audience and blood was spilled. The irate mob tore up the benches, smashed the candelabrums and destroyed scenery before swarming out of the theatre determined to burn Garrick's Southampton Street house to the ground. Only after the shattering of all his windows and the timely arrival of the military, were the crowd dispersed. The failure of *The Chinese Festival* cost Drury Lane over £4,000.

Garrick speedily returned to pantomime, but it was not until four years later he was able to beat Rich at his own game. On Dec. 31st, 1759, *Harlequin's Invasion; or A Christmas Gambol* was presented and with Tom King (later to create the role of Sir Peter Teazle in *The School for Scandal*) as Harlequin, became the greatest success of Garrick's management. Written by Garrick himself with co-author George Colman Snr., it told the story of Harlequin and Co.'s defeat at the hands of the mighty Shakespeare. (Wishful thinking on Garrick's part).

Two things made this production outstanding. One was a mere gimmick. For the first time in over sixty years Harlequin was given a voice, so it could not be called a pantomime. The second had an even greater impact. In the war with France, the British Army had taken Quebec, and shortly afterwards, the Navy had defeated the Brest Fleet in Brittany. Britain was in a fever of patriotism, and Garrick, to commemorate the victories, penned a song that stopped the show dead. With music by William Boyce, Master of the King's Music and musical director of Drury Lane, its rousing chorus is remembered to this day:

"Hearts of oak are our ships,
Hearts of oak are our men,
We always are ready,
Steady, boys, steady!
We'll fight and we'll conquer again and again."

Garrick also went on to conquer. John Rich died on Nov. 26th 1761 aged 69 years and was buried in Hillingdon churchyard, leaving an estate valued at £60,000. Shortly afterwards, Garrick revived *Harlequin's Invasion* and in a specially written prologue, spoken by Harlequin, paid tribute to his old rival.

> "But why a speaking Harlequin?- 'Tis wrong,
> The wits will say, to give the fool a tongue.
> When Lun appear'd with matchless art and whim,
> He gave the pow'r of speech to ev'ry limb.
> Tho' mask'd and mute, convey'd his quick intent,
> And told in frolic gestures all he meant.
> But now the motley coat, and sword of wood,
> Requires a tongue to make them understood."

In the year Rich died, Samuel Foote attempted:

> "From pantomime to free the stage,
> And combat all the ministers of the age"

by devising a production entitled *The Wishes*, wherein Harlequin would be hung in full view of the public. Before the hangman could even get the rope around Harlequin's neck, a great riot broke out in the pit and the furious audience invaded the stage causing Foote to make a hasty exit from the theatre and the curtain to be lowered.

Nevertheless, without Rich's fertile brain, pantomime entered a period of stagnancy. Few new tricks were introduced and though both Patent houses continued to present them, interest was waning. In an attempt to revive it, for pantomime still accounted for the majority of a theatre's income, Garrick introduced the Jubilee pageant he had attempted to stage at the disastrous Shakespeare bicentenery birthday celebration in Stratford on Avon, which had ended with torrential rain causing the river's banks to burst and collapse a tent in which Mrs. Baddeley was singing "Soft thou gently flowing Avon". Fancy dress revellers suddenly found themselves dancing *minuets* up to their ankles in water, none of the advertised fireworks could be made to light, a wall in the Rotunda collapsed stunning Lord Argyle, the Guest of honour, and on leaving the flooded field, 150 of the guests had fallen into a concealed ditch. To Garrick's dismay, he then discovered that the festival had been held five years late, in the wrong month, and not a word of Shakespeare's had been spoken.

This time, fortunately, things went without mishap and the successful great pageant was destined to figure more importantly in a later century. It was not until 1781, however that pantomime found a new direction – and it came from a most unexpected source. The thirty-two years old author of *The Rivals* and *The School for Scandal* – Richard Brinsley Sheridan.

*B*orn in Dublin, 1751, the son of an actor father and a novelist/playwright mother, Sheridan came to England to study Law. After marriage to Elizabeth Linley, he turned his attentions to the stage and his first play *The Rivals*, premiered on Jan.17th, 1775 at Covent Garden theatre, was a resounding success. So much so, that one of his leading characters, the unforgettable Mrs. Malaprop, found immortality not only on stages world wide, but gained a place in the English dictionary, too. *The Duenna* a comic opera, followed a few months later and in 1776, discovering that Garrick was considering retirement and his half of the Patent was valued at £35,000, Sheridan began negotiations to purchase one third of it. The contract was signed on 24th June, and together with his two co-purchasers, Thomas Linley and Dr. Richard Ford, Sheridan became part of the new management. His unbounded enthusiasm encouraged the others to elect him business manager but they soon regretted it, for a more unsuitable person could not have been found. Determined to outshine Garrick's past successes, he mounted lavish, expensive productions and, combined with unerring poor judgement of players, soon had the theatre in severe financial trouble. It was only the presentation of his newly completed *The School for Scandal* on May 8th, 1777 that saved them. Running for twenty nights on its first production, and holding the stage for three nights a week over a period of years, Sheridan's comedy earned more money than any other play had ever done in the past.

Glowing in financial security, for the sum of £45,000, Sheridan bought a half-share of the patent, making himself the principal theatre manager, and following the success of his next play *The Critic* in 1779, turned his attention to politics. Becoming the Member of Parliament for Stafford, he rapidly gained fame as an eloquent speaker, but neglected the business of his theatre so badly that the other investors began to panic. Money was needed, and quickly. For the pantomime of 1781, he wrote *Robinson Crusoe; or, Harlequin Friday,* using the famous Daniel Defoe novel, based on the story of Scottish sailor, Alexander Selkirk who had been marooned from 1704 to 1709 in the Juan Fernandez islands.

Several interesting things arose from this production, the first being that *Robinson Crusoe* had never been used before as a pantomime subject, which makes this the oldest of our now "traditional" titles. Secondly, unlike the pantomimes that had gone before, there was no interweaving of a comical Harlequinade story with an unconnected and serious part, for the two were divided into distinct scenes. The first one dealt with Crusoe and Friday on the island, their rescue of Pantaloon from the savages, and a subsequent departure for Spain. In the second, Friday contemplates suicide because Pantaloon ill-treats him, but a magician appears who gives him a magic baton (the slapstick) and transforms him into Harlequin. With a wave of the magic baton, Crusoe becomes Pierrot and the usual Harlequinade begins. After the adventure is played out, (which includes Clown being strapped to the revolving sails of a Spanish windmill) the penultimate scene is changed to a magnificent Temple where everyone joins in a *grand bower dance.* Though the *Morning Chronicle* claimed that "audiences were in raptures", Horace Walpole (1717-97) was unimpressed. He wrote:

> "How unlike the pantomimes of Rich, which were full of wit and carried on the story! What I now saw was *Robinson Crusoe*. How Aristotle and Bossu, had they written on pantomimes, would swear! It was a heap of contradictions and violations of the costume. Friday is turned into Harlequin and falls down at an old man's feet that I took for Pantaloon, but they told me it was Friday's father. I said, Then it must be Thursday, yet it still seemed to be Pantaloon. I see I understand nothing from astronomy to a Harlequin-farce"

Another critic sneered that "The Drury Lane pantomime written by Mr. Sheridan is proof that even the greatest genius can sink beneath contempt," but *Robinson Crusoe* ran for thirty eight nights and Sheridan's innovation lasted well into the nineteenth century. Other notable things about this pantomime were the teaming of Carlo Delpini (1740-1828) who played Robinson/Pierrot and devised the Harlequinade sequence, and 68 years old Guiseppi Grimaldi who appeared as Friday/Harlequin, for both played important roles in the evolution of British pantomime.

Delpini was an Italian who had worked for Garrick as a Dancing Master, and it was he who, realizing the genius of Rich would continue to overshadow all other Harlequins, had expanded the role of Pierrot the Clown to compensate. From being a very minor "servant" character, Pierrot had gradually been transformed into an overgrown "cheeky schoolboy" type who was proving popular with audiences.

In addition, whilst others based their Harlequinades on magical transformations effected by Harlequin and his baton, Delpini had taken a leaf from O'Hara and Dibdin's burletta *Poor Vulcan* presented at Covent Garden in February 1778, which depicted the quarreling Gods and Goddesses of Mount Olympus journeying to Earth where they find employment – Vulcan as a blacksmith named Crump, Venus, as Maudlin, an ale-house landlady, Jupiter, a country squire, and Mars, a recruiting officer. Using the same principle of character transformation, he had devised the *Crusoe* Harlequinade that so upset Walpole, but at that time, Delpini could have had no idea that his tampering was to change the course of pantomime forever.

Guiseppi Grimaldi, or "Old Grim" as he was often referred to, had arrived in England from the fairs of Italy and France and found employment as the dentist of Queen Charlotte, claiming he could draw teeth or stumps without pain, fill hollow teeth with lead, or replace a bad tooth with a good one "although this operation is so curiously difficult as to be questioned by many, and particularly some of the profession". After leaving the Royal Appointment, he taught fencing and dance, before making his first stage appearance at Covent Garden Theatre, playing Pantaloon to Rich's Harlequin.

According to Henry Angelo, the Fencing Master at the theatre, soon afterwards, Grimaldi approached his employer to propose an extraordinary dance that would astonish and fill the house at every performance. Rich, always on the look out for something unusual showed interest, and after Grimaldi explained that what he had in mind was a dance on horse-shoes, advanced him money for "properties" and eagerly awaited results. Preparations, Grimaldi insisted, must be conducted in secret to avoid a leak to the rival house and the piece would not be rehearsed in public. Only on the opening night could the routine be performed. Rich duly primed the press to expect a breathtaking new surprise, and on opening night, the theatre was packed with patrons eager to sample the new sensation. Grimaldi never appeared – having "danced away on his horse-shoes and returned to France" leaving the embarrassed theatre manager to issue an abject apology.

By early 1758 he was back in England and appearing at the Haymarket theatre doing acrobatic dances, but in October was employed by Garrick at Drury Lane in a ballet called *The Millers* which was presented between the first and second acts of *Richard III*. Said a critic of the time:

> "Grimaldi is a man of great strength and agility. He indeed treads the air. If he has any fault, he is rather too comical."

From then onwards he appeared regularly as Harlequin, Pantaloon or Clown at Drury Lane and Sadlers Wells (the Musick-House-cum-Spa built by Richard Sadler in 1683 which presented non-speaking entertainments), and devised several comical routines that proved highly popular. One featured a dancing skeleton, and another a "petrifying cavern" in which intruders were rendered immobile on entering. Variations of both ideas have been used in pantomimes ever since.

Without question, it was "Old Grim's" ingenuity that prompted Delpini, himself a well known Clown, to expand the insignificant servant role into something much more substantial. As everyone knows, a little self-serving can go a long way.

Eccentric to a degree, Grimaldi greatly amused the rioters during the so-called "No Popery" disturbances in June 1780, for when they ordered him to write "No Popery!" on his garden wall, he hastily wrote in large letters "No Religion at all." His appellation of "Old Grim", however, probably derived more from his morbid turn of mind than his surname, for he spent much of his spare time wandering around churchyards and burial grounds speculating on which diseases the departed had died from and how many had been interred alive whilst in a fit or trance. So much did this affect him, he left instructions that when he died, his head was to be removed before they sealed him in his coffin, and in due course, this is exactly what happened.

A famous womaniser, it was common knowledge he had "littered the Town with bastards", but as pantomime rehearsals took place on Dec. 18th 1779, the news arrived that his 25 year old mistress, Rebecca Brooker had just given birth to a son. The whole Company joined in congratulating the 66-year old Grimaldi, who proudly informed them he would have the boy on stage as soon as he could walk. Just one year and eleven months later, according to his *Memoirs*, Joseph Grimaldi (1779-1837) took his first bow on the stage of Drury Lane Theatre as a little Clown to his father's Harlequin/Friday.

The young Grimaldi quickly became known as "Joey," and remains, even today, the greatest and best loved performer in the history of British pantomime. Circus Clowns are named "Joey" in memory of him, and slapstick routines are known to all professional performers as "Joey-Joeys". The tricks, songs and routines he contrived have passed into pantomime legend, and over two hundred years later it is rare to find a production that fails to include some derivation of a Grimaldi invention in its construction.

On Easter Monday of 1781, he relates, his father engaged him for the pantomime at Sadlers Wells. Dressed as a monkey and secured by a chain around his waist, young Joey was whirled around his father's head at tremendous speed. At one performance the chain snapped sending him soaring over the horrified audience for some distance. Luckily falling into the arms of an elderly patron when he descended, he escaped injury, but the incident found a place in pantomime. For many years now, dummy figures, dressed as one of the cast, have been hurled into the auditorium on elasticated ropes giving audiences an unexpected and sometimes most unwelcome jolt.

The following year, Joey was back at Drury Lane playing a variety of parts such as Little Clowns, gnomes, imps and cats on stage, and entertaining the other performers in the off stage Green Room with songs and dances. "Old Grim" was not amused at the levity, and lifting Joey by his hair, would deposit him in a corner with a baleful glare and the instruction "not to move until he was told". The moment "Grim" had vanished, Joey's tears would stop and his antics re-commence, but when the warning that "Grim" was on his way back came, he'd rush into his corner again and began sobbing loudly as though he'd never moved. This went on for some time, but one night, about to appear as the Little Clown, Grimaldi Sn. caught him in the act and Joey received a heavy beating. With tears streaming down his face, washing away his "inch thick" white greasepaint and giving him a most extraordinary appearance, he heard his cue line being spoken. Terrified of missing his entrance, he dashed on stage and the audience shrieked with laughter at the sight of him. The irate Grimaldi Snr., unable to control himself at the sight of this apparition, began beating him savagely. Joey howled. The audience, thinking it was all part of the show, laughed louder, and "applause shook the house". Newspapers the following day praised both Grimaldis highly, declaring:

"it was perfectly wonderful to see a young child perform so naturally, and highly creditable to his father's talents as a teacher"

The 1783 pantomime at Drury Lane was almost his last. Required to play a cat and unable to see clearly through the badly fitting visor of the headpiece, the four year old Joey vanished down an open trap on stage, falling several feet, breaking his collarbone and suffering nasty contusions to the body. Immediately rushed to a surgeon, he was unable to complete the season, but with surprising speed, recovered enough to appear in the Easter pantomime at Sadler's Wells. For the next few years he appeared at both theatres on a regular basis, earning 15 shillings (75p) a week at each.

As the century entered its final quarter, new entertainments were presented. Philip Astley (1742-1814) an ex-cavalryman and trick-rider had appeared in an improvised ring at Halfpenny Hatch, near the Thames, demonstrating riding and sword play. Discovering he could stand upright if his horse trotted in a circle, he found fame by riding with one foot on the saddle and the other foot touching his head. A hat was passed around the watchers when the performance ended. By 1770, he had made enough money to open Astley's Ampitheatre, or the New British Riding School, on London's South Bank. Here he presented the first British Circus, with tight-rope walkers, equestrian demonstrations, wild animal acts, and jugglers, etc., preceded by the ever popular pantomime. It was Astley who introduced Clowns into the Circus, for by the time pantomimes were dropped from Big Top presentations, Clowns had become an integral part of the Circus world.

One of Astley's Clowns, Dicky Usher, is credited with the famous catchphrase used by Clowns in the Harlequinades of the 19th century. At the end of the Astley pantomimes, when spectators, who could stand in the sawdust ring for half-price, had left the area, new sawdust was laid down for the Circus part of the entertainment. Usher would then leap into the ring and call out "Here we are again" and the Circus would begin. He also caused great amusement by sailing up the nearby Thames in a bathtub drawn by four quacking geese. It was not discovered until many years later, that the tub had been towed by a boat sailing almost unnoticed a few dozen yards ahead.

Emulating the idea, a later Clown advised that he would make his stage entrance in a grand coach, ostensibly drawn by twenty-four tom cats, but in reality simply attached to the long rope upon which a concealed stagehand was pulling at the opposite side. The management thought it an excellent idea and advertised it widely. As loud orchestral entrance music struck up, the coach was pulled on and the panic stricken, howling and spitting animals scattered in all directions. Covered in screeching, clawing cats, the coach and its lacerated Clown were dragged across stage and into the wings to the hysterical laughter and applause of the audience.

In 1782, The Royal Circus was opened in London, a direct rival to Astley, and in 1886, John Palmer's new Royalty Theatre was opened to replace Gifford's old building in Goodman's Field, with the aforementioned Carlo Delpini as its principal attraction.

The Royalty Theatre's pantomimes were ambitious. In *The Four Quarters of the World* a procession depicting America, Asia, Europe and Africa, wended their way around the "orchestra" and Circle before returning to the stage, each pulled by teams of horses, leopards and tigers. Furious at the reception of this spectacle, Sheridan reported Palmer to the authorities as being in breach of the Theatres Act of 1752, and had him closed down.

Almost immediately, it re-opened with another pantomime and Delpini was the Clown. To the delight of both Royal Theatres, Delpini uttered the words "Roast Beef" on stage without musical accompaniment and was jailed. Palmer was hauled before the magistrates who dismissed the case, but the Royal Theatres brought pressure to bear which resulted in them being removed from the Bench for incompetence and fined £100 each.

The dispute had an unexpected backlash. Sadlers Wells, realizing they could be treated similarly, applied for a patent, and as a result, the new Act of 1788 gave them permission, together with The Royalty, Astley's and the Royal Circus, "to exhibit singing, dancing, pantomime and music, on payment of double the usual sums and sureties" from Easter Monday until the 15th of September each year. They were not however, permitted to sell, serve or supply liquors, wines or beer during the performances. All other music houses could present songs and dances only.

In March 1788, aged 75, Guiseppi Grimaldi died of dropsy, and the family's fortunes changed drastically. In his will, instructions had been left that his "effects and jewels" be sold by public auction, and the proceeds divided between his two sons, Joseph and John (born two years after his brother) when they reached the age of 21. A Long Acre lace maker by the name of Hopwood was appointed joint executor, but the boys were never to see a penny of it. After secretly using the Grimaldi money for his own business, Hopwood went bankrupt and fled the country, leaving the family destitute.

Realizing that Grimaldi's family were in serious trouble, Sheridan, unasked, increased Joey's salary to £1 a week for the pantomime season, and agreed to let Rebecca Brooker, whom he had contracted as a dancer at Drury Lane, to take similar employment at Sadler's Wells also, thus doubling her income. The Management at Sadler's Wells, still smarting after the authorities had refused to give them a licence to provide singing, dancing and musical pieces not seen at the Royal Theatres (no piece lasting more than half an hour and no more than two pieces in one evening) throughout the year, as opposed to their usual licence, which allowed them to present these without interference from Easter Monday until September when the Royal Theatres re-opened, at once reduced Joey's salary from 15 shillings (75p) per week to three (15p) in the cause of economy. When his mother protested, she was told politely that "if the alteration didn't suit her, she was at perfect liberty to transfer his valuable services to any other house".

Having little choice, Rebecca accepted the situation and Joey kept his job, playing small parts, helping out in the property room, and assisting the carpenters and scenery painters. Eight year old John Brooker, however, detesting stage life, ran away to sea as a cabin boy in 1789 and for the next fourteen years sailed the world under an assumed name, making no contact with his worried family.

At Drury Lane, Joey fell under the influence of the French tumbler and dancer, Jean Baptist Dubois, a Clown of such value to the theatre that when his wife died in 1796, the pantomime was postponed as a mark of respect. It was Dubois who added colour to the white costume of Pierrot the Clown, and one of his most remarkable routines was a dance in clogs and blindfold on a stage dotted with new laid eggs. To a hornpipe accompaniment, he would leap, pirouette and gambol without breaking or cracking a single one of them. Without a doubt, Dubois's coaching of young Joey was instrumental in the development of Grimaldi's eventual mastery of pantomimic art, and some years later the two clowns shared top billing in the Sadler's Wells pantomime of 1800.

At Drury Lane more problems manifested themselves. Linley, Ford and Sheridan no longer ran the Theatre Royal. Sheridan had bought Ford's part of the patent, and as the company lurched from disaster to disaster, he turned over its management to John Philip Kemble (1757-1823) the actor brother of the famous Sarah Siddons (1755-1831). Kemble was noted for his lack of humour but was an astute businessman and soon got down to the task of reorganizing Sheridan's dealings. Like Garrick before him, he made a clean sweep of all outmoded practices, demanding, and getting, higher standards and greater efficiency, though his struggle to keep Sheridan's constant spending in check made things almost impossible. A further worry developed when it was discovered that the old building, which had stood since 1674, was falling apart. Unconcerned, Sheridan decided to rebuild at an estimated cost of £150,000.

While the theatre was being torn down in 1791, he moved his company to the Haymarket, but even in the smaller theatre misfortune continued to dog his steps. His beloved wife Elizabeth died in childbirth, and as he struggled to come to terms with the blow, he discovered that not only had the re-building estimates been exceeded by £70,000, but the Patent he had paid so much for was not in fact the Davenant one; merely a licence granted by the late Queen Anne. Sheridan had to find the original document, which was still in the hands of the Rich family and buy it from them; an expense he could ill afford. Only by selling shares at £100 each was he able to raise the necessary funding required to complete the theatre and satisfy the authorities.

As all this was going on, young Joey continued to work. Every morning he would walk from their lodgings near Drury Lane to Sadler's Wells to rehearse at ten. By two o'clock, he was back home for dinner. Returning to Sadler's Wells in time for the first performance at six o'clock, he worked until eleven or thereabouts, then made his way back to Drury Lane to sleep, having made some twenty costume changes in the interim.

By 1794, at the age of fifteen, his salary at the newly built Drury Lane had risen to £3 a week and at Sadler's Wells, he was earning £4, perhaps a result of his first personal press notice (after playing Jacky Suds in the 1792 *Mars's Holiday, or a Trip to the Camp* and a Dwarf in the pantomime afterpiece.)

> "The comic abilities of this youth are very great – we wish him his deserved success."

As the Hag, Morad, in Tom Dibdin's *The Talisman of Orosmanes; or Harlequin made Happy* (1796), and appearances in *The Monster of the Cave; or Harlequin and the Fay* and *Blue Beard, Black Beard, Red Beard and Grey Beard* (1798) his reputation began to grow. His proposal to Maria Hughes, eldest daughter of Richard Hughes, part proprietor and manager of Sadler's Wells was accepted and their marriage on Saturday May 11th was followed by a wedding supper at the Wells and a dinner for the carpenters the following day. Their happiness was not to last. Within a year, Maria had died in childbirth and the loss of his wife and child brought the d istraught Joey to the edge of a mental breakdown. It was not until Sheridan insisted he returned to Drury Lane for the Christmas pantomime *Harlequin Amulet; or The Magic of Mona* (1799) he began to pull himself together.

Though Grimaldi's performance as Punch and Clown were first class, the role was almost too much for the grief stricken man. As the monstrous Punch, he had to wear a huge and heavy hump on his back, a weighted chest piece, high sugar loaf hat, hook-nosed mask, and large wooden shoes. The material of his fantastic costume was thick and heavily decorated and in addition, there was a great amount of comic

71

business to perform for the first six scenes of the piece. By the time the transformation scene came along, he was in some distress and the effort to continue as Clown was enervating. Nevertheless, this pantomime earns a place in theatrical history.

James Byrne, the Dancing Master at Drury Lane and who played Harlequin in this production, had been aware for some time that the role of Clown was fast becoming the "star role" of the Harlequinades. In an attempt to draw attention back to where he believed it should be, he redesigned the Harlequin costume, turning it into a skin tight, wrinkle-free cat-suit with diamond shaped coloured patches sewn all over it, outlined with tinsel and spangles. To this was added a white frilled collar, bicorn hat and a soft black domino mask. It was to remain the costume that every Harlequin wore till the end of his days.

In Grimaldi's opinion, Byrne was the best Harlequin he had ever seen, but the character never regained his old popularity. From this time onwards, he gradually became the butt of almost as many indignities as Pantaloon; beaten, blown up, forced through mangles, fired from cannons, or "accidentally" beheaded. (Though like the comical villains in modern-day animated cartoons, always being magically restored in time for the next Clown-inspired disaster.)

Returning to Sadler's Wells for the Easter pantomime *Peter Wilkins; or Harlequin in the Flying World* in which he played Guzzle, the drinking Clown, (Dubois was Gobble, the eating Clown) Grimaldi introduced the new deep pocketed, baggy and multi-coloured costume inspired by Dubois, that immediately made him stand out to the audiences. Also new were the crimson half-moon markings on his cheeks and the wig with its distinctive hairstyle. The most important change, however, was not the costume and make-up, but the character of Clown himself. From being the familiar stupid and clumsy servant of "traditional" Harlequinades, in Grimaldi's incarnation of the role he became a gluttonous, inventive, mischievous and light-fingered schoolboy in the shape of a grown man. The greed on his face at the sight of a table piled high with eatables, convulsed the audience. His attempts at innocence when preparing to commit a crime, reduced them to tears, and his routines with Buttered Slides, Sausage Stealing and Red Hot Poker became essential parts of all future Harlequinades. Grimaldi, as one historian was to say:

"Produced all his effects by acting – by his comic mugs which he drew, by the tortuousness of his pantomimic action, by the naivete of his blunders and by the genuine humour of his practical jokes. He did not call in the aid of acrobatics and dancing upon stilts, walk upon barrels, or play the fiddle behind his back; nor did he seek to gain the applause of his audience by astonishing leaps and feats of strength. He trusted to all the force of his natural humour; and such was his power that he made a success of pieces that were utterly wanting even in the commonest accessories of spectacle"

When the pantomime closed, and not expecting to be called to Drury Lane until December, Joey agreed to take part in a friend's Benefit in Rochester, the first time he had ever left London. His appearance was well received, and his comic songs encored three times each. The Manageress, the eccentric Mrs. Baker, at once offered him two more nights engagement, the money raised to be shared between them, and when he agreed, rushed on stage herself to make the announcement. So great was the crush for admission that hundreds were turned away at both performances and Joey was booked again for the following March at Maidstone. Returning to London he discovered that instead of a new piece, *Harlequin Amulet* would be presented a second time at Drury Lane, and once again the heavy, uncomfortable Punch outfit would have to be donned. This time the production ran until the end of January 1801, and young Grimaldi was more than relieved to say goodbye to it, departing cheerfully for Maidstone where Mrs. Baker was expecting him to appear as Scaramouche.

Maidstone was a repeat of Rochester, with the street outside the theatre so packed with people from four thirty in the afternoon that carriages were unable to pass and had to be re-routed. As a result, the last performance had barely ended before the delighted Mrs. Baker was proposing two further nights at her Canterbury theatre, some twenty miles distant. Having nothing better to do, Joey agreed, and the process was repeated. When he returned to London he had £311 6s 6d in his pocket; more than two year's wages for four days work.

Drury Lane, however, had a shock in store. Without consulting him, they had decided to revive *Harlequin Amulet* yet again, this time for the Easter pantomime, and proudly announced that "Mr. Grimaldi will appear in his original character." The concerned Joey hurried to Drury Lane and spoke to Kemble, explaining he was already engaged to appear at Sadler's Wells and couldn't possibly appear at the same time for Drury Lane. Kemble replied that as a legitimate theatre, Drury Lane had first claim on his services, and Grimaldi must tell Sadler's Wells he could not appear for them. Grimaldi shook his head. He was a man of his word. Kemble shrugged his shoulders, bid him good morning and walked away. The next day, Grimaldi's name was replaced on the posters and a new one inserted. The revival lasted only one night.

As mentioned earlier, Grimaldi was now appearing not only in the pantomimes, but in the musical "plays" that the Wells mounted in order to avoid the "No speech" ruling and it was in one of these productions that he appeared next. *The Great Devil, or The Robber of Genoa* came at the end of the 1801 season, and in it, Joey played Nicola, the robber lieutenant, and a smaller role. In addition he also appeared in the little burletta that followed it, then as clown to the rope-dancer, and finally Clown in the pantomime, making nineteen changes of costume each evening. On June 26th, Grimaldi received a letter from Drury Lane.

Drury Lane Theatre

Sir,
I am requested by the proprietors to inform you that your services will be dispensed with for the next ensuing season."

The philosophical Joey continued to appear in *The Great Devil* but as the production neared its end, once again he met with a serious injury. In the act of drawing a pistol from his boot, the trigger of it caught in the boot-loop, and discharged its contents. Grimaldi's leg immediately became swollen and the audience howled with laughter as he danced around in agony. Somehow managing to finish the piece, he hobbled off stage where the boot was removed to discover the explosion had not only set fire to his stocking which had continued to smoulder, but the wadding from the pistol was still ablaze and resting on his foot. He was quickly placed under medical care and was out of work for some time, being nursed by a small-part actress from Drury Lane named Mary Bristow, whom he married on Christmas Eve.

The Drury Lane theatre began its season on September 30th, opening with *As You Like It*, and the old success *Bluebeard* as the pantomime. One of the highlights of *Bluebeard* had been a fierce broadsword fight which took place during a difficult scene change, and drew loud applause at every performance. For the original production, this had been arranged by Grimaldi, but no-one in the present company knew the routine so Kemble gave the order to omit it. On opening night, the house was crowded and Sheridan himself was occupying a box with several of his friends. When the scene change came, the audience sat in anticipation of the famous fight sequence, only to hear the sounds of heavy sets being moved behind the curtain. Quickly growing restless, they began to whistle and cat-call. Kemble hurried on stage to explain the delay, but the irate audience demanded their fight, even calling for Kemble to do it himself. It developed into a near riot and the rest of the piece was constantly heckled by the audience. The final curtain fell in a storm of hisses and cat-calls. Sheridan, who had been congratulating himself on the excellent takings, was now in a towering rage. The moment the curtain fell, he dashed on stage and demanded to know what had happened to the fight sequence. It was explained that Joey had been dismissed by Kemble at the end of the last season and Sheridan, who was totally unaware of this, once more exploded with fury. He immediately sent a message to Grimaldi's home, requesting him to attend the theatre the following day, and on greeting the twenty two year old performer, not only apologised profusely, but reinstated him with an unexpected rise in salary. Even the autocratic Kemble greeted Joey with deference from that time on.

There was no pantomime at Drury Lane the following year, though the birth of his son, Joseph Jnr. in November made Grimaldi a very happy man. In 1803, however, appearing in the play *A Bold Stroke for a Wife*, on entering the Green Room, he was greeted by a well dressed man who turned out to be no other than his long lost brother, John. After fourteen years at sea, he had returned to London with the sum of £600 and hurried to Drury Lane to see his famous brother. The dazed and delighted Joey quickly introduced him to several of the backstage workers, then after arranging to meet him when the play ended, hurried off to prepare himself.

As the evening went on, John waited in the Green Room, listening to the laughter and applause of the audience. As soon as the final curtain fell, Joey raced off to change then returned to escort his brother to the new home he and his family shared with Rebecca. The room was deserted. Puzzled, Joey searched the theatre and surrounding streets, then remembering the £600 John had been carrying, became very concerned and called the police. Despite a massive investigation, John Brooker was never seen or heard of again and his disappearance remains one of theatreland's greatest mysteries.

When Kemble left to become manager at Covent Garden, a Mr. Wroughton took over his position and it was he who inadvertently caused Grimaldi to sever his connections with Drury Lane. Tobin's comedy, *The Honeymoon* was announced for September 15th, 1805, with dances arranged by James Byrne. So bad was the organization there that no-one remembered Byrne had long since departed, and Wroughton, only discovering this at the last moment, hastily approached Grimaldi who had arranged dances at Sadler's Wells, and offered him the post of Dance Master at an additional salary of £2 per week for the rest of the season. Grimaldi agreed, booked the dancers, devised the pieces, rehearsed them, and within twenty-four hours was basking in audience approval of his efforts.

At the end of the week, collecting his increased salary from Mr. Peake, the treasurer, he was shown a letter signed by Mr. Graham, a magistrate and head of affairs at Drury Lane, confirming the arrangement and congratulated. A few weeks later, on Saturday, October 26th, finding the extra £2 was missing, he asked Wroughton where it was, and was brusquely told that the matter was out of his hands.

The following day, Joey and his wife were walking in Bow Street when they met an old friend who, on hearing the story, persuaded Joey to apply for a position at Covent Garden. Knowing that Kemble was now manager, Grimaldi expressed doubts, but on Monday morning he was welcomed with open arms and before the day was out had signed a contract for £6 a week for the first season, rising to £8 a week in the third. It was also agreed that he could continue working at Sadler's Wells as before.

On returning to Drury Lane where he played Pan in the ballet, *Terpsichore* he was confronted by Mr. Graham, who had heard of the matter, and accused of deserting the company after all their kindnesses to him. Grimaldi replied that if Graham had not broken the terms of his agreement, he would never have approached Covent Garden, but Graham, in front of the whole company, denied an agreement had ever been made. When Grimaldi informed him that Mr. Peake had shown him the letter, Graham was furious, and snapping that Peake was a fool for having done so, stormed off vowing to bring a legal action. On the 9th of November, Joseph Grimaldi left Drury Lane theatre after 24 years of service. One year later, on the 26th December, 1806, at Covent Garden theatre, he became the greatest name in the history of British pantomime.

*T*he Easter pantomime at Sadler's Wells was *Harlequin and the Water Kelpie* for which Grimaldi devised a dance with living vegetables but with his debut at Covent Garden rapidly approaching, he began to worry about which show to do. It was suggested that he might like to try the character of Orson in the play *Valentine and Orson* which had not been performed for many years but would be perfect for him. Grimaldi agreed, and studied hard, making his first appearance on October 10th, 1806. In his own words, it was the most difficult role he had ever undertaken but was a huge success and he was to revive the role again and again for several years.

The pantomime next suggested found little favour with Joey. Instead of the fantastic scenery and splendour of previous years, there was to be little or no "finery", the characters "ordinary" and very little magic involved. In short, a reversal of almost everything that pantomime stood for. Had it not been for Joey's insistence, even the spangles would have been removed from Harlequin's costume.

The management at Drury Lane, hearing through the grapevine that something unusual was in preparation at the rival house and Grimaldi was to star, took the unprecedented step of opening their own pantomime three days early in an attempt to crush them. It was a huge and glittering spectacle, but suffered from an almost complete lack of comedy. On opening night, Dec. 23rd, much to Wroughton's concern, the audience quickly grew restless, hissing and jeering began, and finally, with the place in an uproar, the curtain was lowered mid performance.

A night rehearsal of the new Covent Garden pantomime was held as soon as Christmas Day ended, though the cast were anything but in festive mood. The lack of gorgeous trimmings and showy processions dampened the enthusiasm of all but the quietly confident authors, Tom Dibdin and Charles Farley, and before the curtain rose on Opening Night, a feeling of dread was hanging above the entire company.

The main piece of the evening was *George Barnwell*, a popular old "war horse", but the packed and noisy audience were waiting impatiently for the pantomime after-piece. When finally the stage was ready and the curtain rose on a simple English village green with a violent storm raging overhead, the auditorium grew silent. As scene followed scene, the action of the piece drew more and more laughter and applause, and when the final curtain fell, the auditorium exploded with a frenzy of cheers and shouts that almost rocked the building.

The reception to *Harlequin and Mother Goose; or The Golden Egg* resounded across Britain like no other pantomime had ever done. For ninety-two nights, it played to packed houses, being the whole remainder of the season, and put over £20,000 in the theatre's coffers. On the 88th night, Grimaldi took a Benefit with a triple bill of the play *Man of the World*, a Comic ballet, and *Mother Goose*, which produced the amazing sum of £679 18s.

It should be mentioned here that the *Mother Goose* of Dibdin and Farley, had a far different story to the one we see today, though several elements of it were used in the more familiar 1902 version. Following the Sheridan pattern, there were four scenes in the "opening" and fifteen in the Harlequinade, not counting the "Grand Finale", and though a Patent holding house, there was no spoken dialogue. Musical accompaniment was played and essential dialogue was written on scrolls carried by the principals.

It began, as mentioned previously, with a raging storm, and the figure of Mother Goose descending from the clouds on the back of a gander. As she lands offstage, the storm ends and a rainbow forms. A mixed chorus of peasants enter who sing and dance to celebrate the forthcoming wedding of Squire Bugle (Grimaldi) and Colinette. Colinette then enters with her guardian Avaro. A band of huntsmen, grooms and servants appear from the Hall and are followed by Squire Bugle dressed in hunting pink. Colinette is presented to him, but turns away and greets Colin, who is at the window of a cottage. Avaro pulls her away, indicating she must marry Bugle. She points at the tomb of the Squire's late wife which stands centre. The Squire sings

> "First wife's dead, there let her lie.
> She's at peace, and so am I."

He attempts to lead her to the church, but she pulls away and runs to Colin who has just entered. As the Squire attempts to have Colin put in the stocks, the town Beadle enters with Mother Goose under arrest for being a witch. Bugle orders her to be ducked in the local pond, but Colin rescues her and she casts a spell on the tomb before running off. The tomb opens, and the ghost of Bugle's wife appears. Terrified, he runs away followed by the chorus, leaving Colin and Colinette to express their love in song before they too make an exit.

The second scene, Mother Goose's Habitation, is a nighttime woodland scene, where surrounded by spirits in fantastical costumes who dance as she sings, Mother Goose vows to "plague the Squire and ensure that Colin marries Colinette". Following her exit, Colin enters unhappily and Mother Goose re-appears with her Golden Goose which she gives to him for saving her life, telling him that every day it will lay him a golden egg if he takes care of it.

In scene Three, back at Alvaro's home, the old man is found with Colinette. Colin and the goose enter, and Alvaro demands they leave. Colin shows him a golden egg the goose has laid, and Alvaro at once joins Colinette and Colin's hands. Alvaro then produces a knife intending to kill the goose and get all the gold at once. Colin prevents him, but the Squire appears and Colin, afraid of losing Colinette, hastily agrees to the death of the goose. At once it vanishes, and Mother Goose appears. With a wave of her wand, she changes Colin into Harlequin and Colinette to Columbine, and taking the golden egg, transforms the house into a vast cave by the sea before tossing the egg into the water. She then tells them they must wander the earth forever unless the egg is found again and transforms the cave back into Alvaro's house.

A tap of her wand changes Avaro into Pantaloon and Bugle into Clown, and before leaving, gives Harlequin his magic baton with the warning that he takes better care of it than he did the goose. A few moments later the Goose is seen to fly through the air with Mother Goose sitting on it. Pantaloon and Clown attempt to seize Harlequin but he leaps through the face of a Grandfather clock and vanishes. The clock face is replaced by a Huntsman holding a gun. The Clown opens the door to discover a little Harlequin as a pendulum and calls for the huntsman to fire. He does so, Clown falls over backwards, Harlequin re-enters from the clock, takes Columbine's hand and they dance merrily off. The chase begins with Pantaloon riding piggy-back on Clown, and for the rest of the pantomime, the chaos of the Harlequinade is played out.

In one scene, Clown, in pursuit of Harlequin, enters an inn and sees a table set with a delicious looking meal. Sitting in a chair to eat, Harlequin enters un-noticed and taps the table with his magic baton. The table at once rises into the air. Clown looks round to discover the table gone and wanders around looking for it. Finally seeing it, he sits in the chair again and the table descends. As he is about to eat, his chair, propelled by a long wooden pole emerging from the floor, shoots upwards taking him with it and he yells in fright. Pantaloon enters with the Landlord, and seeing the problem, rushes off for a saw. After much comic business, the chair descends and all three prepare to eat at their own tables. All the chairs fly upwards with their occupants and jig up and down like carousel horses. Harlequin and Columbine enter and sit at a fourth table. Harlequin taps it with his magic baton and a meal miraculously appears, complete with lighted candelabra. After dining, they dance off leaving the others suspended helplessly in the air and calling for help.

Later on, the lovers arrive at St Dunstan's Church where the clock descends allowing them to change places with the two figures that strike the hour. Pantaloon and Clown arrive and Harlequin changes their hats to bells which the figures strike with their hammers. An orchestral scene follows when Clown imitates musicians by playing on a tin kettle and various other domestic items (a kind of early Spike Jones routine) but finally Harlequin finds the golden egg in "The Mermaid's Cave" and the lovers celebrate. Pantaloon and Clown appear and manage to confiscate the magic bat, but at this point, Mother Goose re-appears and Harlequin is able to present her with the egg. At once she forgives them all, the scene is changed to a "Submarine Pavilion", the chorus appear in suitable costumes and everyone joins in this joyful Finale:

> "Ye patrons kind who deign to view
> The sport we'd fain produce,
> Accept our wish to pleasure you
> And laugh with Mother Goose.
> Who humbly begs on bended legs
> That you, good lack, her cause will back,
> And scorn to crack her Golden Eggs."

Despite the huge success of the pantomime, Grimaldi thought little of it, saying "There was not a trick or situation in it to which he had not been accustomed for many years." Even so, the following season it played again for twenty nights with equal success, and was revived yet again in 1808 at the Haymarket. About the only person not to benefit was author Tom Dibdin who declared later he did not even receive from the theatre manager "the usual cheering clap on the back".

It is said by most researchers that *Mother Goose* was the first pantomime to use the "Big Heads" which featured in the "story" part of later productions right up to the 1880s. These were huge papier-mache heads, painted to represent various stock characters, and were worn over the stylized make-ups of the Harlequinade characters to disguise them before the "transformation" occurred. Together with loosely fitting over-costumes, they were quickly discarded at the wave of a wand, to reveal the "magically altered" personage beneath them. There are many prints that show actors wearing these, and back in the 1950s, I remember W.A. Homburg of Leeds having a wonderful collection of "Big Heads" decorating their costume hire shop a short distance away from the now demolished Empire and Theatre Royal.

If *Mother Goose* was indeed the first production to feature "Big Heads" how strange the change to "Harlequinade" characters must have appeared in the 25 years prior to this, for Sheridan's *Robinson Crusoe* began the whole tradition of on-stage character transformations. Presumably the performers had to work their earlier scenes in full "Harlequinade" make-up, no matter what "ordinary" costume they wore, and the "Big Heads" evolved as a solution to this rather unsatisfactory situation.

The season at Sadler's Wells in 1807 opened with the pantomime *Jan Ben-Jan; or Harlequin and the Forty Virgins* and proved so successful that it ran for the whole season. In it, Grimaldi sang a comic song called "Me and my Neddy" which regularly stopped the show, and at the end of the run he was presented with a pocket watch, its face painted with a picture of himself singing the song. Unfortunately, *Mother Goose* at Covent Garden was still running too, so for several weeks, he played at one theatre, then dashed through the streets on foot to appear at the other.

It was an evening in July, however, when his side-splitting antics at Sadler's Wells were responsible for something far more amazing than the box-office returns. Sitting in the gallery with a group of shipmates was a deaf and dumb man who had been afflicted with his disability through a sunstroke related illness whilst abroad. A fellow sailor, busily signed the comedy songs and patter. Following one of Grimaldi's routines and a violent explosion of laughter from the packed house, the gasping and spluttering sailor uttered his first words in years. "What a damned funny fellow." To everyone's amazement, including his own, he had regained both hearing and speech at the same time.

It is often said that trouble comes in threes. On the 15th October a fire at Sadler's Wells caused the death of eighteen audience members, one a ten year old boy who was trampled to death. A year later, on the 19th September, Covent Garden Theatre burned to the ground, destroying its entire contents including the Great Organ willed to John Rich by Handel, and killing twenty two people of whom three were firemen from The Phoenix Fire Office. At the height of the blaze, the immense draft of heated air inside the building lifted the light basket-work feather-covered Goose used in the pantomime and sent it soaring over the watching crowd, wings outstretched, to vanish in the direction of Lincoln's Inn Fields. The stunned management had barely time to draw up plans for the rebuild-ing when on Feb. 24th 1809, Drury Lane Theatre also burst into flames and within hours was nothing but a smouldering ruin.

A famous anecdote about Sheridan relates how he was summoned from the House of Commons with news of the blaze, and with the Duke of York beside him, hurried to the Piazza Coffee House in Covent Garden to watch the destruc-tion of his beloved building. When friends found him sitting at a window drinking wine and viewing the frantic activity outside, they marvelled at his fortitude, but Sheridan report-edly shrugged and said "May not a man be allowed to drink a glass of wine by his own fireside?"

Though fires have brought death and destruction through-out the centuries, a theatre fire seems somehow worse. A matinee or evening performance at which hundreds, perhaps thousands of people are innocently enjoying themselves, is suddenly turned into a scene of indescribable horror. There are several such stories concerning these tragedies, and the world of pantomime contains perhaps the worse of them all. On a Wednesday afternoon December 30th, 1903, the Iroquois theatre in Chicago was presenting a touring version of the Drury Lane pantomime *Bluebeard*, which starred the famous comedian Eddie Foy as Clown.

As a double octet were singing "In the pale moonlight", a wafting border touched an overhead floodlight and in moments burning muslin was showering the stage. Stagehands rushed forward to smother the flames, whilst the audience, consisting mainly of women and children, began to panic and scramble for the exits. 300 sets of cloths and scenery took light as the safety curtain began to fall, but in mid descent it suddenly stopped and buckled under the intense heat. The cast and orchestra escaped backstage but the terrified audience found most of the exit doors front of house locked. Choking smoke and searing flame ripped through the building in a series of explosions and children were trampled underfoot as the frantic adults beat helplessly at the doors. When the fire was finally extinguished, 600 members of the audience were dead. Only one of the 348 members of the *Bluebeard* company lost her life. Miss Nellie Reed, leader of the Flying Ballet, was already in place for the flying sequence, and unable to free herself was so badly burned she later died in the county hospital. The disaster effectively marked the end of British pantomime in the USA for many years.

During the re-building of The Covent Garden Theatre, the company moved to the Kings Theatre in the Haymarket, but on the 18th Sept 1809, the new building opened and the Christmas pantomime was *Harlequin Pedlar: or The Haunted Well* which played fifty two nights, followed by another revival of *Mother Goose*.

Harlequin Asmodeus: or Cupid on Crutches was presented there in 1810, the outstanding sequence in this being Grimaldi's creation of a humanoid figure created out of vegetables that comes to life and holds a boxing match with him. Mary Shelly's *Frankenstein* was published in 1818, and one wonders if Grimaldi's comical creation could perhaps have inspired her?

The 1811-12 pantomime *Harlequin and Padmanaba: or The Golden Fish* was to cause a sensation. For the first time, a live elephant was introduced on stage. It had been purchased by manager Henry Harris for the sum of 900 guineas (£945) and was to be ridden by a Mrs. Henry Johnson while the Columbine, a Miss Parker, "played up" to it. A buzz of excitement ran through theatrical London. Very few had ever seen an elephant, and demand at the Box Office was great. Alexander Johnson, Drury Lane's chief machinist, was

intrigued and sneaked inside the rival house to see the strange beast about which he had heard so much. After some moments of staring hard at the enormous creature, a friend asked him what he thought of it. "Huh" snorted Johnson in disgust. "I should be very sorry if I couldn't make a better elephant than that".

October 10th 1812 saw the re-reopening of Drury Lane Theatre, but Sheridan had gone. Following the terrible fire, the Drury Lane company had taken over the Lyceum Theatre in Wellington Street. A minor theatre, able only to stage exhibitions, firework displays musical items and equestrian displays (Philip Astley used it in 1794 when his own circus was destroyed by fire, and Mme. Tussaud gave the first exhibition of her waxworks here in 1802,) a new licence had been obtained allowing the homeless Royal House to operate there until re-building at Drury Lane was completed. Sheridan approached the famous brewer, Samuel Whitbread, M.P., a relation of his second wife, for help, but Whitbread although sympathetic, had no intention of letting Sheridan run the theatre into debt again. Discovering that £436,971 was owed to creditors, Whitbread formed a Committee, excluding Sheridan firmly, and bought out the Patentees. At a cost of £300,000, the new Drury Lane theatre rose from the ashes and opened on October 10th, 1812. Sheridan never recovered from the loss of his theatre. Drinking heavily, and following a mental breakdown, he died in poverty only four years later.

The year 1812 brought new fame to Grimaldi when in *Harlequin and the Red Dwarf; or The Adamant Rock* he outraged the "Brass" of the Horse Guards, by a comical routine outside a farrier's shop. After watching an Hussar officer in all his finery passing by, Clown attempts to imitate him by donning a pair of red pantaloons, then slipping his feet into two varnished coal scuttles for boots, adding brass candlesticks for spurs, a muff for a cap, plus a false beard and drooping mustache, he clattered about the stage waving a scimitar, chortling with glee at his own inventiveness. The whole house roared with laughter, but the Hussars sitting in the stage box were not amused. A letter was sent to the theatre threatening withdrawal of their patronage if Joey was permitted to continue his "damned infernal foolery". When the contents were made public, the delighted Londoners laughed a second time and clamoured for more even louder.

The ingenuity of Grimaldi was unbounded. Over the next few years he invented routines such as "Bathing the baby", "Bottomless pockets", and the original of the "Sausage gag" so beloved by the audiences of today – even though the start of it has been omitted for years.

Clown and Pantaloon are outside a butcher's shop. They want to buy sausages but have no money. Clown attempts to steal them, but is chased out of the shop by the butcher. A delivery boy arrives carrying a machine which bears the legend "The New American Sausage Machine" which he puts down outside the shop before exiting. Clown and Pantaloon examine it. A snobbish man enters followed by his little dog. He crosses and exits. Clown picks up the dog, pops it into the machine, turns the handle and a string of sausages emerge from the other end. The man returns and whistles for his dog. The sausages hurry towards him and all run off in fright.

From that time on, living sausages have sprung out of pies and ovens in countless pantomimes and a great deal of comic business has developed from the attempts to recapture them. The so-called "Wuff 'n' puff" gag is merely another version of the same routine, using strings of marabou feather which are, of course, fluffier, more brightly coloured and less likely to snag on the steel rings screwed into the French flat facings.

In 1814, Grimaldi had two Benefit nights at Sadler's Wells and during the second one, he relates, *Robinson Crusoe*, was included, with twelve year old J. S. Grimaldi (1802-1832) playing Man Friday to his father's Clown, thus making him the third generation of Grimaldis to appear in Sheridan's creation. Though the old Clown may be correct, (and who should know better?) it must be stated, however, that the younger Grimaldi's official debut was in *Harlequin and Fortunio*, the following year, and *Robinson Crusoe* is not listed as having been performed there in 1814.

Harlequin Whittington at Covent Garden in 1815 became Joey's next big success, and it was here the pantomime had him appearing as Dame Cecily Suet, later transformed to

Clown to sing "All the world's in Paris", a satirical swipe at the craze for fashionable English to holiday in France.

"London now is out of town,
Who in London tarries?
Who can bear to linger here
When all the world's in Paris?"

Although songs had always been part of pantomimes, Grimaldi was now introducing numbers that outlived the show. "An Oyster crossed in Love", "Tippetywitchet" and "Me and my Neddy" were just a few, but the one he introduced at Sadler's Wells in *The Talking Bird*, 1819 was to remain popular until the 20th century. It was "Hot Codlins". Codlins were toffee apples and the song was a fore-runner of the Song Sheet routine in which the final word of each verse is shouted by the audience. The lyrics are set below:

A little old woman her living she got
By selling hot codlins, hot!, hot!, hot!;
And this little woman, who codlins sold
Tho' her codlins were hot, she herself felt cold.
So to keep herself warm, she thought it no sin,
To fetch for herself a quartern of .... (Audience shout "Gin")

Grimaldi, shocked, says "Oh, for shame". Then sings the chorus:
Ri tol iddy, iddy, iddy, iddy,
Ri tol iddy, iddy, ri rol lay.

This little old woman sets off in a trot,
To fetch her a quartern of hot! hot! hot!
She swallowed one glass, and it was so nice,
She tipp'd off another in a trice;
The glass she fill'd till the bottle shrunk,
And this little old woman they say got .... (Audience shout "Drunk")

Another shocked look from Grimaldi, "Oh, how dreadful" and into chorus.

This little old woman, while muzzy she got,
Some boys stole her codlins hot!, hot! hot!
Powder under her pan put, and in it round stones;
Says the little old woman "These apples have bones"
The powder her pan in her face did send,
Which sent the old woman on the latter .... (Audience shout "End")

Grimaldi, even more shocked, rubs his bottom, "How could you?" then into chorus.

The little old woman then up she got,
All in a fury, hot! hot! hot!
Says she "Such boys, sure, never were known;
They never will let an old woman alone"
Now here is a moral, round let it buzz
If you mean to sell codlins, never get .... (Audience shout "Muz")
("Muz" was a nineteenth century word for muzzy or drunk)

A final shocked look from Grimaldi, then everyone joins in the chorus.

A slightly modernised version of the song was used in the show *Joey-Joey* based on Grimaldi's life in the 1960s with the audience joining in wholeheartedly.

At the end of 1819, Grimaldi began to complain of agonising pains in his limbs, possibly due to the numerous injuries he had sustained throughout his career, but perhaps a virulent form of arthritis. At times he wept with pain during the scene changes, though his efforts on stage continued to convulse the audiences. During one performance at Covent Garden, King George IV laughed so loudly he burst the stays in his corset, and was seen to leave the theatre afterwards, still chuckling at his favourite Clown.

By early 1821, Grimaldi's health was causing great concern to the managements. Men were posted to catch him as he stumbled off-stage and several had to support him until his next entrance. Medications proved useless and though he continued to appear, by 1823 he was so ill with spasms and cramps, his role in *Harlequin and Poor Robin; or The House that Jack Built* at Covent Garden, had to be played by his son, J.S. The boy was a great success but the show had a mixed reception, *The Theatrical Observer* said:

"The absence of the King of Clowns leaves a blank in our enjoyment of this piece. But he has abdicated the throne of Fun and is succeeded by Joey the Second, who, though a young disciple of Momus, possesses eminent qualities; He can knock his head against a post with double the force of his revered parent and perform sundry feats of agility in an equally eminent style; but his grin is not so overpowering – his voice does not possess the same racy chuckle, and he neither sings nor eats oysters."

The older Grimaldi continued to weaken, but managed a final Benefit at Sadler's Wells on Monday, 17th March, 1828, (in which the young Joey also appeared) before becoming dangerously ill. On June 17th, after being refused a Benefit at Covent Garden and being barely able to stand, he was carried on stage at Drury Lane, where seated in a chair he performed a short scene from Dibdin's *Harlequin Hoax,* sang "Hot Codlins" and made his final speech.

> "It is four years since I jumped my last jump – filched my last oyster – boiled my last sausage – and set in for retirement. Not quite so well provided for, I must acknowledge, as in the days of my clownship, for then, I daresay, some of you remember, I used to have a fowl in one pocket and sauce for it in the other. Tonight has seen me assume the motley for a short time – it clung to my skin as I took it off, and my old cap and bells rang mournfully as I quitted them forever"

After bidding his audience "That greatest earthly good – Health" he was helped off stage for the last time. Said *The Times*:

> "Never was there such a concatenation of Clowns, Columbines, Harlequins and Pantaloons as here gathered themselves to grace the final exit of one who was so many years "the king among 'em all". He himself performed in only one of the scenes – a barber's shop from the pantomime of Magic Fire in which he played Clown ... and was received with shouts of applause. He was much affected, but although labouring under great bodily infirmity he bore up safely against it and went through the scene with so much humour that the audience laughed lustily as of old; and they were so delighted with that funny song of his about "blue ruin" and "hot codlins" that there was a general call for repetition. But he was too much exhausted to obey the call immediately, and eventually he was allowed to retire without repeating it."

Mother Goose was revived again and again, but without Grimaldi, the magic was gone. In 1831 a Company was sent to America for a New York production under the leadership of William Blanchard, the actor father of writer E. L. Blanchard. E.J. Parsloe had the Grimaldi role of Clown and Squire Bugle, a Mr. Gay (no relation to John) was Harlequin, and Louisa Johnson was Columbine. During a storm as the ship crossed the Atlantic, Parsloe had a nasty fall and badly injured his spine but struggled to continue the engagement. After three nights, playing to indifferent audiences he was taken ill and died the following morning. The production collapsed, and the penniless Gay wandered West where a Native American tribe who were fascinated by his glittering Harlequin costume are said to have adopted him. This is not so unlikely as it sounds. During a visit to America in 1827 the great actor Edmund Kean had been made Chief of a Native American tribe, and on his return to England, had been discovered at his hotel in Covent Garden by a friend, sitting up in bed swathed in buffalo skins, an eagle-feather head-dress and clutching a tomahawk whilst applying facial markings to complete the illusion.

A numbing blow to the frail Grimaldi, was the sudden death of his only son. It has often been said that J.S.Grimaldi died insane, but in actuality he was subject to epileptic fits, probably brought on by a head injury. This would account for the intermittent performances he was able to give. The inquest on Dec. 17th, 1832, revealed he had sharp pains in his side after returning from the theatre where he had been appearing as Scaramouche in *Don Juan*, and had been vomiting violently throughout the night. His Landlady, Mrs. Walker, had tried to nurse him, but he had grown delirious and had to be held down. The Stage Manager testified that the young Grimaldi had slipped down a ladder whilst going down a stage-trap, and there were bruises on his side, knee and ankle to support the statement though these were not considered to be cause of his death. In Frances Fleetwood's fascinating history of the Conquest Family, (W.H. Allen, 1953) it is suggested that the most probable cause of death was peritonitis aggravated by the fall, and in the light of the inquest findings, I am inclined to agree.

The inconsolable Clown was nursed by his beloved wife of thirty years, but in 1834 and without warning, Mary Grimaldi also passed away. On December 18th 1836, Grimaldi completed his memoirs and celebrated his 58th birthday alone. The old Clown now spent his evenings at his local hostelry, The Marquis of Cornwallis, to which the proprietor, George Cook, would carry him on his back and return him home at the close of business. On May 31st 1837, after thanking the landlord for his evening's entertainment and company, Joseph Grimaldi died in his sleep. He was buried in St James' Chapel grounds in Pentonville, his only mourner from the

Harlequinades, the old Pantaloon, Mr. Norman. Dickens was to write later:

> "To those who do not recollect him in his great days, it would be impossible to convey any adequate idea of his extraordinary performance. There are no standards to compare him with or models to judge him by; all his excellences were his own and there are none resembling them among the Pantomime actors of the present day. The genuine droll, the grimacing filching, irresistible Clown left the stage with Grimaldi, and though often heard of has never since been seen."

*F*ollowing Grimaldi's retirement, several Clowns attempted to assume his mantle, the best it seems to be agreed being Tom Mathews, (1805-1899) who had been Grimaldi's pupil and assistant at Sadler's Wells. He was described by Sir Frank Burnand, long time Editor of *Punch* magazine as being a very droll Clown, doing no acrobatic tricks and no dancing, but who "waddled about bow-legged and was always pilfering in the most innocent manner possible." He would:

"knock frequently at shop doors, hiding himself twice, but immediately after the third knock lying down in front of the threshold so as to ensure the tripping up of the incautious and irate tradesman over his prostrate body, when he, the artful, comic, mischievous Clown, would slip into the shop and reappear with all sorts of stolen goods, hams and turkeys under his arms and sausages hanging out of his pockets, just in time to come into a violent collision with the now furious tradesman, whom he would incontinently floor with one of his own hams, and at the watchword "Look out, Joey; here's a policeman coming", given by his faithful but weak-kneed ally old Pantaloon, he would rush off the stage and on again, followed by a mob, when, in the middle of a

regular "spill and pelt" while everybody appeared to be assault-
ing everybody else, he would somehow or other manage to escape
the hands of several constables as the scene changed, and light
and airy music ushered in the Harlequin, masked, with pretty
Columbine, to execute some graceful pas de deux."

The *Theatrical Journal* enthused:

> "He is the soul of the pantomime; the mantle of old Joey has
> fallen on his shoulders. A universal roar proclaims the mirth he
> provokes. What a thief and what a glutton! Mutton pies are
> devoured by the dozen, and then the look of agony on discover-
> ing a dead cat at the bottom of the basket – such a look is worth
> a whole series of choruses. His good nature, too, is boundless
> and deserving of every praise."

So impressed by his talent were two pickpockets, who after
"lifting his watch" in the street, suddenly recognized him, and
returned it with apologies.

Another great Clown was Redige Paulo, (1787-1835) a
French slack-wire walker, who devised a routine set outside an
old clothes shop which inspired several pantomime gags that
are still in use today.

The doddery Pantaloon buys a second-hand handkerchief
from the ragged old shop-keeper. He puts it in his pocket.
Harlequin waves his baton, and the handkerchief flies out of
Pantaloon's pocket and back into the shop. When Pantaloon
looks for it and finds it missing, he sends Clown to buy another. After replacing it in his pocket, Harlequin waves his baton
again, and once more the handkerchief returns to the shop.
This is repeated several times, each repetition getting faster
and faster, with much bad temper. The old shopkeeper is
spotted laughing in the doorway, and Clown and Pantaloon
rush at him and drag him into the street. At a wave of
Harlequin's baton, the shopkeeper disintegrates into a bundle
of old rags and the two run off in fright.

The last Clowns to mention at this point are Richard
Flexmore (1822-1860) who worked mainly at Covent Garden,
and Harry Payne (1830-1895). Flexmore, son of a comic
dancer, made his first appearance as Clown at the Olympic
Theatre in Wych Street, which equestrian Philip Astley had
built in 1806 to present his shows during the winter seasons.
Married to the daughter of a French Clown, his forte was

spoofing the dancers of the increasingly popular ballet troupes of the day. It was Flexmore who changed the baggy costume of Clown into tights and short-frilled trunks embroidered in braids in order to free his legs of any encumbrance, and he is remembered as the creator of the "Cod" ballets featured in many of today's pantomimes. Said one critic:

> "The life and soul of the Harlequinade was Mr. Flexmore, who displays quite as much humour as activity and during all his extravagant feats and unheard of rascalities never once misses sight of the character he assumed from the beginning. In short, he acts the part as well as tumbles and grimaces it. Besides his well known graphic imitations of opera dancers, Mr. Flexmore performed sundry ingenious feats on a couple of wooden horses in capital mimicry of the exploits at Astley's, and instead of "Hot Codlins" which, though duly called for, he was too hoarse to sing, he danced the sailor's hornpipe to admiration"

An amusing anecdote concerns the arrest of an 18 or 19 year old youth at Drury Lane theatre for attempting to defraud the manager of 10 shillings (50p) by claiming to be Flexmore's son. After reading about it, Flexmore wrote a letter to *The Times* saying:

> "Being myself under 28 years of age, I was certainly a bachelor at the early period of 10. I undoubtably have had many sons presented to me during the performances of the various pantomimes in which I have engaged, all of whom have been christened with the kind encouragement of the public; but this unlooked for offspring having, by the conduct alluded to, evinced symptoms of rather a disreputable tendency, I must respectfully decline to father."

Flexmore's leaps and footwork were the equal of any Harlequin, but like Grimaldi, he became so weakened by his efforts he collapsed during a performance of *Little Red Riding Hood* at Covent Garden, and died the following year aged 38.

By a strange coincidence, at the time of Flexmore's collapse, Harry Payne was in the same production. The twenty nine year old son of W. H. Payne, (who had appeared with Grimaldi) was playing Harlequin, a role that by this time had become little more than an acrobatic dancer. As Flexmore, who had been playing the wolf, (prior to his transformation to Clown) lay on the floor, his costume was hastily stripped from him and Harry Payne was pushed on as a substitute, whilst his brother Fred played Harlequin. Payne was later billed as the last of the great Drury Lane Clowns, writing much of his own Harlequinade material, and though not regarded as having much originality, kept alive the Grimaldi tradition of clowning and was extremely popular.

It was no secret, however, that pantomime was dying. Both in London and the Provinces, productions exceeded the number of inventive Clowns, and managements were forced to fall back on Grimaldi's old successes which were not performed particularly well. For a short time, the Harlequins moved into the limelight again, and Thomas Ellar (1780-1842) was easily the most popular of these.

Ellar's transformation from the character of the "opening" to Harlequin was always followed by the extraordinary effect of rotating his head rapidly "as if the masked face was only a whirling teetotem revolving on the centre of his frilled neck". A description of his art by the poet and essayist Leigh Hunt (1784-1859) is as follows:

> "In comes Harlequin, demi-masked, party-coloured, nimble-toed, lithe, agile, bending himself now this way, now that; bridling up like a pigeon; tipping out his toe like a dancer; then taking a fantastic skip; then standing ready at all points, and at right angles with his omni-potent lath-sword, the emblem of the converting power of fancy and lightheartedness. Giddy as we think him, he is resolved to show us that his head can bear more giddiness than we fancy; and lo! beginning with it by degrees, he whirls it around into a very spin, with no more remorse than if it were a button. Then he draws his sword, slaps his enemy (who has just come upon him) into a settee; and springing upon him, dashes through the window like a swallow".

An hilarious anecdote is told concerning Ellar, who had worked with the great Grimaldi, and in 1825 was appearing in a Parisian production of an English pantomime with James (Jimmy) Barnes, (d.1838) the best loved Pantaloon of all and a noted practical joker.

Sharing lodging in the house of a Madame Bambayet, they also vied for her attentions, but Madame B, having seen Ellar's dazzling Harlequin costume, only had eyes for him. Barnes decided to dampen her ardour. As both were keen fishermen and used to go fishing in the Seine during the daylight hours, he took their box of maggots and emptied its contents underneath Ellar's bedsheets. In the candlelit bedroom, Ellar failed to notice them and bone tired after the performance, fell asleep in minutes. The following morning, Madame Bambayet entered the room to see if anything was required and found the floor awash with squirming and rolling maggots. Barnes was awake, and indicating his still sleeping friend, told her it was nothing to be concerned about; poor Ellar was subject to them. The horrified woman let out a loud shriek and as Ellar was jolted into wakefulness, shaking off hundreds more, she scurried out of the room in great haste. Her infatuation ended, she was more than happy to turn her attentions to Barnes and see the back of the bewildered and easy going Ellar.

Another story tells how Ellar took one of his famous leaps through the scenery, to find in mid air that the stage-carpenter who should have been waiting to catch him, was nowhere in sight. Landing awkwardly, Ellar shattered his wrist, but refused to take action against the man because "the fellow had half a dozen children".

Like many a performer in those days, Ellar's popularity was fleeting. Having been poisoned with mercury by a jealous woman, in 1836 whilst appearing in *Harlequin and George Barnwell* at Covent Garden, he passed out on stage in mid performance. Three years later, and desperately ill, he was reduced to playing a guitar in low class taverns in the East End. Wrote W. M. Thackeray (1811-1863) author of *Vanity Fair*,

> "Our Harlequin Ellar, prince of many of our enchanted islands, was he not at Bow Street the other day in his dirty, faded tattered motley – seized as a law breaker for acting at a penny theatre, after having well nigh starved in the streets where nobody would listen to his old guitar. No one gave a shilling to bless him: not one of us who owe him so much."

A Benefit was arranged for him at the Victoria Theatre, but two years later he was dead.

As audience interest continued to wane, the concerned managements looked for inspiration and at Covent Garden in 1830, it was decided to mount a pantomime with a speaking "opening". It was a calculated risk because back in 1814, when the idea had first been tried with *Dr Hocus Pocus; or Harlequin washed White* at the Haymarket Theatre, the first

97

night audiences had booed it off stage and the curtain fell to loud hisses of disapproval. There is, however, a good reason to remember this unsuccessful pantomime. The storyline, what little there was of it, had dealt with the attempt to wash Harlequin's black-masked face white. After submerging him in a tub of water, it was discovered he had absorbed it all and his grossly bloated figure had to be fed though a mangle in order to squeeze out the liquid and restore him to normality (though now wearing a white mask.) Said *The Times* critic:

> "What this might promise is now useless to conjecture. From the ablution of Harlequin, everything of spirit in the piece seemed to have been washed away."

Be that as it may, for two thirds of the 20th century a derivative of the routine was a staple ingredient of Widow Twankey's Laundry in *Aladdin* and though the past thirty years have seen it dropped from many productions because today's sophisticated children have no idea what a mangle is, a comical steam press could surely be substituted if modern directors fancied reviving this "traditional" bit of comic business.

Sad to say, Covent Garden's *Harlequin Bat and Harlequin Pat; or The Giant's Causeway* was just as unsuccessful as its forerunner. The spoken opening was set in Ireland, and concerned the search of King Brian Boru for his bride who had been kidnapped by King O'Rourke. On being transformed for the Harlequinade, instead of a magic slapstick, the Harlequin was presented with a magic shillelagh. The unimpressed critic of *The Times* reported:

> "It was one of the least meritorious we have seen. The announcement had raised our expectations somewhat higher than usual. The advertisements in the playbills that there was to be a speaking opening and the emphatic large letters in which that advertisement was printed had led us to believe that some attempt was to be made which would revive these entertainments which have at former periods been so deservedly attractive. There was not much novelty in these tricks and transformations, and, ... we don't remember any allusion to the follies of the day. The Pantaloon is the best that perhaps has ever been seen; and as for the Clown, Mr. Paulo, he is as good as the rest – better than most of his competitors; but alas! the real Clown departed with poor Grimaldi and we fear the spirit of pantomime has departed along with him"

The piece was never revived.

This time however, audiences were not so judgmental, for spoken openings became general usage at London's Royal theatres *and* in the growing number of provincial ones that were granted licences by their local authorities. We can safely assume that Essayist and critic William Hazlitt (1778-1830) would not have supported the change, as ten years earlier he had dismissed a revival of Garrick's *Harlequin Invasion* with the following acidic report:

> "It is called a speaking pantomime. We had rather it say nothing. It is better to act folly than to talk it. The essence of pantomime is practical absurdity keeping the wits in constant chase, coming upon by surprise, and starting off again before you can arrest the fleeing "phantom": the essence of this piece was prosing stupidity remaining like a mawkish picture on the stage, and overcoming your impatience by the force of ennui. A speaking pantomime such as this one is not unlike a flying waggon"

By 1840 many pantomimes had returned to the style of Rich's presentations of miraculous mechanical changes, but the tricks had been seen before and audiences looking for newer delights had found them in the *Burlesques*, and *Extravaganzas* of James Robinson Planché, (1796-1880).

The roots of *Burlesque* can be traced back to 1611 and Beaumont and Fletcher's *The Knight of the Burning Pestle* which poked fun at the romantic tales of Arthurian gallantry, the hero of the piece being a grocer's apprentice. *The Rehearsal* by George Villiars in 1671 took swipes at the mechanical drama of Restoration plays, while Henry Fielding's 1730 *The Tragedy of Tragedies, or The Life and Death of Tom Thumb the Great* pricked the bubble of seventeenth century tragedies that left the stage littered with corpses.

In *Tom Thumb* the little hero defeats a race of giants and is given in reward, the hand of the King's daughter, Huncamunca. Lord Grizzle, who hoped to marry her, leads an insurrection against the King, but is defeated by Tom who is then swallowed by a cow. The Queen, who is also in love with Tom, kills the messenger who brings her the news. Cleora, a lady in love with the messenger kills the Queen. Huncamunca kills Cleora. Doodle, who loves Cleora kills Huncamunca, Mustacha who loves Huncamunca kills Doodle, and the King kills Mustacha before killing himself, saying:

> "So when the child, whom Nurse from danger guards,
> Sends Jack for mustard with a pack of cards,
> Kings, queens, and knaves throw one another down,
> Till the whole pack lies scatter'd and o'erthrown,
> So all our pack upon the floor is cast,
> And all I boast is- that I fall the last"

The Dragon of Wantley at the Haymarket theatre in 1737, was a spoof on Italian opera, and perhaps the closest thing to a pantomime yet seen. Set near Rotherham in Yorkshire, the villagers are all excited by the news that a dragon has just entered the Squire's residence and consumed all the coffee, toast and butter that had been set out for breakfast. One of the characters, Old Gubbins, asks what is to be done, and his daughter Margery suggests "A valiant knight" named Moore of Moore Hall might be persuaded to kill the dragon. Moore agrees, but his ex lover Mauxalinda tries to kill Margery with a bodkin in a fit of jealousy. She is prevented by Moore and threatened with the Quarter Sessions but pleads:

> "O give me not up to the Law,
> I'd much rather beg upon crutches;
> Once in a Solicitor's Paw,
> You'll never get out of his clutches."

Moore decides to go after the dragon with the words:

> "But first I'll drink, to make me strong and mighty,
> Six quarts of ale – and one of Aqua Vitae"

The dragon is eventually despatched with a kick up the rear by Moore, and as it dies, cries:

> "Oh. Oh. The devil take your toe"

A celebratory chorus is then sung to end the opera:

> "Sing, sing, and roario
> An Oratorio,
> To gallant Morio,
> Of Moore Hall.
> To Margereenia
> Of Roth'ram Greenia,
> Beauty's bright Queenia,
> Bellow and bawl."

The Critic, Sheridan's sublime theatrical burlesque, needs no introduction to theatregoers. It still plays today and remains as funny as ever.

By the close of the eighteenth century, *Burlesque* productions were quite familiar to British audiences, but should not be confused with the various Shakespearean productions such as *Methinks I see my Father* (Hamlet) *Is he jealous?* (Othello) *How to die for Love* (Romeo and Juliet) and *Diamond cut Diamond* (The Merchant of Venice) which were presented as *burlettas* by the minor theatres under the new titles and embellished with songs and dances to escape censure by the authorities. (*Burletta* was defined by the authorities as "*Burlesques* with constant musical accompaniment, and which contained a minimum of five vocal items per act"). These were the closest thing to drama that minor theatres could perform without breaching the law and the application of this rule is remembered by the singing of songs in pantomimes. Had this law never been made, pantomimes could well have developed as plays with dances.

The descendant of Huguenot refugees, J. R. Planché wrote his first *burletta, Amoroso, King of Little Britain*, for a small amateur theatre in Berwick Street. Without his knowledge or consent, it was presented at Drury Lane in 1818 and Blackwoods Magazine described it as "a complete success". The simple plot concerns Amaroso's love for Mollidusta, and Queen Coquetinda's love for Rostando, her cook. A popular item in the *burletta* was the "love" duet between Rostando and Coquetinda:

Coqu: This morning I to Covent Garden went
           To purchase cabbages was my intent,
           But, my thoughts dwelling on Rostando's looks
           Instead of cabbages I asked for Cooks.

Rost: Last night, neglecting fricasses for stews,
           On Coquetinda's charms I paused to muse,
           And, 'stead of charcoal, did my man desire
           To put some Coquetinda on the fire.

The acclaim for *Amoroso* led Robert William Elliston, the actor/proprietor of the Olympic Theatre to ask Planché to provide a speaking Harlequinade/pantomime for Christmas 1818, with songs for the Columbine; the result being *Little Red Riding Hood*. According to the author, the first night (Dec. 21st) was a complete disaster. Every trick failed, not a scene could be opened or closed properly and the curtain fell to a storm of hissing and booing. He reports amusingly, that he sat in a private box with the manager and his family, and listened as the seething Elliston sent an order backstage that not one of the carpenters, scene shifters or property-men was to leave the theatre until he had spoken to them. As soon as the House was clear, the curtain rose again with

> "all the culprits assembled on stage in front of one of the scenes in the piece depicting the interior of a cottage, having a door in one half and a latticed window in the other. Elliston led me forward and standing in the centre, with his back to the foot-lights, harangued them in the most grandiloquent language – expatiated on the enormity of their offence, their ingratitude to the man whose bread they were eating, the disgrace they had brought upon the theatre, the cruel injury they had inflicted on the young and promising author by his side; then pointing in the most tragical attitude to his wife and daughters, who remained in the box, bade them look upon the family they had ruined, and burying his face in his handkerchief to stifle his sobs, passed slowly through the door in the scene, leaving his auditors silent, abashed, and somewhat affected, yet rather relieved at being let off with a lecture. The next moment, the casement in the other flat was thrown violently open, and thrusting in his head, his face scarlet with fury, he roared out, 'I discharge you all'."

The failure of *Red Riding Hood* did not deter Planché. He became not only a prolific writer of pantomimes, comedies and melodramas, but for the 1820 Lyceum production of his *The Vampire; or The Bride of the Isles*, an adaptation of a French melodrama, invented the "Vampire-trap" which became such an important addition to stage machinery for over a hundred years. His interest in historical costuming led to Charles Kemble (1775-1854) requesting him to design and supervise the costumes needed for Covent Garden's production of *King John* in 1823. Came the Dress Rehearsal, and the dismayed cast predicted a riot when the audience saw the result. They were absolutely right, but the riot was of cheers and applause for the stunning effect and the play became the talk of London. Takings of £400 to £600 nightly, soon repaid the costs and *King John* is now remembered as the first play in British stage history to employ accurately represented costumes. Planché's book *History of British Costume*, published in 1834, is still consulted today. A keen musician, he also wrote the libretto for Weber's opera *Oberon* which was produced at Covent Garden in April 1826, the first opera ever having an English text that had not been translated from another language, and it was a singer in this opera who was unwittingly responsible for Planché's role in the evolution of British Pantomime; the formidable Madame Vestris.

Lucy Elizabeth Vestris (nee Bartolozzi) (1797-1856) was married at the age of sixteen to Armand Vestris, a renowned dancer ten years her senior. A vain and vicious man, he was to desert her only a few years later and with his new lover, vanish into Italy to escape his creditors. Making her theatrical debut in 1815 at The King's Theatre in the Haymarket, Lucy Vestris quickly attracted notice for her grace, beauty and "contre alto" voice of the finest order. After a spell in Paris with her husband, during which time they separated, she appeared at Drury Lane in opera and comedy and was the Columbine in the revival of Garrick's speaking pantomime *Harlequin's Invasion*, now retitled *Shakespeare versus Harlequin*, which had irritated Hazlitt so much. Her next piece, the comic extravaganza *Giovanni in London*, (1820) was to firmly establish her as the darling of London.

A revival of a not particularly exciting romp – its theme *Don Giovanni* being too sexually hot for Hades, is returned to the much wickeder place of London where he is redeemed by the love of a good woman – could, according to critics, have been much better written. The success of the show was due entirely to the performance of Madame Vestris in the breeches role of Don Giovanni. It ran for thirty-five nights and made her a household name. Verses, stories and songs about her were circulated, and one enterprising businessman had a profitable season selling plaster-of-paris replicas of the shapely legs that had caused so great a furore and led to the following saucy ballad being published:

Madame Vestris's Legs

1/ Have you heard about this piece of work
All over London town, sir?
It is all about an actress,
A lady of renown, sir;
The case was heard at Marlborough Street,
The truth I will tell you now, sir,
A man had stole the Lady's legs,
Which caused a pretty row, sir.

Chorus: Some villain stole my Lady's legs,
We hope he will get justice
Handsome just above the knee,
The legs of Madame Vestris

2/ Mr. Papara, a gentleman
Of merit was. O fags, sir,
Went unto the Magistrate
About a pair of legs, sir;
He says, kind sir, the legs were mine
And now I do want justice,
They were modelled from a Lady's legs
Whose name is Madame Vestris.

3/ Then sir, says the laughing Magistrate,
I now must ask you, whether
The legs of Madame Vestris
Could not be kept together?
I swear the handsome legs were mine
And hope you'll give the thief a dose,
For it was not in my power,
To keep the legs together close.

4/ I am the man that made the legs,
The model, sir, you now may see,
I made them like my Lady's own,
Exactly just above the knee;
And your worship must commit
the man
And I must ask you, whether
'Twas possible that I could keep
Such handsome legs together.

5/ O, then, says the worthy Magistrate
This case I plainly see, sir.
The legs of Madame Vestris
Are yours above the knee, sir;
And I shall send the thief to jail
In spite of wind and weather,
When the trial does come on,
Bring my Lady's legs together.

6/ Now when the trial does come on
It's true what I report, sir,
You will laugh to see my Lady's legs
Come hopping into court, sir.
If the thief did steal my Lady's legs,
I hope he will get justice,
Was it possible that it could be
The legs of Madame Vestris.

Armand Vestris died suddenly in 1825, and Lucy, relieved at the release from an unhappy marriage, plunged into a series of short-lived affairs with numerous theatrical admirers. It was during this period she was invited by D. E. Morris the despotic and eccentric proprietor of the recently rebuilt Haymarket theatre to appear in another breeches role, Macheath in *The Beggar's Opera* and quickly agreed terms.

Morris is famed for the anecdote regarding an orchestral rehearsal in his theatre where on spotting a player sitting quietly during an orchestral passage, he tapped him on the shoulder and irately demanded to know why he wasn't playing his instrument. The startled man replied that he had several bars rest, to which Morris snapped indignantly, "Rest? Don't talk to me about rest, sir. Don't you get your salary? I pay you to play, not to rest, sir. Rest when you've done your work and not in the middle of it"

Breeches roles might have been created for Vestris. The success of her Macheath in *The Beggar's Opera* led to a reprise of the role at Drury Lane and the verse:

"What a breast! What an eye! What a leg, foot and thigh,
What wonderful things she has shown us!
Round hip, swelling sides, and masculine strides,
Proclaim her an English Adonis."

Her other breeches roles, Don Felix in *Alcaid*, at the Haymarket and Don Carlos in *The Duenna* at Drury Lane drew even larger audiences, though "The Sovereign" remarked sourly:

"This theatrical system of putting the female sex in breeches
is barbarous and abominable"

Vestris however was nothing if not versatile, for she also appeared in the operas of Mozart and Rossini (to which she added, as was the custom, songs of her own choice), and played leading roles in productions of *Hamlet, The Tempest, As you Like it, The Comedy of Errors* and *The Merry Wives of Windsor* with varying success. The song *Cherry Ripe* which she introduced in the 1828 production of *Paul Pry* at the Haymarket can still be heard at Music Festivals all over Britain.

Because of poor managements, by 1829, the financial position at Drury Lane was so bad the theatre could barely function, Covent Garden was so deeply in debt that a special fund was launched to help it, and the Kings in Haymarket had a deficit of £13,000. Returning to London after another successful tour of the provinces, Vestris spotted a notice in *The Times* advertising the availability of Astley's Olympic Theatre in Wych Street. For the sum of £2,000, she signed a contract and on Dec. 6th, 1830, became the first woman ever to manage a London Theatre.

Riding home in her carriage, she saw Planché in Long Acre, stopped, and excitedly hailed him, telling him the news and asking if he had anything she could produce immediately. Although quite busy, with some assistance by his old friend Charles Dance, he revamped an unused *burlesque* and presented it to her. The slight drawback of the Olympic, (as a minor theatre), being unable to present the spoken word without musical accompaniment was easily overcome, for the multi-talented Planché could arrange that too. A piano would tinkle lightly beneath all spoken dialogue. He also suggested that quite unlike the normal practice of using whatever was available, they emulated the earlier *King John* with each costume being "designed individually and collectively to a picturesque and coherent overall scheme". Vestris agreed, but pointed out that a shortage of money would mean a compromise on scenery. The pair finally settled on several items from the Olympic's old stock; "a few clouds, the interior of a cottage, and a well used modern street" making comic references to the latter in the script to "anticipate criticism". As few actors were currently employed, the cast were quickly assembled, and the fare announced.

The *burletta A Roland for an Oliver* starring popular actress Maria Foote would be the main piece of the evening, followed by Planché's *Olympic Revels*. Covent Garden at once objected. The copyright of *A Roland for an Oliver* was theirs. So close to opening night it was a stunning blow for everyone, but the *burletta Mary, Queen of Scots* was quickly substituted and on January 3rd, 1831, the newly decorated and restored Olympic opened its doors. Vestris's new venture was to shake the theatrical world to its core.

*B*efore the dress rehearsal began, Vestris had already broken the first rule of theatrical management by paying her company a week's salary in advance. Never in the history of theatre had this been done before and the other managements were aghast. She had also provided a reasonable break between the final rehearsal and first performance, another broken rule that stunned her rivals. As the entertainment began, the capacity audience were surprised to see the new curtain Madame had installed suddenly part in the middle, each half being drawn up out of sight at the sides and giving a much more elegant appearance than the usual bottom to top scalloping effect.

An even greater surprise was the stunning opening scene designed by Planché. Queen Mary's room in the Castle appeared so authentic it could have been transported from Scotland and rebuilt on the small stage of the Olympic. Furniture had been carefully chosen with the period in mind, and what had not been found in Curio shops had been carved and stained by Vestris's carpenters. The Stuart arms were so clearly depicted, that members of the audience could even identify them on candlesticks and cutlery, and what appeared to be specially woven carpeting covered the floor.

The effect on the public was electrifying. Until that night, stage productions had been performed against painted backdrops, with a minimum of furniture. If one character was to sit during the performance, one chair would be on stage. If two were to sit, then two chairs were set. The characters and action of the play were all that mattered. In the eyes of managements, actors and audiences, what was the point of cluttering the acting area with objects no-one used or referred to?

With regard to costume, performers wore what they liked. Women would wear a favourite gown and display their best jewels, no matter what the character or period demanded, whilst men would often appear in the clothing they wore during the day. Past attempts to display "authentic" costuming were often screamingly funny when one considers the characters the performers were depicting (my own favourite being the 1749 print of James Quin as Coriolanus) but were completely accepted by the audiences of the day. At the Olympic, however, the costumes of the cast had been as carefully researched as the furnishings, and before a word had been spoken on stage, theatrical history had been made.

At the conclusion of the first piece, sustained applause relieved the whole company, but *Olympic Revels* was yet to come and Vestris herself was playing a leading role. The playbills had announced her as Pandora, (a Mettlesome Lady, forged by Vulcan to be passed upon Prometheus, and pleading guilty to the minor offence of uttering notes for her own benefit) This type of punning advertising was to become a feature in *burlesque* and pantomime well into the next century. The three scenes were listed as The Summit of Olympus, with an Olympic Game (at Whist); A street on earth (as unlike Regent Street as possible) and; Prometheus' Work Shop, in Body colours, with the Devil to Pay for Peeping.

Like the later *Orpheus in the Underworld* of Jacques Offenbach in 1858, it portrayed the gods and goddesses of Mount Olympus with somewhat less than reverence, and coupled with the beautiful costumes, the magic of Vestris herself, Planché's witty script and a collection of catchy songs and dances, as the final curtain fell the euphoric audience was shouting for more. Overnight, the one-time run-down building was transformed into the "in" place for London's nobility and every seat was taken for the rest of the season.

Another unexpected benefit came when *Mary, Queen of Scots* was, for some unspecified reason, dropped from the bill. (Maria Foote married the eccentric 4th Earl of Harrington, Lord Petersham, a short time later, so perhaps this had something to do with her sudden retirement from the stage). At the end of the evening's performance, Planché and Charles Dance were leaving the theatre when they overheard several patrons expressing their delight that the show had ended at eleven o'clock instead of well after midnight, which meant that they would be arriving home at a reasonable hour for a change. They at once reported this to Vestris, suggesting that she take advantage of the circumstances and advertise that performances in future would terminate every evening as nearly as possible to eleven o'clock. Madame happily agreed, and when in *Olympic Devils: or Orpheus and Eurydice*, Planché's second *burletta* for Vestris, the final lines were spoken:

> "Since home at eleven you take yourselves,
> It cannot be said that you rake yourselves"

they were invariably greeted with loud laughter and sustained applause.

This new style *burletta* was more to the taste of London audiences than any Drama or pantomime. Drury Lane and Covent Garden were still on the edge of closure, but business at the Olympic was so good that Vestris and Planché felt confident enough to upgrade. Whereas *Olympic Revels* had been staged "on a shoestring", *Olympic Devils* was lavishly mounted with not only beautiful costumes, but scenery to match.

A breathtaking Grecian landscape dominated by the portico of the Temple of Bacchus, opened the show, and the fluted columns of this joined in the general dancing when Orpheus, (played by Vestris) sounded his magic flute. An eerie, shimmering River Styx came next, followed by the spectacular final scene of "Infernal Regions of Tartarus". One of the vocal delights was a quartette sung by Charon, the boatman of the Styx and the three heads of Cerberus, the dog guardian of the Infernal Regions, to the tune of the folk song "Begone dull care".

Vestris ran the Olympic from 1831 to 1839 and made it the most successful theatre in London. Every production filled the theatre and, except for one year when he was legally prevented from working for Vestris, Planché provided an unbroken string of burlettas, each surpassing the previous one in wit, charm and spectacle. In his 1833 *The Deep, Deep Sea*, the legend of Perseus and Andromeda caused laughter when the approach of the sea monster is heralded by this song directed at the King:

Mighty monach, stir your stumps as if Old Nick were following;
A serpent with an awful twist has landed on your shore;
Our gallant soldiers, guns and all, by regiments he's swallowing;
And munching up musicians and composers by the score!

Of council learned in the Law, but *brief* work he is making
Apothecaries just as they were pills, sir, he is taking;
He snaps the parson right in two, as well as his Oration;
And ere the beadle bolts the door, he bolts the congregation!

Mighty monach, stir your stumps, for court and caravansery
Are emptied of inhabitants all crazy with affright;
The monster, he is longer far than any suit in Chancery,
And beats the Court of Aldermen, by chalks, for appetite!

On arrival, the Great Sea Serpent announces himself with this boastful ditty:

All bones but yours will rattle when I say
I am the sea serpent from Americ-ay.
Mayhap you've heard that I've been round the world;
I guess I'm round it now, mister, twice curled.....
When I lie down, and would my length unroll,
There ar'n't half room enough twixt pole and pole.
In short, I grow so long that I've a notion
I must be measured soon for a brand new ocean.

It was Planché's 1835-6 contract with Alfred Bunn, the new lessee of Drury Lane and Covent Garden that led to the next change in pantomime's evolution. Vestris was forced to approach another author, Samuel Lover, for her Christmas piece, and *Olympic Picnic*, a spoof of Cupid and Psyche, was the result. Planché and Dance were not too pleased to find "someone else walking in our sky" so when Planché's contract with Bunn expired he returned to the Olympic with an idea for something different. Instead of featuring Gods and Goddesses in their *burlettas*, why not broach the realms of Fairyland and use the old Nursery Stories as a vehicle?

Vestris was doubtful. Why risk everything they had achieved at the Olympic by changing a winning formula? Planché argued his point strongly, suggesting an English translation of the French story "Riquet a la Houppe", and finally the reluctant Vestris agreed to give it a try. With Charles Dance again assisting, Planché began shaping the new *burletta*.

The idea of a Fairytale subject was not an original one. During Grimaldi's time, nursery stories had often been used as a basis for pantomimes such as *Dick Whittington*, *Cinderella*, *Mother Goose*, *Sleeping Beauty*, and *Aladdin*. None, however, had been more than a ploy to set the Harlequinades in motion, and their outlines were dispensed with as quickly as possible. What Planché proposed was a full length treatment without a Harlequinade, which had never been attempted before. Even at the eleventh hour, the anxious Vestris was seriously considering a cancellation of the piece in favour of reviving an old "classical" *burletta*, but the two writers were quietly confident.

Riquet with the Tuft, though a delightful fairy tale, is not well known in Britain, so a brief outline of it follows.

The Queen of a distant land gives birth to a baby so hunch-backed, twisted and ugly, she can hardly bear to look at him. Her fairy midwife promises her that the child will grow to be very clever and charming and able to share his intelligence with the one who he loves the best. The boy, named 'Riquet with the Tuft' because of the clump of hair he was born with, fulfills the fairy's promise and is loved throughout the land.

In a neighbouring country, the Queen gives birth to twin daughters, the first so beautiful that everyone fell in love with her, and the second so extraordinarily plain that no-one ever would. Unfortunately, the beautiful daughter is born stupid, and the plain one is witty and clever. The fairy mid-wife tells the Queen that the beautiful princess will have the power to give beauty to the one who she loves, and the plain princess will be so charming and delightful, no-one will notice how plain she is.

All the children grow up and one day, the beautiful princess is in the forest crying over her stupidity, when she is discovered by the ugly Riquet.

He asks what is wrong, and when she explains, tells her that he has the power to make her wise if only she will marry him. She agrees on the spot, and at once is given the charm and intelligence of Riquet. Unfortunately, she now realises how ugly and mis-shapen he is, and anxious to escape, tells him she will come back in a year's time to keep her promise, though having no intention of doing so.

On her return to the Palace, everyone is amazed at the change in her, and Princes arrive from all around the world to propose marriage. Though all are handsome, at the side of Esmeralda, they appear stupid and cannot carry on an intelligent conversation. After a year of utter boredom, she flees the palace again and enters the forest. Here she discovers the residents of the neighbouring land preparing for the wedding of Prince Riquet. To her horror, he appears at her side to claim her hand as promised. She confesses he is so ugly she can never marry him and asks him to make her stupid again. He asks if his appearance is all that offends her, and when she affirms, reminds her that the fairy gave her the power to share her beauty with the one she loves. At once she makes her wish and Riquet is transformed to a handsome Prince. The wedding takes place to everyone's delight and they live happily ever after.

Vestris was to play the beautiful Princess Esmeralda and Charles Mathews, later to be her husband, was Riquet. Planché gave the grotesque and mis-shapen hero the following verse:

> I'm a strange looking person, I own,
> But contentment for ever my guest is;
> I'm by habit an optimist grown,
> And fancy that all for the best is.
> Each man has of troubles his pack,
> And some round their aching hearts wear it;
> My burden is placed on my back,
> Where I'm much better able to bear it.
>
> Again, tho' I'm blind of one eye,
> And have but one ear that of use is,
> I but half the world's wickedness spy,
> And am deaf to one half its abuses;
> My motions I own serpentine are,
> Many folks blessed with handsomer legs
> Have ways much more crooked than mine are.
>
> Nature gave me but one tuft of hair,
> Yet wherefore, kind dame, should I flout her?
> If one side of my head must be bare,
> I'm delighted she's chosen the outer!
> Thus on all things I put a good face,
> And however mis-shapen in feature,
> My heart, girl, is in the right place,
> And warm towards each fellow creature!

The final scene of the *Extravaganza*, as Planché called it, was set in Fairyland at the Palace of Queen Mab and a procession of Nursery story characters were introduced, such as Cinderella, Jack the Giant Killer, Red Riding Hood, Beauty and the Beast, Puss in Boots and The White Cat, all garbed in the most breathtaking costumes. At the end of the parade, the Princess stepped forward to lead the company in the final song, set the tune of "A Fine Old English Gentleman"

> Old friends I've the old prayer to make, before it is too late.
> With your old kindness please to view this change in our old state.
> Our old mythology, we thought, was getting out of date,
> And so we've left Olympus old, and all its Gods so great.
> For a fine old English fairy-tale, all of the olden time.
> Now winter old brings frost and cold, we open house to all,
> And while we strive to please the large, we don't forget the small.
> Then "boys and girls come out to play", in answer to our call.
> And with a good old English cheer, Oh, let our curtain fall.
> Upon this good old English fairy-tale, all of the olden time.

Quaint as the above may seem, Planché's Extravaganza was a sensation and dealt another savage blow to the ailing pantomimes of the Patent theatres. Without hesitation, Vestris asked for another Fairy-tale Extravaganza and the following year, *Puss in Boots* (a Mews-ical Fairy *Burletta*) gave her another breeches role, "The Marquis of Carabas", which again took London by storm.

By this time, the unfortunate Alfred Bunn was hopelessly in debt and the problems of keeping Covent Garden and Drury Lane solvent were snowballing. In a desperate attempt to cut costs, he employed several performers and one *corps de ballet* to cover both houses, which only led to more trouble as Planché reports in his memoirs:

> "The audience was sometimes kept waiting a quarter of an hour and upwards at one house, while a performer was finishing his part at the other. On some occasions, indeed, the performer did not stay to finish it, but made his escape before the last scene of the play, leaving speeches that were indispensable to be spoken by another person; and the whole *corps de ballet* was frequently extracted from the last scene of a piece at Drury Lane and hurried over for the commencement of one at Covent Garden".

Author George Raymond in his *Life and Enterprises of Robert William Elliston* (Routledge, London, 1857) adds:

"Actors, half attired, with enamelled faces, and loaded with the paraphernalia of their art, were passing and re-passing as busy as pismires, whilst the hurried exchange of quaint words – "Stage waits" – "Music on" – "Rung up", &c., – would have perplexed the stranger with a thousand surmises ... At the season of Christmas when this state of alternation was at its height, the female figure-dancers pattered from one house to another six times during the evening, and underwent the operation of dressing and undressing no less than eight."

The effort was too great, and after losing control of Covent Garden the hapless Bunn was reduced to presenting animal acts on the stage of Drury Lane, finally declaring himself bankrupt at the end of 1839.

Earlier that year, on July 16th, actor/manager William Charles Macready (1793-1873) concluded his two year lesseeship of Covent Garden and declined to renew it. The proprietors, headed by actor Charles Kemble (1775-1854), younger brother of the aforementioned John Kemble, offered it to Madame Vestris.

It was the chance of a lifetime. With her new husband, Charles Mathews, she had returned from a not entirely successful American tour in the January, and appeared in Planché's *Blue Beard* at the Olympic to great acclaim. On the downside, however, other managements had quickly adopted the Planché and Vestris innovations for their own plays and pantomimes, and serious rivals were appearing on the scene. In addition, Vestris's insistence on the best of everything for Olympic productions had inevitably led to financial problems and though still able to fill every seat in the small house, the costs were beginning to exceed the income. The opportunity to manage the much larger Covent Garden could not be turned down, and Vestris and Mathews accepted.

The news spread through theatreland like a fire, and much gossip ensued concerning the viability of the venture and the unexpected marriage of Lucy and Charles. A well known anecdote tells of three actresses, Mrs. Humby, Mrs. Orger and Mrs. Glover, discussing the matter in the Haymarket theatre's Green Room.

"They do say" said Mrs. Humby, "that before accepting him, she made a full confession of all her lovers. What touching confidence".

Mrs. Orger shook her head. "What needless trouble" she murmured.
Mrs. Glover snorted and commented acidly "What a wonderful memory".

After a shaky start with the almost unknown *Love's Labour Lost*, a revival of *The Beggars Opera*, and sixty two other productions including Planché's exceedingly beautiful *Sleeping Beauty in the Wood*, the first Vestris/Mathews season at Covent Garden was hailed a dazzling triumph. It is possible that the character of Pooh Bah, the Lord High Everything Else of W. S. Gilbert's *The Mikado* was derived from Planché's *Extravaganza*, for the Baron Factotum in *Sleeping Beauty* declares in one of *his* verses:

As Lord High Chamberlain I slumber never;
As Lord High Steward, in a stew I'm ever!
As Lord High Constable, I watch all day;
As Lord High Treasurer, I've the deuce to pay;
As Grand Lord Cup-bearer, I'm handled queerly;
As Great Grand Carver, I'm cut up severely.
In other States the honours are divided;
But here, they're one and all to me confided;
They've buckled Fortune on my back – until
I really feel particularly ill!
Young man, avoid the cares from State that spring,
And don't you be a Great Grand anything.

The second season saw the first production of Boucicault's *London Assurance*; an awe-inspiring *Midsummer Night's Dream* using the music of Mendelssohn for the first time, and thirty two other presentations; *Beauty and the Beast* being Planché's contribution. Towards the end of their third season in which forty productions were mounted including Bellini's opera *Norma*, sung to great acclaim by Adelaide Kemble, and Planché's Extravaganza *The White Cat*, (which featured King Wunsuponatyme and Prince Paragon) one of the greatest injustices of theatrical history took place.

Kemble and his co-proprietors stepped in claiming that although several thousands of pounds had been paid in rent, £600 was still owed, and all scenery, costumes and properties were being confiscated in lieu. There was, of course, no problem. The money would certainly have been paid, but with the amazing success of his daughter Adelaide in *Norma*,

Kemble wanted the theatre back to display her talents himself. On April 30th, 1842, Vestris and Mathews made their final appearance at Covent Garden to a packed house and a standing ovation. As *The Times* reported the following day:

"the stage was buried beneath a carpet of hurled flowers".

Kemble's company collapsed in debt just six months later, and despite frantic attempts to keep the theatre open (including an appeal to Vestris to return, which she rejected), in 1846 the doors of the great playhouse were finally forced to close. After extensive re-building and alteration, it re-opened in 1847 as an Opera House.

In 1843, sustained pressure from theatre managers all over London resulted in the hated Monopolies Act being repealed and apart from the saloon theatres, who were still restricted to musical and variety items until 1911, legitimate theatres – subject to the Lord Chamberlain's approval – were now free to present whatever entertainments they wished. An explosion of plays, pantomimes, *burlesques* and *extravaganzas* swept the one-time "Minor" theatres, each management attempting to outdo its rival in spectacle and ingenuity.

It was a period of confusing and fascinating change for pantomime. Some managements abandoned the by now "traditional" openings of Big Heads and bulky over-clothing by substituting a *burlesque* or an *extravaganza a la Planché* and followed the last scene of it with a Harlequinade played by a totally different cast, though still billing it as a pantomime. Others continued with the familiar speaking opening and silent Harlequinade, silent opening and speaking Harlequinade or speaking opening and speaking Harlequinade. Even female Harlequins (known as Harlequinas) appeared, not to mention Double Harlequinades featuring two of everyone. The following lines from *Little Goody Two Shoes* at Drury Lane in 1862 which featured the popular Charles Lauri and Harry Boleno show that that practice was still being observed even at that late date when Fairy Good Nature announced:

At Christmas, I, of course should generous be;
How many Clowns do you want now, two or three ?
Well, you shall have enough of fun, depend on't,
I'll make you stop to see the very end on't.
First Goody Two Shoes, this reward is thine,
Be happy with your swain as Columbine.
        (Changes her to Columbine)
Little Boy Blue and Stout, one – perhaps more thin –
Touch of Good Nature makes you Harlequin.
        (Two Harlequins appear)
These two attendants with you, you may take
And thus a pair of Pantaloons we make.
        (Two Pantaloons appear)
Be you, the one of poetical renown
Our real Christmas Lauri-ate, the Clown.
        (Changes Charles Lauri)
To play old Harry, Master Green, be mean , oh
Bowl forth as Clown, the Harry called Boleno.
        (Changes Harry Boleno)

Said critic George Augustus Sala, referring to one author's
similar effort:

> "It was a *naivete* worthy of the elder Harlequin himself,
> thinking apparently that by doubling the dose of dullness he was
> presenting them with double their money's worth."

Following the termination of the Vestris/Mathews seasons at
Covent Garden, Planché continued to write for Drury Lane
before entering into an arrangement with The Haymarket
Theatre for the next three and a half years. His *extravaganzas*
for this period were *The Fair One with the Golden Locks* in
1843; *Graciosa and Percinet*, 1844; *The Bee and the Orange
Tree* and *The Golden Fleece* 1845, and *The Invisible Prince*
1846.

Elsewhere, pantomime and *burlesque* continued to flourish
in strange forms. At The Royal Victoria Theatre (now the Old
Vic) in 1847, the public could see *The Birth of the Steam
Engine; or Harlequin Locomotive and Joe Miller and his Men*,
in which the Kings Hupsydown and Wrongsydeup have an
argument about the invention of the steam engine. The Spirit
of Pantomime then enters and changes the scene to a village
near Glasgow where James Watt, a young engineer, is in love
with a certain Miss Latchkey, the daughter of a blacksmith.
He is not the only suitor, however, and in order to settle the

matter of which man will marry her, the Blacksmith announces she will accept the one who devises the greatest invention. Watt returns home and whilst sitting in his chair and gazing into the fire, notices the steam from the boiling kettle is making the lid rattle. Drifting off to sleep, he dreams of an Age of Steam, with machines all over the country producing energy in unlimited amounts. When he wakes again, he invents the steam engine and is reunited with his beloved. Everyone is then transformed into the familiar figures of the Harlequinade and the usual antics begin.

Another odd storyline in a later pantomime was *Harlequin and Old Izaac Walton; or Tom Moore of Fleet Street, The Silver Trout and the Seven Sisters of Tottenham* (1858) which tells of Old Father Thames who, after complaining bitterly that the pollution of his waters have made him ill, rejects the help of the great physician, Board of Works, to seek the help of the River Lee in her "Peerless Pool of the Water Nymphs". She in turn grumbles about the loss of her Silver Trout to fisherman Old Izaac Walton. To solve the problem, they decide to persuade him to marry Maude the Milkmaid, youngest of the Seven Sisters of Tottenham, but their plan comes to naught because the Fair Maid is in love with Tom Moore, Old Isaac's apprentice, who lives in Fleet Street, but refuses to marry him unless he can perform two supposedly impossible tasks. These he manages with the help of a fairy fish and a friendly jackdaw, and when all ends happily, the Harlequinade begins.

The *Daily Telegraph* commented on this with the following:

> "Tell us that some ingenious fellow has dramatised the Plague of London or written comic songs on diphtheria and scarlet fever – (and) we really should be more inclined to believe it than that any venturesome dramatist has made comical capital out of the dirty condition of the Thames and personified the Board of Works"

Reported *The Times* gloomily:

> "Pantomime is no longer what it used to be"

and *The Illustrated London News* agreed with:

> "The Christmas pantomimes have been getting worse and worse for some years"

Inventive minds, however, were still at work. In the pantomime at Drury Lane in 1840, *Harlequin and Duke*

Humphries Dinner; or Jack Cade, the Lord of London Stone (which was the afterpiece to Charles Macready's production of *The Merchant of Venice*) one scene delighted the audience and supplied comedians in future pantomimes with a source of sustained laughter. The Clown and Pantaloon take lodgings in a beautifully furnished room, which, after being "enchanted" by Harlequin's magic baton, proceeds to disappear piece by piece until nothing is left but the four walls. Chairs vanish through the walls or sink through the floor. Fire-irons and fenders vanish up the chimney, curtains disappear, sofas and tables de-materialize, ornaments leap from the mantlepiece, and the huge mirror on the wall falls on Clown's head with a fearful crash leaving him standing in bewildered amazement in the middle of the empty frame. The "Haunted Bedrooms" of modern pantomime are easily recognized descendants of this.

The same year at Sadler's Wells, *Harlequin and Poor Richard; or Old Father Time and the Almanack Maker* showed Father Time sending his hourglass to Poor Richard who has been rejected by his beloved in favour of another. By the power of its magic, the lady preens into a "mirror" and sees a grey haired and long nosed hag performing the same actions. After some moments, she realises it is herself and is horrified. (The comical routine of the Dame seeing what she thinks is her own reflection in a mirrorless frame probably originates from this show). Her lover, seeing the same vision, leaves her, and Poor Richard inverts the hourglass to restore her beauty.

Other titles of this odd period were *Tit Tat Toe, My First Go; or Harlequin N.E.W.S. and the Fairy Elves of the Fourth Estate* based on the printing world of Caxton; *Harlequin William the Conqueror and King Vice of the Silent City; or War, Wine and Love and Queen Virtue in the Vistas of Light and Glitter* (1856); *Hey Diddle Diddle, the Cat and the Fiddle, the Cow jumped over the Moon; or Oranges and Lemons and the Twelve Dancing Princesses* (1861); and the almost unpronounceable *Harlequin and Poonoowingkeewangflibeedeeflobeedeebuskeebang; or The King of the Cannibal Isles* (1845). Small wonder that the play-bills advertising the productions began to increase in size.

By 1847, Vestris and Mathews had taken over the Lyceum theatre and Planché, freed from his Haymarket contract, wrote

The Golden Branch for their Christmas extravaganza. This was followed by *Theseus and Ariadne* and *King of the Peacocks* in 1848, and *The Seven Champions of Christendom* and *The Island of Jewels* in 1849. Though all these shows were hugely successful, it was the young scene painter employed at the Lyceum who stole the applause and created the scenic transformations that were to dominate British pantomimes for the next hundred years; William Roxby Beverley. (c1814-1889)

8

*B*everley was one of the four sons of William Roxby, owner of the Royalty theatre in Tottenham Street, London. As an actor, Roxby had adopted the name of Beverley from the Yorkshire town, and both young William and his elder brother, Henry, followed suit. Both men were skilled artists, but Henry chose to be a performer, becoming known as "Beauty" Beverley because he was the ugliest actor of the time, whilst William found work on the paint frame at the Theatre Royal, Manchester. When the family moved to London, William approached the Vestris Management at the Lyric Theatre and painted the scenery for *The Golden Branch.*

Vestris was notoriously insistent on only the best, and Beverley did not let her down. For the next seven years his outstanding ability with the brushes constantly threatened to overshadow the actual productions, beautifully staged as they were. He had little time for the actors, regarding them as d istractions from the amazing scenery. In his opinion, performers were there merely to "dress the scene" by support- ing draperies or representing statuary that might further enhance his "picture". In the 1848 production *The King of the Peacocks*, he actually produced a backdrop of such startling reality it drew sustained applause and cheers without a soul being on stage. It was, however, for the final scene of *The Island of Jewels*, he created the first of the scenic transformations that established him as the greatest scene painter of Victorian Britain.

The gradual falling of the leaves of a palm tree to reveal six fairies supporting a coronet of jewels had journalists scrabbling for their pens. Wrote the critic of *The Illustrated London News*:

> "Of all Mr. Planché's burlesques, the present is perhaps the most elegant ever witnessed, and the way in which it has been produced the most gorgeous imaginable. An incidental ballet on the subjects of Cupid and Psyche was introduced into the action with fine effect. The concluding scene – the discovery in the midst of an unfolded colonnade of palm trees, nymphs supporting the Crown jewels on a cushion – is indescribably magnificent"

Unfortunately for Planché, the consequent development of Beverley's skills led to demands from the public for more and more spectacular effects. The writer and critic George Henry Lewes enthused after *The Good Woman in the Wood* (1852):

> "Never on any stage was there a scene of such enchantment and artistic beauty as that which concludes the final act of this piece - The Basaltic Terminus on the borders of Lake Lucid. To say that in the long summer afternoons of reverie-peopled boyhood one had dreams of fairyland like this, would be to say that the wide-wandering fancy of a boy was equal to that of a Beverley; but Beverley is the fairies own child: he must be a changeling, his childhood was spent among those regions, and now in his serious and laboured manhood, the dim remembrance of that far-off splendour haunts his soul. The fairies have had millions of worshippers, hundreds of poets, and one supreme artist, and that artist is William Beverley."

The following year's *Extravaganza, Once upon a time there were two kings*, drew even more praise, and writing in the *Journal of a London Playgoer*, Henry Morley was to say:

> "Fairy stories were never more elegantly acted, ridiculous things never were elevated with more grace and finish into an ideal region than when entrusted to the hands of the Lyceum company. As for Mr. Beverley's scenery, our admiration of it makes it difficult to describe. Perhaps it will be enough to say that it is

worthy of his reputation, and that in the final scene of the piece a fairy effect has been created of the completest kind, by lengthening the silver skirts of damsels who appear to hover in the air, grouping them into festoons and giving to their beauty something of a fantastic unearthly character. This perhaps is the crowning triumph of the theatre so far as mere spectacle is concerned. Mme Vestris appeared as the wife of the shepherd monarch, acting with consummate ease and good sense, as she always did and does, and singing with the beauty of voice and articulation which clings to her still"

"As for me" complained the usually placid and even tempered Planché, "I was positively painted out. Nothing was considered brilliant but the last scene. Mrs. Charles Mathews herself told me that she had paid between £60 and £70 for gold tissue for the dresses of the supernumeraries alone who were discovered in "attitudes" in the last scene. Dutch metal was in the ascendant: it was no longer even painting, but upholstery." (The last remark referred to Beverley's painting over scenes with thin glue and then applying gold or silver leaf at enormous cost).

The theatregoing public were dismayed when the ageing but still attractive Vestris was forced to retire in 1854. She had been suffering with a distressing throat complaint for some time which had caused her to miss several performances. Shortly afterwards, in the face of mounting debts, the Mathews company collapsed and the Lyceum passed out of their hands. On August 8th 1856, Lucy Vestris died, possibly of throat cancer, and an era came to an end. As Planché wrote later:

"Since which period, no-one has ever appeared possessing that peculiar combination of personal attractions and professional ability which, for so many years, made her the most popular actress and manager of her day."

On the reputation he had earned with the Planché *extravaganzas*, Beverley was engaged by the extraordinary Edward Tyrrel Smith, manager of Drury Lane, following in the footsteps of another great scenic painter, Clarkson Stanfield (1793-1867), who had created the amazing moving dioramas that so delighted Queen Victoria and enhanced the reputation of theatreland's productions for many years. These were backdrops, some 300 feet in length, affixed to upright rollers at each side of the stage, which when set in motion, afforded views of "moving" objects such as ships in full sail, or horses racing. Primitive and laughable by today's standards, but an amazing advance in stage scenery then.

An amusing anecdote concerning Stanfield tells how, like several others, the painter had often wondered what became of ageing Harlequins. One day, after hearing a less than sprightly Harlequin being told that in future he would have to play Pantaloon instead, Stanfield nodded sagely and muttered: "Ah, I see now. They cut 'em up and make Pantaloons of 'em".

Smith was a great believer in the maxim that money made money, and in order to promote this, hired a £1000 banknote from a moneylender at the cost of £1 per day, in order to casually display it to those with whom he wished to do business. It is said he would regularly attend sales, offer the note in payment knowing full well that no-one could change it, carry off the goods with an offer to pay later, sell them at a profit, then pay the amount owed and pocket the rest.

Another oft repeated story is that sitting in the paint room of Drury Lane theatre where a leg of mutton on a spit was being cooked for lunch, Smith's eye was taken by the slowly turning joint. Drawing Beverley's attention to it, he remarked that a rotating fairy palace which changed colour like the roasting mutton did might make an interesting spectacle. Beverley nodded and replied he would do a design for it, and this is how pantomime transformation scenes came into being.

It is, of course, a fallacy. Scenic transformations had been a feature of the Masques of Inigo Jones and others, two centuries earlier. The 1611 Masque of *Oberon, the Fairy Prince*, for instance, began with "a darke Rocke, with trees beyond it", changed suddenly to a "frontispiece of a bright and glorious Palace" and was followed by another rapid transformation to "the Nation of Fays". These were simple changes, most probably effected by painted flats being swiftly drawn off or slid on to reveal or conceal a painted backdrop, or two sided flats which could be revolved in a trice. In the pantomimes of Rich and Grimaldi, scene changes took place by the use of cloths and mechanical devices, the transformations happening in seconds. What Beverley had discovered was the art of transforming scenery slowly, so that one melted into another with the audience being scarcely aware of it happening, and this he had learned from the *Extravaganzas* of Planché and the stagings of Vestris.

Beverley's skill put new life into pantomime, each scene more beautiful than the last until the final transformation left the audience open-mouthed with amazement. Said one critic:

> "As a stripling in years, although a greybeard in scenic proficiency, William Beverley had not long been in the metropolis before the appearance of his name on a playbill was reckoned sufficient guarantee for the excellence of the scenery. He is the Watteau of scene painting."

Beverley was not the only genius at Drury Lane. Two years earlier, when Smith took over its management, Edward Leman Blanchard (1820-1889) had provided the first of the thirty seven Drury Lane pantomimes he was to write. Vastly underpaid for his remarkable scripts, Blanchard had written his first pantomime at the age of seventeen for a private theatre, and within three years had around thirty dramas, farces and burlesques under his belt. Between 1840 and 1844 he was a "stock dramatist" at the Olympic Theatre, and by the time he died, had written a total of sixty five pantomimes for different London theatres, rarely earning more than £20 a time. Had it not been for his other work as a critic and journalist he would have starved, for several sponging relatives made quite sure he was kept on the verge of absolute poverty.

Known as "The Prince of Openings", his beautifully rhymed and pun packed scripts are a pleasure to read, and his imagination almost unsurpassable. Unlike the two part scripts of earlier days, Blanchard's pantomimes had three sections. The "Dark Opening" in which the Immortal characters discussed modern day trends; the ensuing "Fairy or Nursery rhyme story" that gave the piece its title, and the "Harlequinade" – a format that lasted until the 1880s.

Harlequin Hudibras; or Old Dame Durdon and the Droll Days of the Merry Monarch was the title of his Drury Lane debut, and it opened on December 27th 1852 to a full house.

Reported *The Times*:

> "The combined attractions of new manager, new decorations and two new pieces have done wonders for this disowned among the metropolitan theatres. The pit was crammed to suffocation. Those who bowed in the boxes were evidently distressed by the heat, and how those fared who occupied the top-most seats is very difficult to understand and very unpleasant to imagine ... Oranges were eaten with the customary eagerness and the skin flung upon the heads of the persons in the pit, who sought to return the courtesy, but their performance falling short of their intentions, the occupants of the boxes came in for a share of orange peel. Standing up fights there were too ... but on the whole, the audience behaved decently for a Christmas audience."

After the overture, the curtain rose on the first scene which was set in the "Abode of Antiquity" where Antiquity appears in a watchman's box and flanked by his attendants Mildew, Rust, Cobweb, etc., contemplates the relics of bygone ages – forgotten by humanity – that surround him. The Genius of Improvement arrives in a "carriage of progress", pulled by winged horses with reins of electric telegraph wires, and boasts:

> "To me, for all you have had, some thanks is due,
> I clear the way – and rubbish send to you.
> Thanks to Prince Albert, my task, you see
> Is now much easier than it used to be.
> If there's a prize in science to be won,
> He comes to me – and lo! the thing is done."

To prove her point, the scene is changed to the "New Crystal Palace and Gardens at Sydenham" where the fairies Art, Progress, Peace, Industry, Plenty, etc. dance gracefully, and an immortal welcomes everyone with the dreadful pun on its location:

> Behold my treasures here, there's naught forbid in 'em.
> And all will be revealed, though now it's hid in 'em.

King Charles then enters, disguised as Sir Rowley and attempts to woo Dame Durdon's daughter, Alice, but is surprised by the sudden appearance of her mother who chases him away. Following a comic review of the troops, Charles returns cautiously carrying a small carpet bag and brandishing an umbrella to say:

"All's safe as yet! This is the prudent way,
To be prepared against a rainy day
Oddsfish! A petticoat! There's no resistance
When pretty girls are looming in the distance"

He then begs Alice to hide him from the pursuing Roundheads and she suggests he hides in a nearby oak tree. As the sound of his hunters reaches him, he agrees with the words;

"In such a race, we cannot here crack jokes,
Else this would be an entry for The Oaks.
Well, since it please you, here goes! For a time
I leave my country for a distant climb."

In Dame Durdon's kitchen, Hudibras sees the table set for dinner and producing eating utensils of the usual grotesque size, sits down to dine. The servants spill hot gravy all over him and he flings the wine in his glass at them, but manages to hit Dame Durdon instead. As he mops her down with the tablecloth, Charles dashes in and knocks him over. Chasing Charles off, Dame Durdon covers the battered and bruised Hudibras with yards and yards of sticking plaster. After the triumphant Charles returns to Cheapside and is finally crowned, Antiquity and Genius transform the characters into those of the Harlequinade, which the *Morning Post* praised by saying it provided

"all the possible, punnable and practical references to the changing features of the day. The frailities of the Derby election, bitter
beer, the Wagner excitement and the numerous editions of *Uncle
Tom's Cabin* are all successfully touched upon"

The following year, Blanchard's *Harlequin King Humming Top and the Land of Toys* told the story of a huge humming top whose unhappy son is restored to good humour by means of marbles and football. In the opening sequence, a group of fairies discuss topical happenings such as Spiritualism, ladieswear and steam driven machinery:

Fashion   : In my department, I ought to say,
                   Short sleeves for mantles, now have had their day.
Novelty   : At ladies bonnets, men appear to scoff.
Fashion   : (Rueful) I there admit a little *falling off*.
Invention   : While *I've* invented plans with assiduity,
                   And engines of the greatest ingenuity;
                   (Sadly) But since in fun there's been so great a call,
                   To invent a joke's the hardest thing of all.

Fashion	: That's news indeed: From all it would appear
	You've really had enough to do this year.
Novelty	: Well, what with submarine electric cables,
	Mysterious rappings from revolving tables,
	Sewing machines that steam at work will keep,
	And so enable those who *sew* to reap.
	With other marvels of a late invention
	That now are much too numerous to mention,
	I really think - to quote a famous poet
	I've done the State some service - and they know it.

The combination of Beverley's scenery and Blanchard's script made the 1854 pantomime *Jack and Jill; or Harlequin King Mustard and Four and Twenty Blackbirds Baked in a Pie*, a huge success, though the Olympic's production of Planché's new extravaganza *The Yellow Dwarf* received the best notices not just for the production, but for the chilling performance of E. M. Robson (1821-64), original singer of the Music Hall success, *Villikins and his Dinah* in the title role.

Robson was an ugly little man whose head was far too large for his body, according to Henry Barton Baker's book *History of the London Stage – Its Famous Players 1576-1903* (1904), and his performances frequently gave the impression that he verged on the edge of madness. Suffering dreadfully from stage fright, he was known to stand in the wings awaiting his entrance, gnawing at his arms until they bled. His portrayal of the evil dwarf, however, electrified audiences, and pantomime villains for many, many years were to base their characters on the infamous *Yellow Dwarf*. George Augustus Sala left this description of him in character:

> "In *The Yellow Dwarf*, he was the jaundiced embodiment of a spirit of Oriental evil; crafty, malevolent, greedy, insatiate – full of mockery, mimicry, lubricity and spite – an Afrit, a Djin, a Ghoul, a spawn of Sheitan. How that monstrous orange tawny head grinned and wagged! How those flaps of ears were projected forwards like those of a dog! How baleful those atrabilious eyes glistened. You laughed and yet you shuddered ... you were awestricken by the intensity, the vehemence he threw into the mean balderdash of the burlesque monster ... All this was portrayed by Robson with astonishing force and vigour."

It was a great relief for Planché, who after the scenic excesses of recent years, now felt he was able to rely upon acting for the success of his shows.

John Rich. The father of British Pantomime.
A portrait by an unknown painter, showing the eccentric but generous
actor/manager in later life.
V&A Picture Library.

Right: Rich as Harlequin
in 1753. From an etching
by an unknown artist.
Rich was 61 years old at
the time and is seen,
unusually, without the
traditional black mask
that hid his upper face.
V& A Picture Library.

Below: Joseph Grimaldi,
greatest of all Clowns,
performs 'The favourite
Comic Dance' with John
Bologna as the disguised
Harlequin. A scene from
Mother Goose at The
Theatre Royal, Covent
Garden in 1806.
V&A Picture Library.

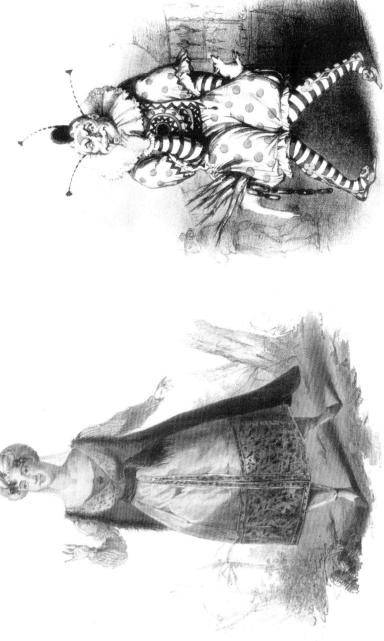

Lucy (Madame) Vestris as Fatima, in Weber's opera *Oberon*, 1826. J.R. Planche having written the libretto, this production marked the beginning of a professional relationship between the pair that changed the course of pantomime and made theatrical history. V&A Picture Library.

Hailed as Grimaldi's successor, Tom Matthews was Clown at Drury Lane, Covent Garden, Sadler's Wells, and also appeared in Ballet and Opera. He died in 1899 V&A Picture Library.

Miss Louisa Fairbrother as Aladdin in the Lyceum Theatre's production of the burlesque *The Forty Thieves* in 1844. She later became the morganatic wife of the Duke of Cambridge under the name of Mrs FitzGeorge and died in 1899.
From a print in the author's collection.

OUR ROUND OF THE THEATRES.

THOUGH evening dress is a bore,
  In Christmas's toils we are
    bound again;
We join the dress-circle once
    more,
  To do the theatrical round again.
It isn't a time with advice
  To come down severely, or
    banter mimes,
So all that we say shall be nice
  Of comedies, dramas, or *panto*-
    mimes.

Obeying the usual call
  Of duty, we give you the gist of
    them
  (Of course, we have visited all—
    You'll see, from the following
    list of them.
Without supernatural aid
  Their numbers, no doubt, had
    resisted us;
But, somehow, we weren't afraid,
  For *Foggerty's Fairy* assisted us).

. "The Garden" has *Little Boy Blue*,
  Bo-Peep (which an interest gives) in it,
And also a wonderful *Shoe*,
  And *Little Old Woman* who lives in it.

THE SURREY.—MAC—THIS IS HIM MACTING.

Who'd acting and gorgeousness gain
  (And *writing*), the best plan to do so is
To drop in one night at "The Lane"
  Where Harris's *Robinson Crusoe* is.

The Standard has *Sinbad*, and that
  Is certainly one in a million.
And *Whittington*, boys, *and his Cat*
  Is capital at the Pavilion.
The *Forty* disport at "The Wells,"
  The pleasure they give is de-
    lectable.
The *Bluebeard* at Sangers' excels,
  The Grecian is more than re-
    spectable.

You'll at the Britannia find
  The wonderful *Dove* that *En-*
    chanted is;
If towards *Mother Bunch* you're
    inclined,
  You'll find at the Surrey she
    planted is.
The Children who're left *in the*
    Wood,
  At the Crystal are dancing a
    sarabun;
Tom Thumb (Alexandra) is good,
  And *Aladdin*'s "all there" at
    the Mara-bun.

They're all good, as pantomimes go,
  Through the list I have pretty well past of them,
And *Little Jack Horner*, you know,
  At the Eleph. and Cas. is the last of them.
Burlesque is again to the fore,
  And rather esteemed of the laity,
At Royalty *Pinto* you'll roar,
  Aladdin's first-rate at the Gaiety.

THEATRE ROYAL MOST-PLACES. "HERE WE ARE AGAIN!"

THEATRE ROYAL SOME-PLACES.—"HERE WE ARE STILL."

London's Pantomime Round-up, according to
Fun Magazine, 1882.

Jack in the Box

E.L.Blanchard's *Annual* for the Theatre Royal, Drury Lane. 1874. Another success for 'the Prince of Openings'.   D.H.Friston''s illustration for *The Illustrated London News.*

Red Riding Hood and her sister Little Bo-Peep

The Covent Garden Theatre's rival production for the same year. Written by Charles Rice, the Theatre Manager. Published in *The Illustrated London News*.

COVENT GARDEN.

OLYMPIC.

LYCEUM.

THE CHRISTMAS

The spectacular scenic displays of London pantomimes,

Christmas 1861. Published in *The Illustrated London News*.

Three London pantomimes of 1883, written by E.L.Blanchard. (Drury Lane) and Frank Green (Sangster's Circus and Her Majesty's Theatre, Haymarket). Published in *The Penny Illustrated Paper*, Dec. 29th of that year.

Two pantomimes by Nelson Lee. Dec. 1884.

Harlequin Crotchet and Quaver; or Music for the Millions
Covent Garden Theatre.

Pounds, shillings and pence; or Harlequin £.s.d.
The Surrey Theatre.

"WE'VE GOT NO WORK TO DO!"

THE "COMIC SCENES" OF THE PANTOMIMES HAVING ALREADY BEEN CUT DOWN TO NOTHING—A *REDUCTIO AD ABSURDUM*—IT IS PROBABLE THAT NEXT YEAR THE REAL PANTOMIMISTS WILL BE OUT OF IT ALTOGETHER, AND EVEN THE CLOWN WILL NOT HAVE THE OPPORTUNITY OF SAYING, "HERE WE ARE AGAIN!"

As the Harlequinade was squeezed out by the Music Hall Element, this poignant sketch appeared in *Punch*, or the London Charivari, Jan 31st. 1885,

The greatest 'Dame' of them all. The immortal Dan Leno.

The Sheriff of Nottingham (Peter Vernon) reads the riot act to 'revolting peasants' in *Babes in the Wood* at Nottingham's Theatre Royal, 1969. Jack Douglas, Audrey Jeans, and George Truzzi also starred.

THEATRE ROYAL, EXETER

Proprietors—THE EXETER THEATRE CO., LTD. Managing Directors—Mr. J. P. G. DAVEY (Secretary) & Mr. PERCY DUNSFORD (Resident Manager)

Commencing BOXING-DAY, DECEMBER 26th, 1934, until SATURDAY, FEBRUARY 9th, 1935. Nightly at 7. Matinees at 2.

PERCY DUNSFORD presents
THE FORTY-SIXTH GRAND XMAS PANTOMIME
ENTITLED

THE BABES IN THE WOOD
and ROBIN HOOD

Entirely new version invented and written by PERCY DUNSFORD. :: Music by EDMUND GAETON.

CAST:

Robin Hood (An Outlaw) .... ENID LOWE	Catchem } (The Robbers) .... { TEDDY FURNESS
Will Scarlet (His Friend) .... NORAH ROBERTS	Killum } { EDDY HOLT
Baron Stoney (Of Stoney Castle) .... REG. MARCUS	Dorothy (Will's Friend) .... SHEILAGH DOCHERTY
Maid Marian (His Ward) .... BABS VALERIE	Friar Tuck .... LEWIS GRAY
Cissie } (The Babes) .... { MARJORIE SMITH	Little John } (Robin's { THOMAS POLLEY
Bobbie } { STANLEY·AXHAM	Much } Friends) { JAMES STUART
Maria (The Babes' Nurse) ...... REGGIE DINGLE	Allan-A-Dale ... ... LOUIS SHADELLO
Sammy (Maria's Son) .... BILLY ROWLAND	Fairy Starlight .... FRANCES MARTIN

Stanley Axham and Marjorie Smith trained by Italia Conti.

THE LONDON FOUR MALE QUARTETTE. :: :: The Robins by The Eldon School of Dancing.

SCENARIO:

Prologue	THE TREE TOPS. (THE BABES' DREAM).
Scene 1 ... **BARON STONEY'S CASTLE**	Scene 7 ... **THE BARON'S BALLROOM**
Scene 2 ... ... THE BARON'S STUDY	Scene 8 ... ... SHERWOOD VILLAGE
Scene 3 ... **THE SCHOOL OF COOKING**	Scene 9 ... **THE BABES' TOY ROOM**
Scene 4 ... THE ROAD TO SHERWOOD	Scene 10 ... ... THE BUTTERFLY DELL
Scene 5 ... ... HUSH. SAFETY FIRST	Scene 11 ... ... THE CASTLE WALK
Scene 6 ... **THE ENCHANTED WOODS**	Scene 12 ... **THE PALACE OF DREAMS**
INTERVAL.	Scenery by Charles Browne and Julian Hicks.

Orchestra and London Chorus under the direction of EDMUND GAETON.

" There's a dear little Cottage close down by the Sea," written by Percy Dunsford. Music by Edmund Gaeton. " Hore-Belisha," by Harry Parr. Other songs by kind permission of B. Feidman & Co., Campbell, Connolly & Co., Francis, Day & Hunter, Messrs. Chappell.

Stage Director ... ... REGGIE CROWE	Property Masters
Assistant Stage Managers .. BILLY ROWLAND & ALFY WILLS	.... CHARLES HUTCHINGS & TREVOR SIMMONDS
Electrician and Effect Master .... W. SWYNFORD	Wardrobe Mistress .... PEGGY WEBSTER

CONTINUED OVERLEAF.

Programme for *The Babes in the Wood*. Theatre Royal, Exeter. 1935.

Two scenes from the Birmingham Hippodrome's *The Sleeping Beauty* in 1966.

'General' Ernie Wise keeps a sharp eye on the guards defending the Enchanted Forest – and particularly the chaotic 'Private' Eric Morecambe.

The villagers greet Prince Michael (Kevin Scott) as he arrives from the New World to seek for the sleeping princess. (Patricia Bredin)

Two scenes from The Theatre Royal, Nottingham's *Merry King Cole.*
1968.

Right: Queen Samantha (Peter Butterworth) has an unexpected meeting with the twin-headed ogre (Edward Bowry).

Below: The Grand Finale with Michael Burgess, Avril Gaynor, Brian Massie, Ken Wilson, Lauri Lupino Lane, Ann Harriman, Robert Earl, Harry Worth, Peter Butterworth, Michael Bevis, Bill Lynton, Julia Nelson, Edward Bowry, Pepie Poupee and Norman Robbins.

Many critics agreed. Pantomimes, they complained, were tired shadows of former glories, and the openings were growing in length. Groaned one in *The Era*:

"In former years, a true lover of Pantomime knew what to expect from each character ... He knew that when the change took place, Harlequin would be agile, the Clown funny, the Pantaloon senile and trusting, the Columbine pretty and graceful. In the present day, the Pantaloon is generally a great deal more agile than the Clown, who is more graceful than the Columbine; instead of the sausage stealing, butter sliding, beadle insulting, police provoking Clown, we have somebody's imitation of celebrated dancers; or worse still, a duet between the Harlequin and Clown on the fiddle. Shade of Grimaldi, a Clown with musical talent."

The mention of music takes us back to Covent Garden, where the new Opera House had opened its doors in 1847 and plunged immediately into financial trouble. Artistic successes there were, but at the end of the 1849 season, another manager had been driven into bankruptcy. From 1850 to the end of 1855 things improved, then the bad luck of the theatre struck again. For the sum of £2000, it was agreed that the so-called Professor J. H. Anderson, (who under the self styled title of "The Wizard of the North" presented Magic shows and poor quality pantomimes), could sub-lease the theatre for six weeks at the end of January 1866.

On December 26th, 1855, Anderson advertised a 'Grand National, Historical & Chivalric pantomime', *Ye Belle Alliance; or Harlequin Good Humour and the Field of the Cloth of Gold* (being a legend of the meeting of the monarchs), with scenery by William Beverley and written by George Augustus Sala, that would feature "two hundred young women, none under the height of six feet two" and a "Great Tournament after the style of Holbein". After packing the house like sardines, the audience discovered that the "two hundred young woman" consisted of four chambermaids in masks with clogs and caps, and the Great Tournament was merely odd pieces of armour perched on hobby horses. Despite Beverley's scenery, it was a total fiasco.

In an attempt to recoup his losses, Anderson advertised a Carnival Benefit to commence on Monday, March 1st which would begin at noon and continue until Midnight. The combined talents of Covent Garden, Drury Lane and The Strand theatres would provide the entertainment and a grand Masked Ball would provide a fitting climax. It was a disaster of epic proportions.

Said the *Illustrated Times*:

> "Judge then the scene presented by Professor Anderson's masquerade, at which there were not twenty persons present in evening dress, the decorations of which would have been discreditable to a barn, the company at which would have disgraced a dancing salon, the whole conduct of which was a disgrace to everyone connected with it ... Less than one tenth of the assemblage was in fancy costume; shooting coats, pea jackets and muddy boots being in great force. The walls were covered in old theatrical "flats" roughly nailed against them while the "flies" and all upper portions of the theatre were left uncovered. There were no extra lamps and the dingily dressed dancers capered in a forced and solemn manner to the music of a dreary band."

The lengthy report goes on to say that at five minutes to five on Tuesday morning, with the last bars of "God Save the Queen" signalling the end of the Ball, firemen discovered the carpenter's shop overhead was on fire. Panic stricken revellers fled the building and within thirty five minutes the blazing roof had crashed down scattering burning timbers in all directions. The place became an inferno, flames illuminating the area for a distance of three miles, and all hope of saving it was abandoned. For the second time in less than fifty years, Covent Garden theatre was a charred ruin. The following day, as Queen Victoria, Prince Albert and the Princess Royal visited the scene, the news broke that because of its multiple "renters", which included the Kemble family, the building had been uninsured.

Two months earlier, at the nearby Adelphi theatre, a French actress was appearing in *Jack and the Beanstalk; or Harlequin and Mother Goose at Home Again*, a burlesque pantomime by *Punch* editor Mark Lemon (1809-70) who had previously written the maligned "speaking" opening of *Harlequin Bat and Harlequin Pat* for Covent Garden.

Madame Celeste, as she was known, was born around 1814, and had appeared in New York at the Bowery Theatre when only fifteen years old. With no other language but her native tongue, when playing in English speaking countries she was only able to appear in roles where speech was unnecessary, but by the age of eighteen, and already a widow, she made her London debut at the Queen's Theatre in Tottenham Street as a dancer. It was not until the 1840s she actually spoke on stage, yet so popular had she become that when The Surrey Theatre advertised her appearance with the promise that audiences would hear her in a speaking role, the place was quickly sold out. The result was four words. "My shee-ild. My shee-ild", but the audience were delighted.

As her English improved, she played a large variety of roles, including a sensational Madame Defarge in Dickens' *A Tale of Two Cities* and later went on to be Joint Manager of the Adelphi, and Sole Manager of the Lyceum. Her fame, however, seems to rest on the title of pantomime's first female Principal Boy, for she played Jack in the "opening" and became Harlequin when the usual transformation took place.

Being a true *burlesque*, the transformation was not the conventional one of "tradition", but came about following the Giant's fall from the beanstalk when everyone began arguing over who was to assume which role in the Harlequinade to come. Jack's father, Sir Gilbert, refused to play Harlequin because his rheumatism would prevent him from dancing, the Giant refused to be Clown because his great size would not allow him to get through the stage's trapdoors, and Jack was too young to play Pantaloon. In the end, the Giant agreed to be Pantaloon, Jack volunteered to be Harlequin, Sir Gilbert accepted the role of Clown and the fairy, Mother Goose announced that she would play Columbine herself. This quite firmly established that the Harlequinade and the "opening" were connected. The piece was a great success and the following year Lemon supplied the Adelphi with *Mother Shipton, her Wager; or Harlequin Knight of Love and The Magic Whistle* which again had Madam Celeste in the breeches role.

Reported *The Illustrated London News*:

"This theatre deservedly takes credit to itself for having originated the composite entertainment of burlesque-pantomime now generally adopted in preference to pantomime pure and simple.

Madame Celeste's accolade as pantomime's first female Principal Boy would seem to be warranted, as Madame Vestris's breeches roles were all in *burletta, burlesque* or the Opera, a different matter altogether. It should be noted though, that breeches roles in pantomime were recorded some years before Madame Celeste ever set foot in England. As early as 1819, Eliza Povey appeared as Jack in the Drury Lane production of *Jack and the Beanstalk; or Harlequin and the Ogre*, but as the role was a child's part and almost incidental to the story, plus the fact that she was not allowed to, or refused to climb the great beanstalk and did not take part in the Harlequinade, perhaps she can be discounted.

Another "breeches player" was Elizabeth Poole, who appeared in three Drury Lane pantomimes *Hop o' my Thumb and his brothers; or Harlequin and the Ogre* (1832), the following year's *Puss in Boots; or Harlequin and the Miller's sons*, and *Old Mother Hubbard and her Dog; or Harlequin and the Tales of the Nursery* in 1838, being Hop in the first, Joselin, the Miller's son in the second, and Cupid in the last. The representations of her in Mander and Mitchenson's *Pantomime, a story in pictures*, (Peter Davis, 1973) emphasize her lack of inches and it is reasonable to suppose Miss Poole was a child actress when she made her first appearance. Like Miss Povey, she took no part in the Harlequinade.

In view of the lack of solid evidence, it is probably safe to say that Planché and Vestris were responsible for the emergence of female Principal Boys in pantomime because role reversal was very much a part of the *burlesque* tradition, and as other managements and authors had quickly adopted the ideas of Planché's *extravaganzas* for their own purposes, there is no reason to suppose they would ignore the attractions of a shapely leg at the same time. Whatever the answer, by the middle of the 1860s, female Principal Boys in pantomime were familiar all over Britain.

*T*he new Opera House in Covent Garden was constructed on part of its original site and part of a plot added to the rear of it. The remaining ground would eventually be occupied by the Floral Hall and used as a concert room. It opened in May 1858 with a performance of the opera *Les Huguenots* and the first pantomime presented was *Little Red Riding Hood* with Richard Flexmore as Wolf/Clown. The opening was established by the fairies Music, Italian Opera, English Opera and Pantomime, and led into the story proper, followed by the Harlequinade.

At Christmas 1859, *Blue Beard; or Harlequin and Freedom in her Island Home* was presented and featured two Clowns and a Miss Craven as the Principal Boy. An hilarious anecdote concerning this production tells of the amazing elephant that had been created in the stage machinist's workshop for Bluebeard's entrance. The body was of covered basketwork, the legs of canvas, feet and head were modelled, tusks carved in wood, and the trunk and tail in covered wirework, all realistically painted. To mobilise it, a member of the stage crew was contained inside each leg, but on one occasion, the "near hind leg" had been drinking heavily and got himself involved in a heated argument with the "off fore-leg" shortly before the performance began.

Still threatening retribution when they got off stage, the inebriated man laborously clothed himself in his "leg" and with Bluebeard perched atop the huge model, the procession began. As they moved onto the stage, the elephant was seen to be somewhat lame in the back leg which dragged behind in a curious manner and finally stopped dead almost centre stage. Despite hissed instructions from the other three, the "leg" refused to move and in a fit of irritation, the off-side rear leg kicked his partner hard. Letting out a howl of pain, the inebriated stage member was heard to exclaim loudly, "I'll punch his bloody 'ead", and lashed out with his feet in all directions. The fore legs, taking the brunt of the attack, joined in with a vengeance and a general kicking ensued. The startled and unseated Bluebeard fell sideways out of the Howdah and crashed to the stage whilst the audience shook with laughter. Before he could stagger to his feet, the carcase of the elephant parted company from its lower region and toppled over leaving the four huge legs to continue their brawl. For future performances, the magnificent elephant gathered dust in the property room and a decorated palanquin was substituted.

Throughout the eighteen forties, fifties and sixties, however, strange storylines had continued to dominate the pantomime scene. Nelson Lee, (1807-1872), who wrote over two hundred of them, contributed *Harlequin £. s. d.* (Surrey Theatre, 1844) in which the immortals (Queen Anne and King Fourpenny) despatch the humble Pennypiece to Earth with orders to do good and by valiant efforts, turn himself into a Pound. After some adventure he becomes a Silver Penny and falls in love with Princess Five Shillings, (daughter of King Sovereign and Queen Half-sovereign of Guinea), who agrees to marry him. The Royal Couple are not pleased at this turn of events and fearing this union could result in a line of lowly Farthings inheriting the throne, order Silver Penny to be boiled alive. Quickly rescued by the Fairy Queen, he is transformed into the character of Harlequin, whilst the Princess, King and Queen become Columbine, Clown and Pantaloon respectively. The Harlequinade, (which was played by a totally different company), then took the tale to its amusing conclusion.

In the same year, at the Covent Garden theatre, his *Harlequin Crotchet and Quaver; or Music for the Millions* introduced audiences to the dainty Semi-quaver, (music seller to the Fairy Court), and her suitor, the dashing young Crotchet. Unfortunately, Semi-quaver is also loved by the villainous Discord, who aided by companions, Racket, Noise, Screech, etc., abducts the lovers and attempts to bribe her father, Demi-semi-quaver, into giving parental blessing for his own marriage to Semi-quaver. The furious old man refuses and, together with the captive lovers, is chained to a music bar in a hidden cave, where "they will never be able to frame a tune again". The timely appearance of the Fairy Queen results in the defeat of Discord and his companions, and a double Harlequinade quickly restores harmony to the world of music.

The ingenious Lee was also responsible for *Romeo and Juliet; or Harlequin and Queen Mab in the World of Dreams* (Olympic Theatre, 1852), another "Shakespearean inspired" pantomime which told how, from the Dismal Swamp of Hemlock and home of chief demon Prussic Acid, the hag Mischief sends her minion, British Brandy, (for which there is no known antidote) to poison Romeo. After Juliet stabs herself, Queen Mab transforms Romeo to Harlequin and Juliet to Columbine for the Harlequinade.

Other intriguing titles of those times were *Harlequin Baron Munchausen and his Comical Cream Cob Cruizer; or The Queen of the Fairy Steed's Haunt* (Astley's Amphitheatre, 1858) which was an equestrian pantomime complete with fairy chariots pulled by pygmy horses, and *The Bottle Imp; or Harlequin the Witch of the Woods, the Beautiful Princess, five Good Fairies and the Magic Ring* (Grecian Theatre, 1865), but the list is almost endless.

Blanchard's *Hop o' my Thumb; or Harlequin Ogre of the Seven Leagued Boots* was the 1865 pantomime at Drury Lane, and marked the final appearance of the previously mentioned

Clown, Tom Mathews, though Lydia Thompson (1836-1908) as Hop continued to delight as Principal Boy.

Having made her debut as a dancer at Her Majesty's Theatre, Haymarket when only sixteen, by 1854, Lydia had appeared at the St James's Theatre in the play *The King's Rival* and was "Little Bo-Peep in the Haymarket Theatre's pantomime of that year, *Little Silver Hair; or Harlequin and the Three Bears.* In 1862 she was playing in burlesque at The Prince of Wales Theatre for the Bancrofts before her pantomime debut at Drury Lane that Christmas in *Goody Two Shoes; or Harlequin and Cock Robin.* Seven years later, she caused a sensation when she took a troupe of girls to America for the burlesque *The Forty Thieves* at New York's Niblo's Gardens and packed the house nightly. Said Richard Grant White in *Galaxy*:

> "She was one of the most charming comic actresses it had been my good fortune to see. She played burlesque with a daintiness which few actresses of note are able to flavour their acting, even in high comedy ... she was the embodiment of mirth and moved others to hilarity by being moved herself. It was as if Venus, in her quality of the goddess of laughter, had come upon the stage"

Thompson had a great following in America, and "Lydia's Blondes" as the girls were known, had a devastating affect on its male youth. During their Chicago engagement, the drama critic of *The Chicago Times*, Wilbur F. Story, made derogatory remarks on what he assumed were the troupe's morals, and Lydia, together with Pauline Markham, one of her girls, stormed his office demanding an apology. After insulting them again, the critic produced a gun and threatened to shoot, but Pauline disarmed and held him while Lydia laid into him with a horse-whip. The amused Magistrates fined her two cents for the offence, but following an appeal by *The Chicago Times*, reluctantly increased the amount to 2,200 dollars – which "The Blondes" considered very cheap for the satisfaction they felt. In the end it cost them nothing, as sympathisers happily paid the fine.

Lydia remained popular with American audiences for twenty years, not to mention throughout Europe. In Riga and other Baltic towns, her portrait was displayed opposite that of the Tzar in many homes and in Cologne, students freed the horses drawing her carriage, and pulled it through the streets themselves.   She continued to work in pantomime and *burlesque* until shortly before her death.

Another huge pantomime success in America was *Humpty Dumpty* at the Olympic Theatre (March 1868) featuring comedian George L. Fox (1825-1877) in which he appeared as Clown. Adapted from an English production, it had a cast of sixty, plus a *corps de ballet*, was in seventeen scenes, and played for 1268 performances in New York alone taking over one million dollars at the box office. At the end of the run, a tour of the piece raised another million, after which it returned to New York to take another half million. Fox, who successfully presented pantomimes for several years, developed "softening of the brain" and died aged 52, but the form lived on in America before vanishing from the scene at the end of the 1800s. None, however, came near to equaling the fantastic success of *Humpty Dumpty*.

Though Blanchard continued to dominate the pantomime scene in London, the work of Henry J. Byron, (1834-84) a *burlesque* writer, had been drawing attention for some time and was to have a large influence on the British pantomime. Born in Manchester, his original intention was to be an actor but ended up as the first editor of the humorous weekly magazine, *Fun*, which he helped found in 1861. Byron wrote over one hundred *burlesques*, and though his rhymes were not as polished as Blanchard, his atrocious puns made Victorians laugh for over thirty years.

A good example of his work is seen in the following short exchange from *Puss in a New Pair of Boots* at the Strand Theatre (1862). After Will, the deceased Miller's son, is told that his only inheritance is a cat, he exclaims:

Will : What! Left his youngest child a cat! It's true.
     Well, that's a *feline* sort of thing to do.
Puss: I am, as you perceive, sir, an I-*tail*-ian,
     But never scratch my friends, though I'm a *naily-un*;
     It's only foes that ever raise my fur.
Will : Well, really. You're a charming *furry*-ner.
     What can you do?
Puss: My pictures, folk applaud;
     They say they're scratchy, but resemble *Claude*.
     I'm not much of a linguist, my good friend,
     But I've a-*tal (i)* on at my finger's end;

I can't dance well amongst young ladies, yet
I come out very well in a puss-et.
I sing at times like any cat-a-lani.
Will : Your favourite opera is?
Puss: Il *Purr*-itani.

The *Claude* referred to is Claude Gellee, also known as Claude Lorrain (1600-1682) who was the first painter to specialize entirely in landscapes. Pusset, as near as I can ascertain, is the weaving walk of a cat around people's ankles. *Catalani* was Angelica Catalani (1780-1849) the most phenomenal opera singer of her day. In 1807 alone, it is reported she earned twenty-one thousand, seven hundred pounds in addition to the various items of jewellery bestowed on her by admirers. Possessor of an incredibly powerful voice, she was once appearing in York when a London music lover was asked if he would be travelling there to see her perform. "No need" he replied. "I can stay here and listen to her. "Puritani" is, of course, the Bellini opera. See how knowledgeable the burlesque audiences needed to be in those days?

Another dig at the fashion for opera is sung by King Noodlehead IX in the same *burlesque*;

At the Opera, and at Covent Garden as well,
I have always observed that the expiring swell
Tho' you'd fancy just there he'd be shortest of breath,
Sings a difficult song just before his own death
And I've likewise remarked that the young hero-ine
Walks about in a low dress of thin white sat-ine
Defying the fog, and the cold and the damp
And also rheumatics, and likewise the cramp.
With a diddle, diddle, diddle,
Chip chop chooral I-ay
That's how they arrange things at the Oper-i-ay.

Though Byron only wrote eight pantomimes in his entire career, his *burlesques* gave pantomime two enduring features. His *Cinderella; or the Lover, The Lackey, and The Little Glass Slipper* at the Royal Strand Theatre in 1860, introduced us to Buttoni, a page, and his one act *Aladdin or the Wonderful Scamp* gave us the cheerful Widow Twankay.

As a pantomime ballet in two acts, Cinderella had been performed at the Theatre Royal, Drury Lane, 1803, and was a mixture of dancing, recitatives, arias and choruses. The following year, it appeared again, this time as "a grand allegorical pantomimic spectacle", and opened in the January, with James Byrne as Prince (later Harlequin), Grimaldi as Pedro, (later Clown) and the spiteful sisters a Mrs. Byrne and Miss Vining. Cinderella, (later Columbine) was played by Miss Decamp. At this point, there was no Fairy Godmother, no Dandini, no Baron, Baroness, Buttons or Broker's Men.

The "opening" was set on Mount Ida where Venus and her court are gathered. Cupid fires an arrow into the heart of the Prince who has just seen Cinderella in a dream. The Prince sends invitations to a ball in the hope that his dream-lady will attend. Cinderella, helped by the servant Pedro, looks after the house for her two vain sisters who mock her as they leave for the ball. Venus arrives and changes pumpkin, mice and lizards into a coach, horses and footmen then changes the rags of Cinderella and Pedro to fine clothing. As they leave for the ball, she warns them they must return home before midnight. The Prince and Cinderella meet and he gives her a diamond ring and a silk scarf. At midnight, Cupid moves the hands of the clock back to give them another hour, but as the clock begins to strike the real time, Pedro's clothing changes back causing confusion. As he jumps over tables, etc., Cinderella whose clothing has also reverted but un-noticed, slips away, losing her slipper in the process. The Prince finds it and kisses it. The ragged Cinderella is ignored by the Prince's men who are searching for her, and Pedro, carrying the pumpkin, finds her and they go home. The sisters return and the Prince's announcement is made.

On Mount Ida, Venus and her court rejoice. The Prince enters with the slipper, but it fits no-one until Pedro introduces Cinderella to the Prince. He recognises her and fits the slipper on her foot. She produces the other slipper and Venus enters with the rest of her court and marries them. Princess Cinderella then forgives her sisters and introduces them to two noblemen. All are then transformed into the characters of the Harlequinade in the usual manner.

Rossini's sparkling comic opera, *La Cenerentola*, an Italian version of the Cinderella story, opened at The King's Theatre, Haymarket, in January 1820, and besides providing the heroine with a father, the Baron Monte Fiascone, introduced Dandini, valet to the Prince of Salerno. The magic was left in the hands of Alidoro, the Prince's old tutor and the sisters remained more vain than ugly.

In March of the same year, *Harlequin and Cinderella: or The Little Glass Slipper* became the Easter pantomime for Covent Garden, and featured a Baron Pomposini, a Baroness, (played by Grimaldi) and a Fairy Godmother with the name of Finetta (which was the name the Countess d'Aulnoy gave Cinderella in her collection of fairy tales in 1721, pre-dating the English translation of Perrault's by some years) Pedro was still the unrequited lover of Cinderella, but this time did not accompany her to the ball. Nor did the Prince find her slipper, and the Fairy Godmother was not the gentle old lady depicted in todays versions. She was an imperious character who punishes Cinderella for not leaving the ball on time by revealing to the Prince that Cinderella is the maiden who so enchanted him, and until the missing slipper is found, they will never be able to marry. She then transforms Cinderella into Columbine, the Prince to Harlequin, Baron and Baroness to Pantaloon and Clown, and lovesick Pedro into Dandinee, (sic) vowing they will stay in these characters until the slipper is recovered. Following the usual ten scene Harlequinade, the Fairy Godmother announces;

> The slipper found, your task is o'er,
> The pow'r to punish, is no more ...
> In Finetta's Temple, this pair shall prove
> The joys that wait on constant love.
> Here Cinderella this prize shall win,
> And in Wedlock's bonds be join'd with Harlequin.

Until 1860, this version provided the basis of all other Cinderella productions, but Byron's *burlesque* came much closer to what today's audiences would expect to see. Both Prince Poppetti and his valet Dandino were played by women and it was in this production that the characters first exchanged clothes to impersonate each other after the following pun-filled exchange;

> Dandino   : This coat, you will admit, is not the best cut,
> And neither is my waistcoat quite the *West Cut.*
> I must di-vest myself of that affair:
> These buckles aint the thing for *Buckley* Square.

Prince	: You shall be decked in gems of vast expense.
	And be a *gem-man* in a double sense.
	Your servant, I will wait, clean boots, wash glasses;
	Thus serve a nob, an' *observe* all that passes.
Dandino	: Then you'll obey me till you've found La Donna?
	You *pledge* your princely word?
Prince	: *A-pawn* my honour.

Even more excruciating is the following conversation between Cinderella and the Prince;

Cinderella	: Cinders and coals I'm so accustomed to,
	They seem to me to tinge all things I view.
Prince	: That fact I can't say causes me surprise,
	For *khol* is frequently in ladies eyes.
Cinderella	: At morn, when reading, as the fire up-burns,
	The print, from stops, to semi-*coalums* turns
Prince	: Who is your favourite poet? Hobbs?
Cinderella	: Not quite.
	No, I think *Cole*-ridge is my favour-ite.
	His melan-coally suits my situation;
	My dinner always is a *coald coal*-ation.

Not much better is the exchange between Buttoni and Cinders when she tells him she often dreams of wearing fine clothes and dancing a waltz with the Prince.

Cinderella	: I wake, alas, to life's far different round
	In these, the dullest vaults that could be found.
Buttoni	: (Aside) Alas! With all her *vaults* I love her still!
	Oh, make me happy, Miss, do say you will,
	Oh, don't be deaf as *post*, Miss, I beseech you;
	Let the memorial of this sad page reach you;
	Don't stop its course by letting pride prevail,
	Or wrong de-*livery* of this *mourning male*.

After two hours of such pun packed doggerel rhyme, one imagines the audience would totter out into the street exhausted, but many returned time and time again, eager for repeat performances.

There was of course, a comic Baron Balderdash ("a slightly damaged edition of *The Last of the Barons*, bound in calf, three vols. in one, by no means lettered, and very generally cut"); the aforementioned Buttoni, listed as "a page of *Last of the Barons*, with Clorinda, one of the Baron's trio of daughters, (the others being Thisbe and Cinderella) being played by a man. Having no Harlequinade, the production ended as usual with a "Gorgeous Transformation Scene".

The addition of Buttons to pantomime versions of *Cinderella* was not immediate, but the Pedro character (who changed names frequently as the years rolled by) assumed the characteristics of Buttons in the Byron version. The 1893 Lyceum *Cinderella*, written by Horace Lennard and featuring the lovely Ellaline Terriss actually replaced him with a black cat, played by Charles Lauri, the famous animal impersonator.

Lauri was the son of a Clown and from an early age had specialised in "skin" roles. He had been a bear, a wolf, a "flying" bird, and countless other animals, but as a cat or dog was considered the "best in the business". He frequently amazed audiences when playing cat roles, by leaving the stage and clambering up to the dress circle where he would stroll along the narrow balustrade "purring" at the children in the front row and "washing his face" with apparent unconcern at the sheer drop behind him.

As the "Babes" pet dog in *Babes in the Wood*, audiences were reduced to tears when he was "killed" by the villains and in 1894, William Archer, critic of the *World* wrote bitterly;

> "As embodied by Mr. Charles Lauri, Tatters is the most popular and sympathetic character in the pantomime and his untimely end is too harrowing to be borne. Children ought not to have their feelings wrung and their pleasure saddened in this way."

Such was his support from the public, Tatters was hastily brought back to life again in subsequent performances.

An amusing story tells of a rehearsal involving Lauri and a speciality double act known as the Tender Brothers. Being possessed of particularly thick skulls, their act consisted of hitting each other over the head with solid wooden staves, axes, building bricks, and other such weapons, without any adverse effect. Lauri, who was playing a dog, thought up a piece of business that would cause the audience to sympathise with him and hate the two villains even more, so approached the easy-going "Brothers" with his suggestion. When they arrived at the Dame's door to evict her, he would dash out of his kennel and bite their legs. In return, they were to hit him with their sticks and he would beat a retreat, howling and whimpering. When the scene arrived, Lauri dashed out and one of them gave him a gentle (for them) tap over the head. To Lauri it was like being hit by a sledgehammer and as the horrified "Brothers" looked on, he staggered dazedly off-stage before collapsing in a heap. It was several days before he metaphorically left his kennel again, and his idea was quietly dropped.

When the production of *Cinderella* crossed the Atlantic in 1894 for a ten week run at the Abbey Theatre, New York, it was greatly acclaimed, but unfortunately, in mid performance, the actor playing Lauri's role collapsed and died. With the combination of the devastating fire at Chicago's Iroquios Theatre just a few years later, pantomime was declared "jinxed" and within a very short period, vanished from the American theatre scene for more than three quarters of a century.

By 1920, however, the name Buttons was well established, as was that of Dandini and Prince Charming (who had moved rapidly through Precious, Poppetti, Vanilla, Plenteous, Lovesick, Prettifello, Paragon and Pastorelle), though the Baron's Family name is still flexible, veering these days between Hardupp and Stoneybroke (after several years of de Broke, de Bankrupt or something similar). Whilst the wicked stepmother is rarely seen today, the Ugly Sisters continue to change their forenames from year to year, usually spoofing the latest television celebrities.

Aladdin, first presented as a pantomime on December 26th, 1788 at Covent Garden, is the second most popular of our "traditionals", but again, was a far different story to the one we know now. There was no Widow Twankay, no Laundry, no Wishee Washee, no Chinese policemen and not until the Easter presentation of a "melodramatic romance" on the subject at Covent Garden in 1813, was the mysterious African Magician of the Arabian Nights story given the name Abanazar. (Grimaldi also appeared in this as Kasrac, the dumb slave of the mighty magician, but as the production was not a pantomime, was not required to play Clown). Mrs. Charles Kemble played Aladdin, and her mother was Ching Mustapha, the widow of a tailor.

In 1856, The Royal Princess' Theatre presented a burlesque-pantomime entitled *Aladdin and his Wonderful Lamp; or the Genie of the Ring* in which Aladdin, his mother *and* the Princess were all played by men, but Byron's burlesque at the Strand Theatre in the Easter of 1861 proved to be the definitive version, for almost all productions of *Aladdin* that followed have been based on his original storyline.

Taking his cue from the Clipper Ships that transported tea from the East, he named Aladdin's mother Twankay after a variety of coarse leaf used for making green tea, whilst the Vizier's son (who often turned up in the pantomimes of the 1930s and 40s as a kind of secondary Principal Boy), was Pekoe, a more refined type of leaf.

By 1870, Widow Twankay could be found in almost all pantomime treatments of Aladdin, though it was another twenty years before she could be found in her famous laundry. In Blanchard's 1885 version she runs a newspaper shop before being lumbered with the Emperor's dirty laundry, and prior to that she appeared to be simply "A washerwoman of mangled feelings". It was not until late 1896, that Widow Twankey, in the shape of Dan Leno, could be found wrestling with a mangle on her own premises. (Courtesy of Drury Lane) together with Wishee Washee, who had made *his* first appearance just ten years earlier. The Chinese policemen also made their first appearance around this time, and are the last of the familiar characters of British pantomime to arrive on the scene.

Not that policemen had been neglected in pantomime. The upholder of the law had been a source of fun from the days of the Commedia dell' arte, and though not playing a leading role in the proceedings, *Il Sbirro*, the policeman, was often directed by Pantaloon to track down the fleeing Harlequin and Columbine. In the days of Rich, he generally found himself outwitted by means of the magic slapstick, and as Clown became more important, the unhappy butt of practical jokes.

In the 1807, *Harlequin in his Element*, Grimaldi had great fun by locking the "Watch" in his own watch-box before waking up the entire neighbourhood, the helpless law enforcer unable to silence him. In a later production, Grimaldi would steal various pieces of clothing such as boots, a coat, a dressmaking stand, etc., and construct a dummy out of them. As Harlequin passed by, he would touch the dummy with his magic baton and transform it into a policeman who then arrested the Clown for stealing.

When Sir Robert Peel formed his police force in 1829, they were decidedly unpopular with a great section of the public, so pantomime Clowns could always raise audience laughter by inflicting "pain" on an unsuspecting stage "Peeler". Nine time out of ten, the wrong end of Clown's "red-hot" poker would end up in the hand, pocket, ear or mouth of a self-important policeman leaving him hopping around in agony, and for as long as the Harlequinade flourished, outwitting a policeman was an expected part of every Clown's repertoire. The bungling "Keystone Cops" in the days of silent film were off-shoots of early British pantomime comedy and though *Aladdin* is now the only pantomime to sometimes feature Policemen, their counterparts live on as Broker's Men or Captain and Mate, etc. in other pantomimes.

At the end of the nineteenth century and up to the latter end of the twentieth, the Chinese Policemen were named as Ping, Pong, Pang, Hi, Lo, or something similar, though the idiocies of political correctness have once again taken their toll and most managements omit them from productions altogether. It is perhaps worth noting that when my own version of *Aladdin* was presented in China in the early 1990s, the management supplemented my two Chinese Policemen with several extras as "audiences loved to see them dashing about and causing chaos."

The pantomimes of Blanchard and his imitators were not to everyone's taste. To the older generation, the longer "open-ings" and shorter Harlequinades had caused them to lose much of their appeal and spectacular transformation scenes were no substitute for old time inventive comedy. An open let-ter to Clowns by a contributor to *Chambers' Journal* in 1864 complained:

> "Do you ever reflect upon the painful fact that English boys are now growing up wholly ignorant of the nature and efficacy of the Buttered Slide? But how should they do otherwise when pan-tomime after pantomime ignores its existence? ... Again, the "spill and pelt"; to what has *that* degenerated? Why – *once* in an

entire evening, a knot of long-striding youths and screaming maidens hurry pell mell from wing pursued by a policeman or two and a mere handful of high flying carrots. What a falling off. We have no longer the *organized* mob – image-men, fishwomen, greengrocers, crockery sellers, bakers, police – running in Indian file across the stage – out at one wing, round at back of flat, and in again at the other, for you and Pantaloon to spill and pelt and bring every scene to a conclusion amid a protracted eruption of vegetables, crockery, images and fish ...

What has become of the red-hot poker? ... I don't believe there is a living Clown who can give his heart the slap and say honestly: "I never rob the people of this famous usage." ... Every Clown can be practically funny. Be the enemy of mankind and you become the audience's dearest friend. Be *cruel* – brutally, increasingly, perpetually cruel, and lo! you are intensely funny. In "spill and pelt", take care that people really *are* hit. Never mind hurting the *supers*-supers have no more right to feel pain than eels have ... Look to your legs. Why, they're getting *straight*; you aren't knock-kneed nowadays; neither do your calves grow at the side of your shins. Shew us your tongue oftener ... As for sausages, it is *years* since a legitimate chain of them has been seen at a West End theatre"

The complaint, as usual, fell on deaf ears and apart from theatres cautiously starting to drop the plays that normally preceded the pantomimes owing to the latter's greater lengths, there were no drastic changes until the next decade, though a surprising name emerged in 1867 when the aforementioned Edward Tyrrel Smith commissioned a 31 year old writer to provide the pantomime for his recently acquired Lyceum Theatre. The result was possibly the longest title ever seen on a theatrical poster; *Harlequin Cock Robin and Jenny Wren; or Fortunatus and the Water of Life, the Three Bears, the Three Gifts, the Three Wishes, and The Little Man Who Woo'd the Little Maid*, and the writer, who received £60 for it, was W. S. Gilbert.

*W*illiam Schwenck Gilbert (1836-1911) had been amusing the public since 1861, when following the publication of a short article in *Fun*, he had been invited by Byron to become a regular contributor. With the success of *The Bab Ballads*, his dramatic criticisms and general journalism, he had been able to forsake his unrewarding law practice and concentrate on writing. The burlesque *Dulcamara; or The Little Duck and The Great Quack*, presented at the Theatre Royal, St. James, on 29th Dec. 1866, was his first production for the stage and earned him the sum of £30. His second stage piece, *La Vivandiere; or True to the Corps* was another burlesque, first presented at the St James's Hall in Liverpool and followed by a 120 performance run at the Queen's Theatre, London in 1868. A third *burlesque, The Merry Zingara; or The Tipsy Gypsy and the Pipsy Wipsey* entertained audiences at the Royalty Theatre and prompted the *Illustrated London News* to report:

> "It is remarkable, even among punning extravaganzas, for the abundance of its puns which came down among the audience like a sparkling shower."

Gilbert's commission to write the Lyceum pantomime came as a direct result of this, and following the traditions of the time, he peopled his script with the most unlikely characters. For the evil Immortals he supplied The Demon Miasma and his offspring, Malaria and Age, plus a collection of attendants, Want, Misery, Pestilence, Satana and Demonio, while for the good Immortals, there were Fresh Air, The Fairy of the Fountain, and Fairies Health and Happiness. Cock Robin and Jenny Wren were a pair of love-birds, and The Three Bears their wicked enemies. In the opening scene, The Demon Miasma's Dismal Swamp, Miasma summons up his minions to issue instructions:

Miasma	: Gather round me, serpents,vipers, toads,
	Scorpions and beetles from your dark abodes;
	Infect the earth, the water and the air;
	Spit pestilential poison ev'rywhere!
	With sulphurous fumes all human nostrils fill -
	You understand? It is Miasma's will.
Pestilence	: (Whining) My sphere of action's cramped as it can be;
	Chloride of lime has nearly done for me.
Misery	: Poor people live so cleanly and so neatly
	I find my little game played out completely!
	E'er from cheap lodging-house, back I'm sent:
	Now poor folk lodge by act of Parliament.
Miasma	: What's this I hear? My deadly tools
	Restricted now to fens and stagnant pools?
	Have I no home - no friends - no footing - none?
	My occupation, like Othello's, gone?
	I'm nearly stamped out in this cursed nation.
	My epitaph: He died of ventilation.

In revenge, Miasma decides to kill the bird life of the forest, notably Cock Robin and Jenny Wren, but the fairies foil the attack and change the pair into The Little Man and the Little Maid. In a later scene, the Little Maid goes exploring the forest and finds the home of the Three Bears, who enter disguised as Courtiers. During a dance with them, First Bear squeezes her too tightly and she protests, only to discover the terrible truth;

First Bear	: Concealment and disguise away we tear – (Does so)
	I am your ancient enemy, First Bear.
	Of my determined enmity you have heard -
Second Bear:	I am the Second Bear!
Third Bear	: And I the third.

148

The Bears decide to bake her in a pie, but fortunately, a rescuer is at hand who successfully fights them off. As the Three Bears nurse their wounds, Miasma appears in a cloud of fumes which causes the Little Maid and her rescuer to faint from the stench. Cackles the Demon;

Miasma : So perish all who brave Miasma's will;
    My noxious fumes their open nostrils fill;
    Fresh Air alone will bring them to, that's clear.
    And that's a thing that never ventures here!
    That she can penetrate this wood I doubt.
Fresh Air : (Entering) I beg your pardon, you can't keep her out;
    Where're she goes all decent men of sense
    Rejoice to feel her gentle influence.
    For cleanliness is her prevailing feature.
Miasma : Cleanliness? Ugh, you disgusting creature.

When the proceedings are brought to a conclusion with the usual Transformation scene, the second cast entered with the Harlequinade to end the evening.

As one can gather from the above, Gilbert's pantomime was no worse than any other of its day, but the end result was a disaster. As Gilbert himself wrote in the *Era Annual* several years later:

"It was written in about four days. ... Mr. Smith had bought a vast crystal fountain and this property was to be the principal scenic effect of the pantomime. Four scenes had to be introduced to give time to set this absurdity, and three scenes to strike it. Most of these scenes were written by the stage manager, who, when I expostulated, told me they were much better written than mine, and Mr. Smith agreed with him ... The rehearsals were, of course, a wild scramble. Everybody was going to introduce a song or a dance (unknown to me) and these songs and dances were rehearsed surreptitiously in corners. ... It had occurred to Mr. Smith that it would be a good idea to have the scenery painted at Cremorne (of which he was lessee) and carted up to the Lyceum. The scenery was all behind – at least, it was none of it behind – it was all at Cremorne. At about four o'clock on Boxing Day, instalments of the scenery began to arrive. ... When the curtain rose on the piece, about three complete scenes had arrived. Two of these were scenes that had been introduced to set the fountain. ... Then came a ballet scene – all perfect except the cloth. Then came two more scenes to set the fountain, and the three scenes introduced to strike it. The last of these ... was a forest scene. It was to be followed by the transformation scene; but the transformation scene was not

149

ready, so a lady who rendered invaluable service on this eventful evening went on and sang "Not for Joe". Then came a pause. Then an excited dialogue was heard at the wing.

Mr. Smith. "Go on, somebody, and do something! Here. You go on!"

Voice. "Please, sir, I'm on for the comic scenes"

Mr. Smith. "Bless the comic scenes. Cross the stage at once"

And immediately a plum pudding on two legs hopped to the centre of the stage, turned to the audience, bowed politely, turned to the opposite wing and hopped off.

Mr. Smith. Now the ballet. Quick. The Fish Ballet.

Voice. (In expostulation) A fish ballet in a forest?

Mr. Smith. (Maddened) Is this a time to talk of forests?

... A "Fish Ballet" entered (very shiny and scaly, but otherwise not like any fish I have ever met) and danced a long ballet, which they themselves thoughtfully encored. ... Then came the clever and hard-working lady with another song (from last year's pantomime.) At last, the Transformation scene – that is to say, some of it. Only one half of the scene – the O.P. half – was there; tinselled fennelly branches, with large half – opened oyster shells beneath each branch, each shell containing a beautiful young lady ... but the other half of the scene – the P.S. half – alas! it hadn't arrived it was at Cremorne. There was no attempt to fill up the deficiency. One half of the stage was complete, the other half was empty. ... The Harlequinade went well, but poor Mr. Smith's fountain was never seen"

One may think, knowing Gilbert's sense of the ridiculous, his description of events could perhaps be a slight exaggeration, but one hundred and twenty-one years later, in 1988, I was in a very similar production which reduced the entire cast to hysteria and gave me two displaced ribs in the bargain.

The failure of Gilbert's pantomime did not deter Smith from trying again. The following year, 1868 *Harlequin Humpty Dumpty; or Dame Trot and her Cat* took the stage and if for nothing else, will be forever remembered by historians as the production that introduced the famous Vokes Family.

Frederick Vokes and his wife had a shop in Henrietta Street, Covent Garden, from which they supplied "Grand Fancy Costume Ball, Theatrical and Historical Dresses". Their children, Jessie, Frederick Jnr., Victoria and Rosina all took to the stage in turn, Jessie making her debut aged four years at the Surrey Theatre, (being taught dancing by Flexmore, the Clown), Victoria at the age of two, Rosina as a baby in arms and Frederick spending his early years working for the infamous "Wizard of the North", Professor Anderson as a conjuror's assistant. Though all could act well, their fame came from dancing, and after they had been shaped into a troupe by an aunt, made their collective debut in Paris presenting short "entertainments" before touring Canada, the U.S.A. and Britain with huge success.

Fred Vokes was undoubtably the star of the troupe and his extraordinary dancing skills gave him the title of "The man with the elastic legs".

> "Mr. Vokes" (wrote the *Daily Telegraph* critic) "dances as few men in this world probably could dance or would wish to dance. The extraordinary contortions of limb in which his dancing abounds, contortions which in Mr. Vokes's hands - or rather legs – are not lacking in grace – are highly suggestive of the impossibility of his suffering at any time from such accidents as dislocation."

The following year (1869), at the invitation of lessee F. B. Chatterton, the family moved to Drury Lane for the pantomime *Beauty and the Beast* and with the exception of 1873 when they were touring abroad, remained there for the next ten years, much to Blanchard's dismay. His beautiful scripts were badly mauled by the cavorting troupe, whose gyrations continued onstage even when others were speaking or singing, and a certain amount of ill-feeling appeared in the rest of the company. The Public, however, had taken the Vokes to their heart and cheered them heartily, which only led them to greater excesses.

For the 1870 pantomime *The Dragon of Wantley*, a fifth member was added to their dancing troupe, and though no relation, adopted the name of Fawden Vokes. Elastic legged Fred was Moore of Moor Hall, Jingo, his squire, was Fawden, Lady Joan, the Principal Girl, was Victoria and in the minor role of Madge, her attendant, was Rosina. Jessie Volkes was principal dancer and leading Water nymph. The Fairy element was provided by Mother Shipton, the kindly Witch of Knaresborough, who emerging from her famous cave at the pleas of the villagers, announced herself like this;

> Now let me hear what you desire to find out.
> One at a time, and each one speak their mind out.
> My marvelous perception, so to speak,
> Shall penetrate the middle of next week;

And, though it much more wonderful appears,
Pierce the dark mystery of three hundred years,
Prophesies published as the Act directs...
All copyright, with registered effects.

From this point on, the Volks' danced their way through every scene as though possessed, but still found the energy to invade the Harlequinade too, Fawdon being one of the Harlequins, and Jessie and Rosina two of the Columbines.

By 1871, when *Tom Thumb; or King Arthur and the Knights of the Round Table*, went into rehearsal, the troupe had conspired to commandeer every principal role and after the opening night *The Times* was to report:

> "The great weight of the work fell on the Vokes family, and this talented clan, both as singers and dancers and in the comic business of pantomimists, exert themselves to the utmost and earn whole acres of laurels. The manner in which first the crown and then the wig of Mr. Fred Vokes as King Arthur persisted in tumbling off while that monarch indulged in unusual gyrations excited tumultuous laughter ... nothing in the way of dances came amiss to the airy monarch whose legs and arms seem to spin round on pivots and who seemed at once to simulate the actions of the cockchafer and the grasshopper. He was well assisted by Mr. Fawdon Vokes as the court fool who had apparently danced himself out of his mind in his infancy and had lived on tarantula spiders ever since. All the Misses Vokes ... were fully equal to the occasion. When they didn't dance, they sang and danced simultaneously and then all the Vokeses jumped on one another's back and careered – so it seemed – into immeasurable space"

In the 1874 *Aladdin*, Fred was Abanazar, Fawdon was Kasrac, his slave, Victoria was Aladdin, Rosina the Princess, and Jessie the Genius of the Lamp. At the end of the performance, they took a family bow and did a specially devised dance as they did it. The following year, *Dick Whittington* found another "adopted" Vokes in the cast, Walter, who played the Cat, and in 1876, Mrs. Fred Vokes had joined the troupe for *The White Cat*. Poor Blanchard was in despair and even the critics began to wonder how much longer the talented, but undisciplined Vokes would continue to disrupt the Drury Lane pantomimes. Wrote George Augustus Sala in 1878:

> "... they are sublimely indifferent as to whether the story of Cinderella be a Sanskrit myth or a Greek fable. They brought the

house down, metaphorically speaking, over and over again;
The only wonder is that physically speaking, they did not bring
down the wings and sky borders and the very planks of the stage
itself. Impulsive Mr. Fred Vokes as the Baron Pumperknickl ...
accompanied by Mr. Fawdon Vokes as Kobold ... disdained to be
shackled by the preliminary dreariness of an incantation scene
in which some tiresome magician relates a prosy prologue for the
edification of supernumeraries in monstrous masks. Scarcely
had the curtain risen and a number of children disguised as wild
boars begun to disport themselves in a woody glade in the Black
Forest, then Mr. Fred Vokes, attended by Mr. Fawdon Vokes
skipped onto the stage and both began to throw their arms and
legs about in the most wonderful manner."

Said another:

"They dance exactly as they have danced for years past. ... If they
want to retain their hold upon the public, they should get someone to concoct for them new modes in which to display their
exceptional powers"

And a third:

"They were on stage far too long"

Indeed they were, and halfway through the run of Cinderella,
Chatterton found out he was in debt to the tune of £36,000.
The Vokes Family, not having received their usual salaries on
the Friday night, promptly went on strike and Drury Lane theatre closed down on Feb. 4th, 1879, "in consequence of
unforeseen circumstances".

The failure of Chatterton, however, was the beginning of
pantomime's greatest days, for as luck would have it,
Augustus Harris (1851-1896), the twenty seven year old son of
a theatre manager was looking for a venue and Drury Lane
theatre passed into his hands. Quite how Harris managed it
is a miracle in itself. When he approached the Drury Lane
committee and told them of his plans for the theatre, he had
precisely £3 and 15 shillings (75p) to his name. The
Committee asked for a deposit of £1,000, and Harris agreed to
the terms. By borrowing the money from various sources, he
raised the sum of £2,750, and this tiny amount was to bring
him fame and fortune.

Opening on November 1st, 1879, with Shakespeare's
Henry V, against all advice he concentrated on the military and
battle scenes, crowding the stage with horses, waving banners,

clashing swords and other visual effects. The result was electrifying, and packed the theatre night after night. Said *The
Era*;

As audiences clamoured for admittance, Harris was working
on his Christmas pantomime, due to open on Dec. 26th.
Blanchard had provided the script for *Bluebeard* and Beverley
was working on the scenery, but Harris was far from happy
with his cast. Because of his late arrival on the scene, he had
been forced to fall back on the talents of the Vokes Family, and
was not impressed.

To the dismay of Blanchard, Harris tore apart the beautifully crafted script, removing everything he felt that held up the
action, which in *his* opinion, was anything you couldn't *see*.
The horrified Vokes' Family discovered that Harris was no
Chatterton and their terpsichorean excesses were slashed to
the bone. Whatever remained was wrapped in unrelenting
spectacle and Harris directed everything himself.

The result was the most glittering pantomime ever seen on
a stage, the transformation scene alone taking several minutes
to unfold with its myriads of gauzes, cloths, flats and costume
changes, the subtle differences drawing sustained applause
from dazzled and ecstatic audiences. There was even a
double Harlequinade, with many extra characters, including
Arlequin Parisienne, Panette, and Polichenelle. At the close of
the evening, Harris appeared on stage and asked the audience
if they were satisfied. The answer was most definitely "Yes".

With the bit firmly between his teeth, Harris knew he had to
surpass himself next year, and did. Following a phenomenal-
ly successful season including operetta, Shakespeare, and a
specially written play, *The World*, which featured in its five acts
and nine tableaux a bomb explosion that sank a liner leaving
survivors bobbing around on a raft, the interior of a lunatic
asylum, an exact duplicate of the great Aquarium at
Westminster and a Fancy Dress Ball, *Mother Goose and the
Enchanted Beauty* became his second pantomime for Drury
Lane.

In place of the Vokes Family, Harris had selected performers from the Music Hall for his stars.

Arthur Roberts, (1852-1933) the comedian whose saucy
song "I'm living with mother now " had lifted a number of eyebrows.

Stand me a cab fare, duckie, do now, there's a dear.
Or buy me a hot potato, for I'm feeling awfully queer.
Your eyes look dreadful wicked, but kissing I couldn't allow.
I might have done so a few months ago, but I'm living with
mother now.

James Fawn (1849-1923) remembered for his song "If you
want to know the time, ask a policeman", dancer Fred Storey,
singer Ada Blanche and Kate Santley who had begun her
career in Shakespeare before turning to Music Hall and
Burlesque, were only just a few of his star studded cast. Many
theatregoers were horrified and prophesied disaster. Music
Hall entertainers in pantomime? Had it really come to this?

To the audiences of today, accustomed to beautifully
dressed television versions of Music Hall shows such as *The
Good Old Days*, or the polished, elegant, touring theatre
companies with a genial Chairman introducing each act with
a torrent of hyperbole, it is difficult to imagine what all the
fuss was about.

The real Music Hall was a far cry from these cosy images as
any reader of its history will confirm. Originating in the "song
and supper" rooms in the early 1800s, by the 1840's there
were several all male establishments in London where food
and drink could be bought and vocal entertainment, usually
bawdy, supplied by the landlords or patrons, though later,
professional singers were brought in which allowed landlords
to step down and act as Chairmen.

One of these establishments was "Evans", late "Joys" in
King Street, Covent Garden, which was infinitely respectable,
and frequented by such luminaries as W.S.Gilbert, Charles
Dickens, Thomas Hood, and H. J. Byron who met their friends
there for chops, devilled kidneys, baked potatoes and a drink
or two, followed by entertainments of religious or operatic origins performed by Abby choristers. On the other hand, just a
few hundred yards away, *The Coal Hole* in The Strand was per-

haps the most notorious room in London where songs of such indecency were sung, even military men were known to walk out in disgust.

With the passing of the 1843 Theatre's Act, London's Saloons were given the choice to become legitimate theatres unable to sell drink in the auditorium, or Concert Rooms able to sell drink, but not to produce stage plays. Some, like the "Britannia" at Hoxton, the "Grecian" in City Road and the Stepney "Effingham" took the former option, but most preferred to derive the major part of their income from the sale of alcohol and food with variety as a sideline. (Richard Preece of *The Grapes* in Southwark Bridge Road named his entertainment room there "The Surrey Music Hall", making him the first person to use the term "music hall".)

Charles Morton, later known as "the Father of the Halls", had run several "gentlemen only" saloons before taking over the Canterbury Arms in Lambeth, and after tastefully refurbishing the place, began to hold his Mondays and Saturday "gentlemen only" Free and Easies. No vulgarity or obscenity was allowed, and he was soon asked if wives and sweethearts could be welcomed there too. Morton agreed, setting aside a "Ladies Thursday" which quickly became popular.

To accommodate the crowds, he was forced to build a new hall behind the Canterbury, making this seven hundred seater the first specifically built Music Hall in England and it was opened on May 17th 1852, performances being given nightly to all comers. Suddenly Music Hall became a craze, and buildings sprang up like mushrooms all over London. They were cheap, cheerful, and appealed to the working classes who wanted nothing more than a drink, a laugh and a knees-up at reasonable prices. By 1890, Music Hall performers were their idols, their saucy songs and risqué references to working class life and morality raising gales of laughter from appreciative audiences.

There was little elegance in the lives of the lower paid, so a "sad tale" told by a washer-woman, a rag-picker, a costermonger, a hen-pecked husband or a battered wife could always strike a chord with the listener. Comedienne Bessie Bellwood, for instance, would always give as good as she got, and on one occasion, held a slanging match with a heckling coal-heaver in the audience that left him dazed and speechless and had the rest of the patrons cheering her command of down-to-earth language until they ran out of breath. You wouldn't have got that with Sarah Siddons.

It was the middle and upper classes who attended pantomimes at Drury Lane and Covent Garden. That common Music Hall performers should be invited to bring their coarseness and innuendo to a Royal Theatre was an absolute outrage to them. Decent parents would never take children there again, they vowed, but Harris was unconcerned. On Opening Night, many who would normally have attended did not, though Music Hall supporters who previously would never have attended a Drury Lane pantomime were there to replace them. There was no opening play and *Mother Goose* occupied the entire evening.

It was still not the version we know today, but Blanchard had done another attractive "book", of which Harris discarded almost half. It had fifteen scenes, twelve leading up to the transformation, and three following for the Harlequinade, which Harris had again double cast. All were breathtakingly beautiful and included three ballets, two for children and the third a showpiece for the international dancer Emma Paladino. The showstopping scene was once again the transformation, this time "The Fountain of Love" and as before, when Harris appeared and asked if the audience were satisfied, the answer was in the affirmative.

Over at Covent Garden, *Sindbad the Sailor* was a more "traditional" offering, the goggle-eyed Big Heads drawing particular praise from one critic remembering former days and being profoundly disenchanted by Drury Lane's efforts. "We can better spare slim legs than Big Heads in a pantomime" he declared firmly. After praising the rest of the show (which featured Herbert Campbell, Arthur Williams and Fanny Leslie (1857-1935), a male impersonator, in the title role) he then went on to rhapsodise over the performance of Harry Payne as the Harlequinade's Clown who provided:

> "Genuine clowning, – some hearty, sly, wicked, humorous, sausage-filching, authority defying, pantaloon - deceiving clowning. Willingly would most of us spare some of the earlier portion

> of our now tediously spun-out Pantomimes for the sake of a few
> really good, genuinely funny and novel scenes between Clown,
> Pantaloon, Harlequin and Columbine (like these.)"

Harris however ignored the non-too subtle hint and the Christmas of 1881 saw *Robinson Crusoe* sail into Drury Lane, again with a star studded Music Hall cast, Arthur Roberts as Mrs. Crusoe, James Fawn as Timothy, Fanny Leslie as the hero, and Harry Nicholls as the villainous Will Atkins. All the Pirates were played by girls and one scene depicted a view of the Thames from both sides as the departing ship sailed away. There was a highly realistic storm and shipwreck followed by a glittering undersea ballet, an astounding transformation scene by Beverley entitled "The Fairy Wedding Cake" and the first of Harris's *processions a la Garrick* which came to dominate all his pantomimes; a procession of Trades Guilds down a London Street. There were over one hundred adults in the chorus, plus almost two hundred children in addition to a huge cast. It ran for 122 performances and the only criticism came for Blanchard when the *Illustrated London News*, complained bitterly that for the first time, the word Harlequin had not been included in the title of the piece.

The victories of the British troops in Egypt inspired Harris's production the following year. The subject was *Sindbad the Sailor*, which though penned by Blanchard, who Harris dismissively referred to as "The Old Man of the Sea", was literally torn apart to accommodate the talents of Arthur Roberts, James Fawn, Herbert Campbell, Harry Nicholls, Nelly Power, Vesta Tilley, Fred Storey, Constance Loseby and Charles Lauri. Harris's procession was a pageant of every King and Queen of England from William the Conqueror down to Queen Victoria, every costume detail correct down to the smallest item. It involved over three hundred "supers" and took six minutes for them to cross the stage.

The intended hit of the show, however, was the enormous Roc which had to lift Sindbad (played by Nelly Power) and cost £1,000 to construct. Unfortunately, on opening night, things didn't go to plan. The Roc filled the entire stage and had only to lift Sindbad a few feet off the ground before the front cloth came in. When the cloth fell, stagehands rushed to clear behind and set the next scene which should have taken ten minutes. It was one and a half hours before the cloth rose again because the enormous bird was wedged in position and couldn't be moved. Twelve carpenters had to saw and hammer it apart before the pantomime could continue and Harris was forced to appear with an apology for the delay. Though beautifully dressed, most of the cast were inaudible and by the time the final curtain fell, the disgruntled audience felt distinctly cheated. Nevertheless, it went on to play for 102 performances. Wrote Blanchard in his diary:

> "To Drury Lane to see Sindbad, which though expensively got up, is a very dreary music hall entertainment; and for the misprinting and grossly interpolated book, I am in no way responsible. It was deservedly hissed at various portions – hardly anything done as I intended it, or spoken as I had written: the music hall element is crushing out the rest and the good old fairy tales never again to be illustrated as they should be"

W. Davenport Adams, the critic and historian agreed wholeheartedly. In the February issue of *The Theatre* 1882 he commented

> "I admit the extreme ability of certain music hall comedians. ... I object, however, altogether, to the intrusion of such artistes into the pantomime. ... They bring with them not only their songs, which when offensive in their wording, are sometimes made doubly dangerous by their tunefulness; not only their dances, which are usually vulgar when they are not inane; but their style and manner and "gags" which are generally the most deplorable of all. ... Pantomime is dead, and *burlesque* of the most deteriorated type has usurped its place"

It was perfectly true, of course. The old style of pantomime had almost completely vanished at Drury Lane. Harris had already removed the (by now) "traditional" dark opening and plunged into the "Village Square" the moment the curtain rose, (though the ghosts of them still remain in the *Prologues* of a few modern pantomimes). The flood of "speciality acts" from the Halls had replaced forty percent of the script, and most of the comic business of the Harlequinade had been performed by the artistes in the "fairy tale section" before the transformation scene even began. Referring to the *Aladdin* of 1885, Blanchard wrote:

> "The pantomime not at all following the text I have written.

Augustus Harris seems to have placed it very brilliantly on the stage, but it is more dazzling than funny, and I get very weary of the gagging of music hall people, and with eyes dazzled with gas and glitter cannot stay till midnight when the Harlequinade only commences and which few now seem to care about. Oh, the change from one's boyhood! Left to be rattled through as rapidly as possible and without, I fear, any adequate rehearsal"

Poor Blanchard was right. Harris's gargantuan displays of opulence cast their shadow over everything else. The performances now lasted in excess of four hours and were still expanding, but audiences clamoured for more. To satisfy the demand for tickets without having to extend the run and disrupt his following productions, for his 1883 *Cinderella*, Harris had introduced twice daily performances, an innovation, as we know, that has continued to this day. Even Covent Garden found it impossible to compete with him, and in 1887, following its production of *Jack and the Beanstalk*, ceased to stage pantomime for thirty three years.

Sighed a weary subscriber to *Punch* in 1886:

In Pantomimes, in ancient days, we gave enthusiastic praise
To Harlequin and Clown;
But now the "Spectacle" 's the thing, and ballet-dancers in a ring
The talk of all the Town.

Now long processions throng the boards, of Beauties, or of Kings
and Lords,
And mimic war they wage;
It seems to me that very soon poor Columbine and Pantaloon
Will vanish from the stage!

We miss the dear Clown's buttered slide, no longer does he
deftly hide
Unhappy Bobbies' hats;
He's not so agile as of yore, his wondrous jumps delight no more,
And who has seen "the spratts"?

The Comic Scenes are shortened now, more time for dancing to
allow,
And "scenic changes" please.
We've "Dreams of Beauty", "Realms of Bliss", I wonder do the
children miss
Each old amusing "wheeze"?

The glories of the Stage today are won in quite another way,
But I would fain forego
Each gorgeous and expensive "set" for fun that I shall ne'er
forget,
More humour and less show.

160

> We're great upon historic dress, we see much female loveliness
> In costumes of the time:
> But surely, when all's said and done, there's far too little honest
> fun
> In Modern Pantomime !

Blanchard whole-heartedly agreed. His last pantomime *Babes in the Wood*, was presented in 1888, though almost nothing of the original remained. In his diary he wrote:

> "Looking over the ghastly proofs of the Drury Lane annual in which I find my smooth and pointed lines are turned into ragged prose and arrant nonsense, I shall consider the payment due to me an equivalent for the harm done to my literary reputation"

He died just a few months later, never knowing that his final mutilated script had provided a role for Grimaldi's only eventual rival in popularity: The Champion Clog-dancer of the World, George Galvin, better known as the immortal Dan Leno.

*B*orn at No 4, Eve Court, the site of which is now buried beneath St Pancras Station, George Galvin (1860-1904) was the second son of itinerant entertainers known as "Mr. and Mrs. Johnny Wilde" and travelled around the country with them as they struggled to earn a living. Galvin senior died of drink related problems when George was four years old, and a few months later, Mrs. Galvin married William Grant, who was working the Halls under the name of Leno. As the Leno family, they continued to tour, and, in 1864 under the billing "Little George, the Infant Wonder, Contortionist and Posturer" the young Leno made his debut at the Cosmothica Music Hall, Paddington.

By 1867, George and his elder brother, Jack, were appearing as a dancing double-act, but stage life had no appeal for Jack, and he left to find work as a tradesman, his place being taken by the boys' uncle, Johnny Danvers, who was one month older than George. Two years later, George made his debut as a solo artiste, billed for some reason as "The quintessence of Irish Comedians" and the following year became "Dan Patrick Leno, Descriptive and Irish Character Vocalist".

The change in name came about because the Leno Family were usually engaged as a troupe, but, by giving George a new name, he could get solo billing and be paid a separate salary. Nevertheless, whatever money he was fortunate enough to earn, it went straight into his step-father's pocket. Like Dan's real father, William Grant was a drinker and this led to an amusing anecdote.

The Leno's (father and step-son) and Johnny Danvers had found work in Manchester, where Leno senior and Johnny dressed as devils and popped up and down through a variety of trapdoors whilst being pursued by Dan in the guise of a shillelagh wielding Irishman. Having imbibed a bit too freely, Leno senior miscalculated and in vanishing down a grave trap, his head came into violent contact with the surround before he landed in a crumpled heap several feet below the stage. As the horrified Dan stood alone, a tearful Johnny popped out of the star-trap to continue the mock fight and chase, and as the two boys raced around the stage, managed to sob that Leno senior was "killed". A moment later he vanished down the grave trap and Dan at once leapt after him to find his step-father covered in blood but alive and semi-conscious.

Without pausing to rid themselves of make-up and costumes, the two boys hauled Leno senior into a cab and drove to the nearest doctor's house. When the maid opened the door to their frantic summons and saw a devil and an Irishman supporting another devil with blood streaming down his face, she hastily slammed the door shut and shrieking with terror, fled down the hallway looking for sanctuary. Fortunately, the doctor himself had heard the commotion, and after a hasty examination was able to satisfy them that the injury was only superficial. At which news, with the wound cleaned and dressed, the devilish trio returned to the theatre and continued with their act.

By 1880, Dan had been in showbusiness for sixteen years and had incorporated Northern clog-dancing into his repertoire. As he would later boast he "could put more beats into sixteen bars of music than a drummer can with his drum-sticks". At Wakefield, in Yorkshire, he entered a clog-dancing competition winning not only the purse of silver on offer, but a leg of lamb as well. Shortly afterwards, another competition at The Princess's Music Hall in Leeds was to win him a gold and silver belt, valued at £50, and the title of "Champion Clog-dancer of the World". It was not the only thing he won, for the same year he met Miss Lydia Reynolds, a 17 year old singer from Sunderland and, three years later, married her.

The troupe continued to work the Halls for the next two years, Dan and Lydia still appearing as solo acts. In 1885, Dan made his first London appearance as a solo comedian and clog dancer at Forester's Music Hall, Mile End, earning £5 for the week. Dressed as a down-trodden, working class woman he sang two songs written for him by Harry King, "Buying milk for the twins" and "When Rafferty Raffled his Watch". The songs were never published, but according to J. Hickory Wood's biography *Dan Leno* (Methuen 1905), the chorus of the latter ran as follows;

> The fender was chained to the fireplace;
> The poker was chained to the hob;
> You bet your life if they'd been loose,
> They'd both have been on the job.
> The tables and chairs were tumbled downstairs;
> We'd plenty of Irish and Scotch;
> And the divil's own row there was that night
> When Rafferty raffled his watch.

To Dan's surprise and dismay, although the songs went down very well, the clog-dance which followed them was a wash-out. Londoners had no idea what a clog-dance was and had no particular desire to find out. Though he quickly became a favourite of Music Hall audiences all over the city, the clog-dancing part of his act was quietly dropped.

A short time later, discovering that Dan had never seen Drury Lane Theatre, Johnny Danvers escorted him there. After gazing at it in silence for some time, Dan walked up the steps and knelt on the topmost one. A few moments later he came back down and taking his uncle's arm said "Johnny, I shall act there some day".

As luck would have it, the Middlesex Music Hall was also in Drury Lane and Dan was invited to perform. George Conquest (1837-1901) manager of the famous Surrey Theatre (and before that, The Grecian), saw him working and at once offered

164

him the role of Dame Durdon in *Jack and the Beanstalk* for the 1866-7 season. With the exception of Drury Lane and Covent Garden, the Surrey and the Britannia were London's greatest pantomime houses and when Lydia was also hired to play "Mercury" with the pair being jointly contracted for the sum of £20 per week, the couple had something to celebrate.

Like the Britannia, (built in 1856 by Sam Lane, and where his widow Sarah continued to appear until well into her seventies), the Surrey Theatre was not a run of the mill pantomime house. In the early 1870s, when most theatres were settling down to presenting versions of the familiar subjects we see today, *Aladdin, Cinderella, Dick Whittington*, etc., these houses continued with the older style pantomimes boasting fantastic titles such as *Spitz-Spitz the Spider Crab; or the Pirate of Spitzbergen* and *Bhlutzherrhanbothrumh; or The Dwarf of the Diamond Dell.*

Though not as lavishly dressed as the others, both theatres could boast far more memorable productions in terms of comedy and innovation. While the Britannia, or "old Brit" utilised the talents of the famous Lupino family (who had arrived in England in the early 1700's and had at least one descendant still appearing in pantomime during the 1960's), the Surrey could safely rely on the ingenuity of George Conquest and his extraordinary talented family.

George Augustus Conquest was born on May 4th, 1837, the first child of Benjamin Oliver (1804-1872) a singer of comic songs (under the name of Conquest) and lessee of a converted cotton factory known as The Garrick Theatre in Leman Street, Whitechapel. By 1851, Benjamin was running the Eagle Tavern and Grecian Saloon in City Road, still remembered by the famous rhyme;

> Up and down the City Road,
> In and out the Eagle,
> That's the way the money goes...
> Pop goes the weasel.

The last line being a reference to the habit of the local tailors of pawning (or "popping") their "weasels" (fore-runners of electric and gas irons that needed heating over flames before use) when short of a few shillings for drink and entertainment.

Six years later, the twenty year old George Conquest was not only attracting critical attention in the pantomimes the re-named Grecian Theatre so successfully presented, but had met and married Miss Elizabeth Osmond. From then onwards, together with partner Henry Spry, he was to write all the Grecian and Surrey pantomimes up to his death in 1901.

George's talent for acrobatic leaps and odd characterizations came to the fore in 1862 when his startling abilities caused one reviewer to write:

> "The extraordinary performance of Mr. George Conquest as Number Nip in the pantomime "The Spider and the Fly" has crowded the theatre since Christmas. As a pantomimist, Mr. Conquest must take rank with the highest in his line and...would have driven playgoers of a hundred years ago out of their wits."

Ten years later, *Nix, the Demon Dwarf; or Harlequin, The Seven Charmed Bullets, the Fairy, the Fiend, and the Will-o'-the-Wisp* introduced a new element to the Grecian pantomimes: an ape-like and bodiless head representing Nix, the Demon Dwarf, which appeared to float across the stage on its beard and could roll its eyes, poke out its tongue and pull grotesque faces. It was built by Conquest himself, taking around nine months to perfect, and when struck by one of the charmed bullets fired by the Principal Boy, proved to contain the even more alarming Fiend (played by Conquest) who once released went on to cause problems for the lovers. Breathtaking entrances and exits though numerous trapdoors combined with acrobatic leaps and dives earned him enthusiastic applause, and the famous head of Nix brought an offer of £200 from the American showman Phineas Barnum (1810-1891) which Conquest refused.

Benjamin Oliver died in 1872, and the Grecian theatre passed into George's hands. The following year he not only introduced the new "Flying apparatus" to Grecian pantomimes, but appeared in Blanchard's *Puss in Boots* at the Crystal Palace in the afternoon and his own *The Wood Demon* at the Grecian in the evening, playing the Giant in each. In the former, he transformed himself from a Giant to a Dwarf, but in the latter, it is reported, he began as "a blighted, lightning-stricken, withered old tree-trunk with branches waving weirdly above his head ... the trunk opens and out steps a giant of most portentous size – an ogre so real that the babes in the pit begin to cry. By a wonderful compression, the giant is changed into a little dwarf, as broad as he is long. Next he becomes an animated pear, and then – hey presto-a vivid green version of the Brighton Octopus is dancing about the stage; and with this, the first part of Mr. Conquest's performance may be said to be ended"

There were now clear signs that George Conquest was beginning to specialise in the so-called "skin" or non-human roles of pantomime which had been an important part of them since Rich's days, and whose ancestry pre-dated Rome.

In Rich's production of *Harlequin Hydaspes; or the Greshamite* in 1719, a comical lion appeared. Dragons and ostriches had been followed by camels, cows, cats, dogs, and almost every other kind of animal, but one could always depend on Conquest to surprise. Over the next seven years he appeared as an Oyster (*Snip, Snap, Snorum* 1874), a gigantic crab whose claws extended from one side of the stage to the other (*Spitz-Spitz, the Spider Crab* 1875), an Octopus and a Giant Ape (*Grim Goblin* 1876), a steamed pudding and a huge parrot (*Roley Poley; or Harlequin Magic Umbrella* 1877) a giant Porcupine with moving quills (*Hokee- Pokee, the Fiend of the Fungus Forest; or the Six Links of the Devil's Chain* 1878), and a monstrous Toad (*Harlequin Rokoko, the Rock Fiend* 1879). In all of these, which he designed and created himself, he also appeared in acrobatic characterizations making leaps of twenty to thirty feet (made possible by the use of adjustable springs which could hurl him from below, on, or above stage) that drew gasps of amazement from the watchers.

On one occasion, he relates, his leaps were to be taken from all three levels, but feeling tired at the rehearsal, he only tried the under-stage machine, and told the man in charge of them to put the same number of springs in each. The following afternoon, he did his first leap from the above-stage position and suddenly found himself rebounding past the trapeze on which he should have landed, the hanging bordercloths, the burning-hot gas lighting battens and rocketing upwards towards the grid-iron in the roof area. Frantically he grabbed at the ropes, but only succeeded in turning himself upside down before friction tore them out of his hands and he soared even higher. At the last moment, his impetus gave out and he began to fall again, but this time head first. Fortunately he landed with his chest across the trapeze and managed to grab the ropes. From there, he needed to take a 25 feet leap to the stage to conclude his performance.

In 1880, Conquest gave up the Eagle Tavern and its Grecian Theatre, (which eventually became General Booth's Salvation Army Hotel) and set sail for America with his family and company, intending to present *Grim Goblin* in New York. It opened in August at Wallack's Theatre with George and 22 year old George Jnr. in leading roles. Again the spectacular leaps featured heavily, but this time worked on a counterweight system. On the first night, George senior was twenty feet above the stage when a rope snapped and he crashed to the ground with multiple injuries and a shattered leg that surgeons advised should be amputated.

The show closed for two days as George Jnr. rehearsed his father's role, and another actor took over his, but in the meantime, examination of the rope revealed it had apparently been sliced through by some sharp implement, though this was strongly denied by the theatre management. By a strange coincidence, when the pantomime resumed its run, at the very same point in the production, the rope supporting George Jnr. snapped, and he too fell stageward, luckily landing on his feet shaken but unhurt. Sabotage again was suspected but the management somehow contrived to have the incident hushed up. It seemed far more than coincidence, however, when shortly afterwards, his little sister, Ada Conquest (who played the Fairy), was also injured when a severed "flying" rope resulted in a broken nose and several missing teeth. Within a month of their arrival, the Conquests re-packed their things and returned to England. Cared for by his family, George Snr. slowly recovered, but his acrobatic days were over: for the rest of his life he was to walk with a permanent limp.

In the Spring of 1881, he took the lease of the Surrey Theatre in Blackfriars Road and continued its policy of presenting high class melodrama and pantomime. His first

Pantomime there was also the first in which none of the family appeared. Conquest himself was not fit, George Jnr. was elsewhere, and his brothers, Fred and Arthur, were too young. Entitled *Mother Bunch, or the Man with the Hunch; or The Reeds, The Weeds, the Priest, the Swell, the Gypsy Girl and the Big Dumb Bell*, it was loosely based on the Victor Hugo novel *Notre Dame de Paris* and featured the characters of Squashimodo and Claude Frollico. To make up for the lack of "flying", the whole was superbly costumed and the scenery outstanding.

By the following Christmas, however, George Jnr. had returned, his father had trained two new young acrobats and once again, the flying harnesses could be used. George Jnr. played Tiny, the Giant's monstrous page in *Puss in Boots, the Ogre, the Miller, and the King of the Rats; or Pretty Princess and the Queen of the Cats*, which had a cast of twenty two principals and over a hundred "supers". There were eleven scenes in all for the "opening", commencing with "The Rat's Run under the Mill" and culminating with the transformation scene "The Fairy Home of the Anemones". The Dame role in this pantomime was the Widow Oatmeal (played by Harry Monkhouse) who introduced "herself" with the following couplet:

> I'm a lone lorn woman, which is, I'm a widder
> To be disposed of to the highest bidder.
> I'm not a new lot, truly, but every particle
> Is perfectly sound. I'm a genuine article.

And later:

> Turned out of house and home, how I'm afflicted.
> I'm a wretched tenant who has been evicted,
> By my brother-in-law. I'd send to "Old Harry", him;
> How can I be revenged? I know. I'll marry him.

Here is a prototype of the modern Dame, a woman of uncertain age, firmly convinced of her own charms but prone to giving "herself" back-handed compliments, a role to be brought to its peak only a few years later by George Snr.'s discovery of Dan Leno.

The Surrey pantomime of 1886 had a strong cast, including Dan's old friend Johnny Danvers and comedian Tom Costello

(1863-1943) remembered for his song *At Trinity Church I met my Doom* who played Mephistopheles Muldoon. George, of course, directed, and during the second performance invited both Dan and Lydia back for the following year's production as Principal comedian and Principal Boy respectively. *Sindbad the Sailor and the Little Old Man of the Sea; or The Tinker, The Tailor, The Soldier, The Sailor, Apothacary, Ploughboy, Gentleman, Thief* had Dan in the role of Tinpanz the Tinker, and Conquest himself as the Rock Demon, his first and last appearance on the Surrey stage. During his entrance through a trapdoor, concealed inside a huge jar which for some reason toppled over on his arrival, Conquest suffered a broken shoulder-blade and had to be replaced. Both show and Dan, however, were huge successes and *The Stage* reported:

> "Full of dry genuine humour, Mr. Dan Leno does not fail to accentuate the funny lines of his part of the Tinker. Every movement being a signal for laughter and his dance on the rolling vessel is a sight to see".

Most importantly for Dan, Augustus Harris was in the audience one evening and at once offered him the Drury Lane pantomime of 1888 at a salary of £28 per week. With George Conquest's blessing, the diminutive Leno bade the Surrey goodbye and as the wicked Baroness in *Babes in the Wood and Robin Hood and His Merry Men and Harlequin who Killed Cock Robin* made his Drury Lane debut the following Christmas.

Though not the leading role in the pantomime, which featured Harriet Vernon (1852-1923) as a strapping Robin Hood and Herbert Campbell (1846-1904) and Harry Nicholls as a pair of improbable Babes, he made a large impression on the public, and Harris promptly booked him for the next three pantomimes. Lydia, in the meantime, had retired from the stage to await the arrival of their second child.

The death of Blanchard had meant little to Harris, who for the last few years, together with Harry Nicholls, had savaged the old writer's scripts and cobbled together replacements with the surviving pieces. For the 1889 production, he and Nicholls had taken things a step further. In *Jack and the Beanstalk*, in addition to the original spectacular massed meeting of all the

Gods and Goddesses on Mount Olympus to decide what to do about the Giant, they introduced a second procession, this time set in the Giant's library, when all the principal characters of Shakespeare's plays stepped out of the books to wend their way across stage. To make room for this added pageant, dialogue and comic "business" were pushed aside, though Leno as Jack's mother, Mrs. Simpson, was highly praised for the routine in which "her" efforts to sing a serious love song were foiled by a chorus of screeching cats outside the window. (This routine was originally performed by Grimaldi).

The following year, in *Beauty and the Beast*, Leno played Beauty's father, Sir Lombarde Streete, Vesta Tilley was Principal Boy and Campbell and Nicholls played Beauty's elderly sisters. For the second time, there were two processions, plus a huge "Flower" ballet, and for good measure, Harris also added a full sized sailing ship that was so heavy, tram-lines had to be laid down to enable an army of stage-crew to tow it from one side to the other.

At the end of the run, Harry Nicholls left the cast, and Leno was teamed with Campbell for the 1891 *Humpty Dumpty; or The Yellow Dwarf and The Fair One with the Golden Locks*. As the King of Hearts, the nineteen stone Campbell was a striking contrast to Leno's slender Queen, and for the next twelve years they were to *be* the Drury Lane pantomime. Joining them for this production was Marie Lloyd (1870-1922) who played Princess Allfair, and Harry Relph, better known as "Little Titch" (1867-1928) in the title role, though for this show he was not to wear the famous extra-long dancing boots that so delighted the Music Hall audiences. Again, no expense was spared and a double procession was staged.

Having decided that nothing succeeded like excess, Harris continued his spectacular pantomimes with enthusiasm. For the 1892, *Little Bo-Peep, Little Red Riding Hood and Hop o'my Thumb*, again with Leno, Campbell, Lloyd and Relph, and adding Ada Blanche and Marie Loftus, (1857-1940) his first procession displayed two dozen different sports and pastimes, while his second introduced every Nursery Rhyme character known to the public at large. In later productions there would be processions of "Remarkable Women of all Ages",

"Shakespearean heroines", "Nations of the World", "British Territories" etc., each involving hundreds of "supers", and as his obsession with parades grew, a story circulated London concerning one of the comedians in his pantomime who approached him for permission to add a joke to the official script. Harris asked to hear it first and the comedian began "There's an English sailor and a French sailor--" but before he could go on, Harris jumped in with the required permission. "We can have a procession for it" he beamed happily. "Sailors of all Nations". Small wonder he earned the title of "Druriolanus"

It was not all success, though. Marie Lloyd, was already drawing disapproval from audiences. As Red Riding Hood, she had shocked many by clambering out of the bed in one scene and instead of kneeling to say her prayers, as directed, began to search vainly underneath it for a chamber-pot. In 1893, after appearing in her third pantomime for Harris, *Robinson Crusoe*, and drawing further complaints for her rendering of the song "A saucy bit of cracklin'" she left the Lane to find greater fame and freedom in Music Hall. *Crusoe* also proved to be Harris's greatest failure. In an attempt to outdo himself, he overloaded the production with so many Music Hall stars and their "Acts", the pantomime collapsed and he lost £30,000.

The shock of this made Harris draw in his horns and for *Dick Whittington* (1894) there were no processions, just a handful of music hall artistes and the comedy was placed firmly into the hands of Herbert Campbell and Dan Leno. The critics applauded the return to the fairy-like extravaganzas of older times, and "the virtual elimination of the sordid music hall element" with the *Daily Telegraph* commenting:

> "By those who assume the music hall elements of Pantomime to have been overdone in past years, the present Pantomime may be regarded as a step in the right direction. There is certainly very little of the music hall entertainment of the distinctive type in it. What there is, is summed up in the proceedings of Mr. Herbert Campbell as Eliza the Cook and Mr. Dan Leno as Jack, the idle apprentice"

The following year's *Cinderella*, was equally restrained, with Harris resisting the temptation of starring Leno and Campbell as the wicked sisters and installing them as Baron and Baroness. The sisters were played by women. Harris being Harris, however, created a sensation by sending Cinderella to the Ball in a representation of the very first motor car ever seen on a stage. Having been introduced to Britain just one year earlier, at the time of his production there were no more than twenty "horseless carriages" in the entire country. Built specially for the production and decorated with gold leaf, the car was driven by an electric motor stored in its floor and fed by a rather visible long thick cable that trailed off-stage to a power point in the wings. Watching the car move sedately away trailing its long cable behind it, Leno convulsed the audience by ad-libbing "Oh, look. The Great Sea Serpent's going as well"

Aladdin was planned for the following Christmas, but on June 22nd, the theatre world was shocked by the news of Harris's death. For seventeen years he had dominated the British theatre scene, managing and writing at Drury Lane, running the Covent Garden Opera seasons, presenting pantomimes at the Crystal Palace, touring companies around the country, had once owned *The Sunday Times*, and, as Sheriff of the City of London, arranged entertainments for the visit of the first German Emperor for which service he had later been knighted. It was inconceivable that the genial Guv'nor had presented his last show at the age of forty four. A memorial drinking fountain, topped by a bust of "Gus Harris" was fixed to the front of Drury Lane theatre, paid for by Public Subscription. It can still be seen today, and is, I believe, the only one of its kind in the world.

Oscar Barrett, a one time composer of music for the Drury Lane pantomimes, and director of the Lyceum's record breaking *Cinderella* of 1893 which I mentioned earlier, directed *Aladdin* (1896) for Harris's widow, with stage manager Arthur Collins (1863-1932) assisting. Not a great success, having too much of Barrett's music on offer and being far too long, it was considered almost dull by Drury Lane standards, though Leno (as Widow Twankey) and Campbell brought the house down by appearing in a hot-air balloon, supposedly floating over London, where they attempted to cook a bloater and boil a kettle on a single spirit stove dangling outside the basket. At the penultimate moment, the balloon lurched and their breakfast fell through the air to land at the feet of a passer by in Cheapside, who picked it up and proceeded to devour it as he exited, much to the fury of the starving couple.

It was almost the last pantomime in the old theatre. A rumour swept London that the playhouse was to be demolished and the site merged into Covent Garden Market. Arthur Collins quickly applied for the remainder of the lease which had ten more years to run, only to discover that a payment of £1,000 was required to transfer it. Unable to find the money, his hopes were dashed, but a chance meeting with a theatre-loving Australian merchant reversed the situation and Collins not only got the remainder of the lease, but an eighty year renewal. On May 28th, 1897, Drury Lane Theatre became a Limited Company with Arthur Collins as its first Managing Director.

The script for *Babes in the Wood* (in which Ada Blanche starred as Robin Hood, with Leno and Campbell as the "Babes", Reggie and Chrissie) was written by Arthur Sturgess, and Collins quickly proved that the pantomimes of the new regime would be just as spectacular as those of Augustus Harris, though employing much more style, pace, and imagination. Several unusual practices were brought into play. Until Oscar Barrett directed the Lyric's 1893 *Cinderella*, pantomimes had been watched at a single sitting, even though some were four hours long. Barrett had divided his production into two Acts by providing an Intermission which allowed his audiences to stretch their legs and seek refreshments. Though no other theatre had taken up the idea, it appealed to Collins, and from his first pantomime, the vast transformations or parades that had concluded the story prior to the Harlequinade were brought forward to mark the end of Act One.

Rhyming couplets for "mortal" characters were gradually discarded in favour of prose, though the "immortals" continued to speak in verse in order to emphasise their "other-world" origins. Unlike Harris, who had allowed the comedians free range in order to concentrate on his spectacular effects,

Collins insisted they worked to a set script and his writer devised the action and dialogue around the talents of the particular artistes. Even so, like his old Guv'nor, he never knew when enough was enough. A Collins pantomime often ran for almost five hours, ending after one in the morning with a ten minute travesty of the once glorious Harlequinades that had filled the theatres for so many years. On leaving the theatre one evening, the wife of composer Herman Finck asked him "What time is it?" Finck wearily replied "You mean what *day* is it".

George Bernard Shaw (1856-1950) was not impressed by the new style presentation. In a devastating attack in the *Saturday Review* he wrote:

> "To the mind's eye and ear, the modern pantomime as purveyed by the late Sir Augustus Harris is neither visible nor audible. It is a glittering noisy void, horribly wearisome and enervating like all performances which weary the physical senses without any appeal to the emotions and through them to the intellect. I grieve to say that these remarks have lost nothing of their force by the succession of Mr. Arthur Collins to Sir Augustus Harris. ... The spectacular scenes exhibited Mr. Collins as a manager to whom a thousand pounds is as five shillings. The dramatic scenes exhibited him as one to whom a crown piece is as a million. If Mr. Dan Leno had asked for a hundred guinea (£105) tunic to wear during a single walk across the stage, no doubt he would have got it, with a fifty guinea hat and a sword-belt to boot. If he had asked ten guineas worth of the time of a competent dramatic humourist to provide him with at least one line that might not have been pirated from the nearest cheap-jack, he would, I suspect, be asked whether he wished to make Drury Lane bankrupt. It is piteous to see the wealth of artistic effort which is only swamped in the morass of purposeless wastefulness that constitutes a pantomime."

Somehow Collins survived the attack.

His second pantomime *The Forty Thieves* added more innovation to the familiar story when Ali Baba (Johnny Danvers) and family arrive in London, laden with the treasure they have stolen from the Robber's cave, and set up home in The Red Lion public house. The irate Robbers, led by Abdallah (Dan Leno) and his sweetheart, The Fair Zuleika, (Herbert Campbell) follow them, and after a visit to London Zoo, all but Abdallah and Zuleika (who is too plump), hide themselves in

beer barrels in the courtyard of the Red Lion where Principal Girl, Morgiana, discovers them and drowns them in a mixture of hot beer, arsenic, paraffin and castor oil. The penniless survivors attempt to tunnel their way into a bank but miscalculate and find they have arrived inside a cell at Newgate Prison.

Sturgess was again the author of the 1899 pantomime *Jack and the Beanstalk*, with Leno as Dame Trot, Herbert Campbell as the King, and Nellie Stewart as Jack. It was in this pantomime that the Giant was given the name Blunder*boer* to mark the beginning of the Boer War which had started only twelve weeks earlier. At the end of the pantomime, when the dead Giant lay sprawled across the stage, crushed cottages and public buildings beneath him, one of the villagers opened a pocket of Blunderboer's tunic and out marched over four hundred children dressed as artillery, horse, and foot soldiers of the British Army, each wearing the new khaki uniform that had just replaced the familiar scarlet and black. A direct answer to Kruger's boast that "he could put the little British Army in his pocket".

In the November of 1900, Collins was thrown into confusion when his assigned scriptwriter proved unable to deliver. Desperately seeking a replacement, he made contact with a writer from Manchester who had already provided the Garrick Theatre with its successful *Puss in Boots*.

Sleeping Beauty and the Beast, a skillful blending of two other pantomime stories, was written in two weeks, and another great pantomime name arrived at Drury Lane; J. Hickory Wood.

*W*ood, real name John James Wood, (1858-1913) had been an insurance clerk in his home town and wrote sketches, lyrics and recitations for popular entertainers before penning his first pantomime, *Cinderella*, for a Liverpool theatre. The Garrick's *Puss in Boots*, for which Leslie Stuart, composer of the musical *Floradora* had supplied several numbers, was only his second stage work, but Collins recognized a kindred spirit and Wood was to write the Drury Lane pantomimes for the next ten years. The role of Queen Ravia was played by Dan Leno and King Screwdolph was Herbert Campbell. Fred Emney Snr. was Martha, the Nurse, Madge Lessing, the Princess Beauty, and Elaine Ravensberg the unfortunate Prince Caramel.

The First Act tells the usual story of *Sleeping Beauty* and concludes with a general awakening after a series of beautiful tableaux depicting the seasons of the year. In the Second Act, far from the Citizens of Prapsburg being delighted to see them again, no-one can remember them, the Kingdom having been replaced by a Republic many years earlier. Even more distressing, the Crown Jewels are locked away in the City museum, and the villainous President refuses to hand them over. Princess Beauty and Prince Caramel prepare to marry, but the evil Malivolentia reappears unexpectedly and transforms him into The Beast.

The King and Queen disguised as burglars, break into the museum and steal the Crown Jewels, but their escape is delayed when the car they have hired breaks down and finally falls to pieces. (The "disintegrating car" became a standard pantomime routine and was still going strong in the 1960s, even crossing over into Circus and film). The couple finally escape by using the "Twopenny Tube" which they enter through a tree after an altercation with a railway conductor. Unfortunately their efforts have been in vain for the President has substituted the real Crown Jewels for paste, so Queen Ravia decides to cheer up their heartbroken daughter by taking home a rose from the magnificent garden they have wandered into. As she plucks it, there is a flash and the hideous Beast appears who promises not to harm them if Beauty returns the rose herself and promises to marry him of her own free will.

Things get worse when the President throws them into jail but to save them, Beauty agrees to marry the Beast. After she departs, the President puts a tax on bicycles and a Revolution (led by the Nurse) breaks out. The President is overthrown and the King and Queen are restored to the Throne. Beauty returns the rose and kisses the Beast who at once is transformed back to Prince Caramel and all ends happily. The short Harlequinade that followed featured Whimsical Walker, the last Clown ever to appear at Drury Lane, and the pantomime played for 136 performances, interrupted for four days in January 1901 by the death and funeral of Queen Victoria.

The 1901-2 *Bluebeard* introduced Campbell as the murderous Bluebeard, and Leno as the plain but determined Sister Anne, eager to coax him into matrimony. As she explains:

> "I'm the very wife for you. I shall make you an excellent wife – oh!
> You've no idea. See - there you are – a millionaire! Here am I – a
> lovable womanly woman. You absolutely don't know what to do
> with your money. I do know what to do with your money, and I'll
> do it, see? ... You'll wonder however you managed to get on so

long without me. ... Men don't usually *fall* in love with me – not *suddenly* – I sort of grow on them – they glide gradually into love with me – but when they're once there, they're there for ever. I'm a sort of a female rattlesnake. I weave spells round them – like – you know – those fog horns you hear on the river – of course I don't mean that I'm a fog-horn – but you know – tut, tut – Sirens. That's it. I'm a *Siren*."

Bluebeard remained unimpressed, and a later attempt to woo him with her harp playing only resulted in her hair becoming hopelessly entangled in the strings of it, while her desperate attempts to free herself but continue playing sending her crashing to the floor intertwined with both harp and music stand.

In another scene, Leno and Campbell were scripted to play a game of table tennis (or ping-pong as it was then called). This was duly set up for rehearsal, but within a few minutes, the partners had hit upon the idea of replacing the bats with frying pans, the balls with potatoes or dumplings and the net with an onion bag. The result brought the place down and this routine has been part of pantomime's "kitchen" scenes ever since. Perhaps the most unusual feature of this production was the presentation of it in three acts instead of the now familiar two, but the innovation was rarely repeated in future pantomimes.

The 1902-3 pantomime was Leno's greatest triumph. Wood and Collins created what we now accept as the definitive version of "Mother Goose". From "her" very first entrance in a tiny cart drawn by donkeys, Leno's "Mother Goose" had the audience in convulsions. A speeding motorcar collided with the cart, spilling the shabby old lady onto the ground and allowing the geese she was transporting to escape and scatter in all directions. Dashing around the stage, attempting to recapture the indignant birds, right the cart and help the braying donkeys to their feet, she rages at the motorist and his passenger:

M. Goose : Oh, if I could get at your eyes, I'd scratch them out! Yes! You do well to cover yourselves all over in scrap iron when you rush about the country like this! Come out of your meat-hasteners and talk to me, if you dare. Oh! I forgot! They're sure to be foreigners! Vour avez smashe mon carri-age, and I demande le damage- see? It's very evident they're not French ! Itsen das cartzen splitzen - donner

	und blitzen! So ! And they're not Germans, either. Senors!
	El Carto pieco. Broko! El Demando Compensationo..!
	Caramba! Caraggio Caracas Cocoa! Well! I don't believe
	they know *any* language !
Man	: Why cawn't you talk English ?
.M. Goose	: That sounds a familiar accent.
Man	: We aint no foreigners! I druv a Brixton 'bus for twenty
	years.
Passenger	: Yus ! And mine was a priviliged keb in Euston station.
M. Goose	: And I've been wasting my education over them like this!
	Police!

In his penultimate pantomime Leno created the greatest and most difficult Dame role of all, but the effort it took brought problems. Having suffered from increasing deafness for the last two years, he suddenly became strangely irrational, exploding into anger for unknown causes then dissolving into tears of remorse. His legendary generosity prompted him to distribute huge sums of money and jewellery to absolute strangers and at the end of the run, after convincing himself that he was the son of a Scottish marquis and should be playing in Shakespeare, suffered a complete mental breakdown and was admitted to a nursing home in Camberwell. On his second day there, he asked if the clock was right. When told it was, he replied "Well if it's right, what's it doing in here?"

During the next few months, he fought to regain his old form and by August, his doctor considered him well enough to return home. Though Collins had taken the precaution of booking comedian Harry Randall to partner Campbell in the spectacular *Humpty Dumpty* at Drury Lane, when Leno reappeared in London he seemed in good form and the parts were quickly reshuffled to allow him to play Queen Sprightly. He received a five minute standing ovation at his first entrance, but repeatedly fluffed his lines and had to be rescued by the other performers.

Theatregoers however remembered two hilarious scenes, one the now-famous "Tree of Truth" sequence that had huge acorns dropping on the Royal Couple's heads every time a lie was told, (Many other variations of this were developed in later years including "The Tiddly Tree", "A little bit of Heaven" etc.) and the second, an exchange between Queen Sprightly and her female Cook, played by Harry Randall, part of which is reproduced below:

Cook :	What shall I send you up for lunch today?	
Queen :	I think we'll have the cold beef	
Cook :	Oh, I never thought you'd want to see that little bit again.	
Queen :	Little bit? It was a great big joint yesterday. and what we ate hardly made any difference to it.	
Cook :	All I know is – that the bit you sent down wasn't worth keeping – so I gave it to the cat.	
Queen :	Oh. Then you can send us up the pheasants.	
Cook :	Pheasants?	
Queen :	Yes! The brace of pheasants the King shot.	
Cook :	Oh, those. Now it's a pity about those pheasants. They didn't keep.	
Queen :	Why the King only shot them yesterday.	
Cook :	I can't help that. They must have been high when he shot 'em. I gave them to the cat.	
Queen :	Same cat?	
Cook :	Same cat.	
Queen :	Well ... we'd better have a bit of fish, then.	
Cook :	It's funny you should ask for that ... but the cat walks in its sleep.	
Queen :	The cat ate the fish?	
Cook :	That's it.	
Queen :	Same cat?	
Cook :	Same cat.	
Queen :	Well ... we must fall back on the pickled pork.	
Cook :	Now isn't that curious? Only half an hour ago ...	
Queen :	You gave it to the cat.	
Cook :	I gave it to the cat.	
Queen :	Same cat?	
Cook :	Same cat.	
Queen :	Well in that case, there's only one thing we *can* eat. Serve up the *cat* for lunch.	

As the show continued its long run, Leno became more and more erratic, throwing off - stage tantrums, locking himself in his dressing room and ignoring the worried pleading of his friends. On the last night though, he had pulled himself together and stepped forward with Herbert Campbell to sing the following duet:

In the panto of old Drury Lane
We have both come together again.
And we hope to appear
For many a year
In the panto of old Drury Lane.

181

It was never to happen. Herbert Campbell was killed in an accident on July 19th, and Leno died of a brain tumour on October 31st. On the day of his funeral, November 8th, traffic was halted, shops closed and mourners lined the three mile route to Lambeth Cemetery where he was laid to rest. Wrote *The Times* in his obituary:

> "They were a complementary pair. Mr. Campbell's humour was as broad as Mr. Leno's was fine, but there was no question which was the greater comedian. Mr. Leno had not only a rich fund of comedy in his own quaint face and personality, but had that far rarer gift – the intelligence to make use of it. He had imagination. He was not content to trade solely on what nature had given him. He could hardly walk, and certainly never danced, without raising a smile. to find anything like a close parallel to his style we should probably have to go back to the Italian *Commedia dell' Arte*, or to any of the farces in which the actors extemporized their parts."

To which Max Beerbohm in the *Saturday Review* added;

> "So little and frail a lantern could not long harbour so big a flame"

The 1904 pantomime, *The White Cat* was a disaster. As a concession to the carping of "too many Music Hall performers", Collins had hired James Welch, a comic actor from the legitimate theatre to play Prince Patter, one of the three sons of King Ivory of Oddland (Johnny Danvers), the others being Fred Eastman as Prince Plump, and Queenie Leighton as Principal Boy, Prince Peerless. Marie George was naughty Cupid, Jeannie Macdonald was Princess Aurora and Harry Randall had the Dame role of her godmother, the aged Fairy Asbestos. Despite a funny script with many original touches, such as the comic fairy making her first entrance on a "flying wire"; the introduction of the "Missing Link" (a recent talking point), one of the most beautiful Finales ever seen at Drury Lane and a best selling gramophone record of Queenie Leighton singing the hit song of the pantomime (surely a "First"), it fell victim to a sustained attack from *The Daily Mail* which declared it "Not fit for children" and invited the public to write to them in support, saying:

> "Pantomimes here in the past have been such a joyful medley of fairies and colour and music that thousands of old friends must

Every other reviewer awarded it top marks and the performances of Harry Randall and Marie George were singled out
for additional praise. *The Morning Post* declared the show
better than any recent pantomime in almost every respect, but
the *Mail* campaign caused James Welch to leave the show after
only ten performances, party bookings to collapse and parents
to take their children elsewhere. Collins was left with no
choice but to cut the run short.

Examining the published script, it is difficult to see what
outraged the *Daily Mail* and Mr. Cooper. It is even more difficult to imagine why the subject is no longer seen in today's
pantomime cannon, for Wood and Collins had to my mind (as
a modern day pantomime writer) produced a show that is far
more interesting than *Robinson Crusoe* or *Goody Two Shoes*.

Based on a story by the Countess d'Aulnois, the
Wood/Collins version tells of the comical King Ivory whose
three sons wish to succeed him when he retires. Unable to
decide which one it shall be, he tells them he has heard of a
Golden Net so large it can contain the whole world, yet so fine
it can be drawn through a wedding ring. Whoever finds the
net and brings it to him shall have the Crown of Oddland.
Eagerly the three princes depart in search of it.

In an Enchanted Garden, far away in Ollapod, Princess
Aurora is guarded by her elderly Fairy Godmother, Asbestos,
whose magic skills are somewhat rusty through lack of use.
The arrival of Hecate, an evil witch who wants the princess to
marry her hideous son, creates havoc and after threatening
that should she refuses to marry him within a year she will
suffer a dreadful fate, departs again. The three princes (two
comedians and the Principal Boy) arrive in Ollapod where the
Golden Net is supposed to be hidden, and Cupid, seeking a
husband for Princess Aurora, fires his arrow at Prince Peerless
before leading him to the Enchanted Garden. The young couple are immediately attracted to each other and Cupid tells
him that the Golden Net is simply love. In the meanwhile, the
love-starved Asbestos, in a variety of disguises, attempts to

coax the other princes ... or any other single male ... into wooing her.

Prince Peerless returns to Oddland, followed by his brothers, and tells his father of his success, but as he cannot produce the Golden Net of Love, the King decides his throne will go instead to whichever of his sons can produce the most beautiful bride. Peerless hurries back to the Enchanted Garden for Aurora, but Hecate has already carried out her threat and the princess has vanished. As he searches for her, the other two brothers plot to win the throne by trickery. Cupid leads Peerless to the Palace of the White Cat, who promises to help him find his missing sweetheart if he will take her home with him and do as she says. The Prince agrees.

Back home, the King has decided to marry the most beautiful bride *he* can find and keep the throne himself, but by accident ends up with Fairy Asbestos who has been rejected by every other male in the Kingdom. The two brothers then return, one of them dressed up as the bride-to-be of the other, but their plan fails when their stupidity gives the game away. Prince Peerless returns with the White Cat and is mocked by the Court and his family. Seeing how unhappy the taunting makes him, the Cat tells him to kill her with his sword but he refuses, saying he loves her far too much to do her any harm. Cupid then fires an arrow at the Cat and the spell is broken. Aurora re-appears and the couple are re-united. The King keeps his Crown as Aurora already has several Kingdoms of her own, and all ends with general rejoicing.

Given the usual Collins treatment, the gorgeous costumes, breathtaking scenery and parodies of popular songs of the day, its failure remains a complete mystery.

For the next seven years, the Drury Lane pantomimes returned to what had become standard fare pantomime. *Cinderella, Sinbad the Sailor*, (the "d" was dropped), *Babes in the Wood, Dick Whittington, Aladdin*, and *Jack and the Beanstalk*, drew the crowds with its now familiar Music Hall and Musical Comedy star names in principal roles, but in the 1911 production of *Hop o'my Thumb* were two things of interest. For the first time in many years there was no Dame role in the pantomime, and the Pender Troupe, who had appeared on stilts as giant storks in the previous year's *Jack and the Beanstalk*, played most of the roles in the short Harlequinade. It was with this talented family of acrobats and jugglers that the young Archibald Leach, better known as actor Cary Grant, (1904-1986) found his first job in show-business.

In 1912, came another change. Written by George R. Sims, C.H. Bovill and Arthur Collins, *The Sleeping Beauty* featured Florence Smithson (the Musical Comedy star who had created the role of Sombra in *The Arcadians* at the Shaftesbury Theatre in 1909) in the title role, George Graves (the original Baron Popoff from the London production of *The Merry Widow*) as the Duke of Monte Blanco, comedian Barry Lupino as Finnykin, The Poluski Brothers as contemporary detectives Blake and Holmes, and most surprisingly, the well known concert singer, Wilfrid Douthitt as Prince Auriol. Though *The Times* enthused about the delightful singing of the romantic leads, the combination of a male Principal Boy and (for the second year running) no role for a Dame, brought a flood of complaints.

The production was hugely successful, however, with much of the laughter coming from George Graves who awoke from *his* sleep to find he had been used as a scarecrow for the past umpteen years, and had mice nesting in his pockets, mushrooms between his toes and a golf-ball from the local links embedded in his ear. The scene in which he attempted to wall-paper a room in the Castle spawned a tidal wave of "decorating scenes" which are still in use today.

The following year Collins revived it with additional scenes, re-titling it as *The Sleeping Beauty Re-awakened* using almost the same cast, and following the outbreak of World War I in 1914, staged it a third time as *The Sleeping Beauty Beautified*, this time with Bertram Walliss (the romantic lead from Lehar's *The Count of Luxembourg*) as Prince Auriol and Ferne Rogers as Princess Marcella. In view of the circumstances, a special Epilogue was spoken at the end of the pantomime by Puck, the fairy:

Here Love has won, but on the greater stage,
The demon Hate, a wicked war doth wage,
To conquer Hate and Love's fair course to win,

In Freedom's name, Love bids you all, "Fall In".
Here are we all, sonny, here are we all,
The friends who are brave and strong,
The boys of Britain and the lads of Gaul,
To right the Belgian wrong,
With the hero sons of the northeren snow
At bay with the raging Hun,
For his broken faith we will break the foe,
And fight till Right has won.

The whole company then joined in with the recruiting song "Fall in" which was written by Sir Frederic H. Cowen. The brief Harlequinade that followed had Whimsical Walker as Clown and Jessie Vokes (perhaps related to the famous Jessie Vokes who had died in 1884) as Columbine.

Collins again used a male Principal Boy (Eric Marshall) in the 1915 *Puss in Boots*, but when it was repeated in 1916, Madge Titheradge took his place. With men in demand for the Armed Forces, female "Boys" returned to pantomime, and forty more years had to pass before any further attempt was made to displace them.

For some time, Drury Lane had dominated the British pantomime scene, but a dangerous rival was emerging. Six years earlier, the freehold of the Lyceum Theatre had passed into the hands of the eccentric Melville brothers, Walter and Frederick. Born in 1875, Walter was one year older than his sibling and together with their younger brother Andrew – who later became manager of the Grand Theatre, Brighton – had worked in the family theatres ("The Grand" and "The Queen's") in Birmingham until the death of their father. With the help of their inheritance, Walter and Frederick became owner managers of both Terriss's Theatre in Rotherhithe and The Standard, Shoreditch, before buying the Lyceum in May, 1910 for two hundred and forty thousand pounds. For the next twenty eight years, without backers and using only their own money, they were to write and produce most of the melodramas and pantomimes presented there without ever experiencing a failure.

A Melville pantomime was almost unique. Curiously old-fashioned, with large sections of the scripts remaining in rhymed couplets throughout the brother's reign, they also retained a small Harlequinade when almost every other theatre in Britain had long forgotten them. On the other hand, only the best in comedy and spectacle was good enough and each year the Lyceum's reputation for solid value in entertainment continued to grow. The glittering and original scenery was built in the theatre's own workshops in Holborn - the brothers insisting on the "Palace" set being constructed before work began on anything else – but unlike most other managements, all the costumes were hired (usually from Clarksons in Wardour Street) and returned at the end of the run. Vitality was the keyword and though the pantomimes were anything up to four hours in length, the time sped by in a torrent of hurled pastry, smashed eggs, gallons of whitewash, bags of flour, dazzling dance routines, bouncy songs and wince-promoting puns. Witness this exchange between Sarah, the Cook, Idle Jack and Alderman Fitzwarren in the *Dick Whittington* of 1912.

Cook :	(Grabbing Jack) Come to work. This idling cease.
Jack :	(Struggling free) Take your hands off me, they're covered with grease.
Cook :	Your conduct's dis-*grease*-ful. You should have a whipping.
	Observe how the tears from my eyes are a-*dripping*.
	Can't you see for love of you I pines ?
Jack :	I'd rather have beer; I can't stand your w(h)ines.
Cook :	(Indignantly) Beer indeed ! You already look moppy.
Jack :	I've got a stiff leg, that's why I'm so *hoppy*.
	I do like beer, because there's no bones in it.
Cook :	You'd drink it the same if there were stones in it.
	I thought you loved me.
Jack :	That's not true.
Cook :	(Wailing) Oh ! how I love him. I do. I do. (Sobs on his neck)
Jack :	(Struggling) Get off my collar-bone. You've broken it, drat you.
Cook :	(Stung) Take back those words...or I'll chuck the things at you.
Jack :	(Grandly) All is over. I love one fairer.
	My heart is a desert.
Cook :	(Pleading) Let me be your Sa(ha)rah.
	Anything on earth I'd do for you;
	I'll do the washing and cooking too.
	Ignore your faults...and I know you've got many.
	I'll darn all your socks.

Jack :	I haven't got any.
Cook :	A loving wife to you I'll be.
	I'll work till I drop.
Fitz :	(Entering) Then do some for me.
	Get back inside, you lazy, idle lot.
	(To Sarah) Get thee to the kitchen.
Cook :	(Grimacing) I'm catching it hot.
Fitz :	(To Jack) And as for you, you idle apprentice,
	You make me feel quite *non compos mentis*.

Though this particular script was written by Newman Maurice, the Melville brothers were more than capable of concocting their own confections as this extract from their 1922 *Robinson Crusoe* shows.

Mrs. Crusoe:	I'm Mrs. Crusoe, a lonely widow, as you can plainly see.
	With not even a gentleman lodger to keep me company.
	I take in a little washing to pass the time away,
	My only serious trouble is, the customers don't pay.
	And Robinson, my elder boy's a sailor, so you can see
	Whenever I want to see him, well, he's always out at sea.
	And when he's come back home again,
	and he's not upon the sea,
	He's forever going out to see when he's going out to sea.
	So I really never see him. I simply seem to see
	The sea. You see? I see the sea,
	And that's about all that I see.
	So when I say "I see the sea", the sea I see's the sea, you see?
	(Irritated) Ooooh. I'm so muddled up with all those sees, so
	hang the sea. (Looks aghast at what she has said)

Bland as the above would be to today's audiences, the Melville pantomimes made between ten and twenty-five thousand pounds profit each year and the final one *The Queen of Hearts* in 1938 made over sixty thousand, partly because of the amazing collapsing Castle of Playing Cards which was probably the most startling set ever to be used in a pantomime. It (or a copy of it) was still being used in 1965 when I played in *Humpty Dumpty* at the Birmingham Hippodrome, and drew horrified gasps and sustained applause at every performance for eighteen weeks. Walter Melville died in 1937 and his two brothers the following year, leaving a total of £546,000, one of the largest theatrical fortunes of the day.

With road improvements forecast in The Strand, the Lyceum was scheduled for demolition, but a change of plan brought a halt to this. For some years it became a Dance Hall, then for many years it lay empty. Only in the final decade of the 20th Century was it returned to the theatregoers it had served for so long.

By a strange quirk of fate, all three of London's great pantomime houses were to sever their connections with it in the very same year. In 1920, with the management unwilling to curtail the run of the highly successful play *The Garden of Allah*, which ran from June 1920 to April 1921, Drury Lane theatre had repeated the previous year's *Cinderella* at Covent Garden. It was the first pantomime to be presented there since the 1887 *Jack and the Beanstalk*, and almost at once caused problems.

On the posters, large lettering proclaimed "The Drury Lane Pantomime", but the much smaller lettering "at Covent Garden" was generally missed. Thousands of pantomime lovers booked advance tickets at the Lane's Box Office only to discover later they were scheduled to see *The Garden of Allah*. On what was expected to be the first night of the pantomime, crying children and irate parents packed the foyer and surrounding streets, complaining bitterly. Though a solution was quickly found, with the generous Covent Garden management honouring the mis-booked tickets, pantomimes at Drury Lane ceased to be a regular feature.

The following year, the theatre was closed for renovations and it was not until 1929 when Julian Wylie presented *The Sleeping Beauty*, with G.S. Melvin as principal comedian, that pantomime made a brief reappearance. It was a resounding success, but five years were to pass before Wylie returned with *Cinderella*, which starred Ethel Revnell and Gracie West as the Ugly Sisters, Billy Danvers as Buttons, Phyllis Neilson-Terry as Prince Charming and Dan Leno Jnr. as the Baron. It was reputedly the best *Cinderella* ever presented on a British stage, but shortly before Opening Night, in the middle of supervising six pantomimes, Julian Wylie had a heart attack and died aged fifty-six.

Only two more pantomimes were staged at Drury Lane. Prince Littler presented the 1935 *Jack and the Beanstalk* with Binnie Hale as Jack, and Shaun Glenville as Dame – script supplied by Marriot Edgar, author of the comic monologue "The Lion and Albert" – and in 1938, Wylie's successor, Tom

Arnold, delivered *Babes in the Wood*, the final pantomime in Drury Lane's history, with the beautiful Fay Compton as Robin Hood.

In the same year Covent Garden presented Francis Laidler's *Red Riding Hood* with Nelson Keyes as Dame, and when their respective runs ended, both theatres had unknowingly said goodbye to the entertainment they had created and which had sustained them for over two hundred years.

*S*ince the days of John Rich, provincial theatre managers had followed London developments avidly. In 1748, for instance, the ban on selling tickets at unlicensed theatres had been bypassed in Exeter by granting free admission to plays and pantomimes on the receipt of tooth powder wrappings. By a strange coincidence, the tooth powder cost exactly what the price of a theatre ticket would have been had the management been allowed to sell them, and to the frustration of the magistrates, this rather expensive commodity (which could be purchased from the local printer), enjoyed record sales.

In later years, managements had followed the 1835 example of the Adelphi theatre by following the letter of the law *exactly*. Being forbidden to sell tickets "at the door", they sold them through specially constructed small windows that looked out onto the street. This is probably where the term "Box Office" came from, for the takings were kept in a box on the floor beneath the window. Normally, the manager or a trusted accountant would have sat by the door taking money as patrons entered.

After gas lighting had been introduced at Covent Garden around 1816, it could be found in many provincial theatres a few months later, so it's not surprising that their pantomimes, though mostly re-written and localised versions of London "originals", were in no way inferior to their contemporaries. Entertainers were always looking for work and all the latest songs, tricks and inventions were employed to keep them one step ahead of rivals.

In 1819, emulating the famous Grimaldi, who would often use live geese, hens and other animals in his performances, an enterprising provincial Clown appeared on stage carrying a small piglet and after tying a baby's bib around its neck, proceeded to feed it from a huge bottle of milk topped with a large rubber teat. The audience watched with some fascination as the tiny animal appeared to consume several pints of the liquid and squeal hungrily for more. Only those backstage knew it never received a drop, for beneath the bib was a rubber tube carrying the milk away to a second bottle beneath the stage, ready for the next performance. This illusion still exists in its modernised form, and over the past 19 years as Dame I've worked it occasionally using a huge tea-pot and a very small cup ... one of those daft routines that never get written down but produce gales of laughter in the right place.

Curious titles continued to attract audiences and *Harlequin Templar, or Richard Coeur de Lion taking in Bristol on the way to Palestine* was presented at Bath in 1850, while *Little Tom Tucker and the Fine Lady of Banbury Cross; or Harlequin Taffy the Welshman and the Old Woman who Lived in a Shoe and Little Silver Bell the Fairy* could be seen at the Theatre Royal, Bristol in 1867.

Towards the end of the 19th century, however, and almost un-noticed, a change was taking place that would have a profound effect on pantomime. Many towns had their own small theatre, and others were having them built. Some cities could boast eight or ten, each competing with its rival to present the best pantomime in the area. Managements spent fortunes on glittering scenery, dazzling costumes and the latest effects, but as the Drury Lane versions grew more and more lavish and provincial theatres struggled to keep up with them, the strain began to tell.

Though the annual pantomime made enough money to carry the average theatre through the year, storage space became a major problem. While much of the scenery could be altered, cut down, repainted and used the following year, the hundreds of increasingly elaborate and expensive costumes used in each show were a different matter. The only solution appeared to be to hire as many as possible, cut out the parades and reduce cast numbers, though managements worried that if this path were followed, audiences may feel cheated and stay away altogether. Many theatres experimented by quietly dropping the Harlequinades, (which had, in any case, dwindled to almost an afterthought) and this at least saved on scenery, but as they entered the 20th century, growing numbers threw in the towel completely and ceased to stage pantomime at all.

Realizing the potential for further profit making, some managements, like Edward Marriss of the Shakespeare Theatre in Liverpool took a company of two dozen or so principals (plus chorus) for one week runs in nearby towns and cities as soon as the run in their own theatre had ended, while others hired "vacant" theatres for a complete season to re-create pantomimes presented in their own theatres the Christmas before, thus getting double usage out of sets and costumes. As the practice increased and theatre chains grew larger, a new breed of producer emerged.

By acquiring huge storehouses where scenery and costume could be kept in good condition, they were able to present a dozen or more pantomimes every year at little comparative expense. If rotated in order, construction expenses plummeted and by adding one new show each year, refurbishing the oldest, or selling it off to a smaller management, maximum profit could be made from each.

Francis Laidler (1870-1955) was one of these new "Pantomime Kings". A Yorkshireman who staged his first pantomime in 1901, he went on to produce and direct over two hundred and fifty more. Based in Bradford, he planned all his productions there and constantly scoured the seaside pierrot troupes for new talent. "If they have any ambition to shine in pantomime" he would say "they cannot do better than learn their business in a concert party". On his travels he signed up those fabulous "Dames" George Lacy, G. S. Melvin, and Sandy Powell, to name but a few.

Sandy, who was 22 at the time had been appearing in pantomime for six years, and such was his personality, Laidler booked him to appear as Peter the Page (the Buttons character) in *Cinderella* at the Theatre Royal, Leeds. As this character, he planned to introduced a piece of "business" he had invented that is now quite common; the gag of leaving something by the proscenium arch and asking the audience to warn him if anyone tried to steal it. In this case it would be Peter's umbrella. Laidler was totally against it. In his pantomimes, an artiste never involved audiences in the on-stage proceedings, but after much pleading, and a promise to remove the gag if it didn't work, the great man reluctantly agreed. That it was never removed and now appears as a pantomime standard gag (in countless variations) all over the world, proves that even the greatest Producer, and Laidler truly was one, can sometimes be wrong.

I saw many of his pantomimes in Bradford and Leeds during the 1940's and early 1950's, and one of the regular delights of his productions was the Flying Ballet in which eight or ten girls disguised as butterflies, birds or fairies, etc. flew gracefully through the air on wires, sometimes soaring out into the darkened auditorium then returning to the stage in a colourful explosion of glittering sequins and diamonte. A scene from his *Babes in the Wood* at the Theatre Royal, Leeds, when circling "forest birds" showered autumnal coloured and glitter dusted leaves over the sleeping "Babes" to hide them, was a magical piece of theatre, and in almost half a century of watching and appearing in pantomime, I have rarely seen it repeated.

Julian Wylie (1878-1934) was another of the new movement. Originally from Lancashire, Wylie had been an accountant with a taste for theatre and particularly the art of the stage magician. On arriving in London, he became a business manager for David Devant, the famous magician and rapidly became a first class technician. After some time he opened an agency and eventually went into partnership with revue producer James Tate, husband of music hall star Clarice Mayne. Shortly after the first world war, the two men began to stage the kind of pantomimes where storylines were the most important feature and music hall excesses were considerably pruned.

Using skills he had developed during his Devant days, Wylie devised a scene change that electrified audiences and caused his partner who had not been present at rehearsals to blink in astonishment. It occurred in their production of *Aladdin* and came in the scene where Abanazar the magician finally gets hold of the Magic Lamp. It was a full set scene, and when Abanazar commanded the Geni to "transport the palace and all within it to the middle of the desert", there was a blinding flash, and in less time than it took for the audience to focus their eyes again, the beautiful grounds had been replaced with rolling sand dunes and desert palm trees. Never before had a full set change been achieved so rapidly and though nowadays it would pass without comment, it set a standard for other managements for many years.

After the death of Tate in 1922, Wylie continued alone, but the rules they had established remained firmly in position. "It must be an entertainment for the whole family" he said in an interview "There must be something in it that everyone can enjoy. The story must be kept as the chief thing and treated seriously, played for all it is worth with no liberties taken". If he could have seen into the future, he would have wept.

Within a short period, Wylie had pantomime productions all around the country. Not that his skills lay only in that direction. He also brought J. B. Priestley's *The Good Companions* to the stage, both here and in New York; the musicals, *Mr. Cinders*, (which featured the still popular song "Spread a little happiness"), and *Balalaika*, plus several plays and summer shows. On the technical side of theatre, in the early 1930s he was involved with Strand Electric in the development of Ultra Violet lighting which has been a popular feature of many stage productions for years. It is pantomime, however, for which he will ever be remembered.

Following closely in his footsteps was Tom Arnold, who in his early days had worked for music hall magnate Sir Walter de Freece and learned a great deal about the theatre while doing so. He made a considerable amount of money in touring productions, and following the unexpected death of Wylie, the quietly spoken Yorkshireman purchased all his theatrical interests. For over thirty years he was to present pantomimes, musicals and ice-shows with equal success. In 1936 he spent £20,000 on a single production of *Mother Goose* at the London Hippodrome, and at one period during the second World War, was providing employment for over 3,000 people.

An amazing scene in an Arnold pantomime of the early 1940's was the "Phantom Guard" which I believe was performed by a troupe called "The Zio Angels". A ghostly legion of mist enshrouded "guards" appeared to materialize from nowhere and march remorselessly downstage before the unbelieving eyes of the audience. At a given moment, they turned their backs on the watchers and marched upstage again to gradually vanished into the mist. The effect was achieved, so I was told by one of the cast a number of years ago, by using several gauze drapes that were drawn away, one at a time, from the back of the stage, the removal of each gauze giving a little clearer view of the oncoming marchers. By the time the last gauze had gone, they were in full view. As they turned and marched upstage again, the process was repeated in reverse. Again, a routine I have never seen since, but one that remains firmly in my memory as a piece of pure pantomime magic. Many years later Tom Arnold gave me my first major pantomime job at the Birmingham Hippodrome, and I worked for his company for the next four years. He died in 1969.

Emile Littler (1903-1974) was the youngest of the pantomime "Kings". Two years younger than his brother Prince, who also presented pantomime, Emile had been employed at the Birmingham Repertory Theatre as an A.S.M. before leaving for New York as a stage manager for the play *Yellow Sands*. Returning to England in 1931 he became manager and lessee of the Birmingham Repertory Theatre, marrying the superb Principal Boy, Cora Goffin, in 1933 and entering management of his own in Birmingham the following year when he staged his first pantomime.

Like the Melville brothers, he wrote his own scripts and had a fondness for subjects usually avoided by other managements. *Goody Two Shoes*, *The Old Woman who Lived in a Shoe* and *Jack and Jill* were all particular favourites, the latter boasting a particularly strong cast when staged at the Prince's Theatre, Birmingham in 1940. Arthur Askey was Big Hearted Arthur, Cora Goffin was Jack Horner, Billy Bennet was The Crooked Man, the wonderful Bert Brownbill as Dame Horner, and the zany O'Gorman brothers as Johnny Green and Willie Stout. It ran for eighteen weeks and Arthur told an amusing story about the production.

Like most directors, Emile liked to keep an eye on the antics of the comedians who could sometimes get out of hand. A quick handwritten note to the offender was followed by similar ones to all others involved in the scene, with a reminder to keep to the script. Having so many "offenders" that season, notes were arriving on almost a daily basis, but the comedians soon put a stop to it by rushing to the front of the stage when they saw him appear at the back of the Stalls and shouting "Any letters, Mr. Producer"? No one laughed louder than Littler.

He is remembered for introducing new pantomime stars such as Douglas Byng, Sir Henry Lytton, Billie and Renee Houston, Stanley Holloway and Dave Burnaby, but like Tom Arnold, also produced musicals such as *Dear Miss Phoebe*, *Blue for a Boy* and *Zip Goes a Million*, and was knighted for his services to theatre. He ceased to present pantomimes in 1963 and died in 1974.

The Northernmost "Kings" were Messrs Howard and Wyndham who began producing as early as 1883. Though presenting the familiar titles, they always tried to be a little different. Their *Dick Whittington* of 1893, at the Theatre Royal, Newcastle-on-Tyne, in which Vesta Tilley played the title role, had no King Rat, but boasted a Storm Fiend (played by Mr. J.H. Seaton) who sinks the ship, and featured two fairies Suga-Kandi and Lollipop. The "magic" element however was almost non-existent, for apart from a dozen lines or so, the trio barely appeared. Like all Howard and Wyndham productions it was beautifully dressed and staged and had a superb transformation scene ("The Home of the Golden Butterfly"), plus a two scene Harlequinade.

Cinderella at the Theatre Royal, Glasgow, in 1931, had a second Principal Boy and Girl (Conrad and Mopsa) plus a Wicked Witch who kidnapped Cinderella on her way home from the Ball and imprisoned her in a magic toyshop. She was, of course, rescued by the glamorous Fairy, Sylvania, and even Santa Claus played a role in the events. The Baron's page was a very Scottish Andy.

Though the "Kings" eventually dominated the British pantomime scene, many theatres continued to stage in-house productions. The Grand Theatre, Leeds; the "Alexandra's" of Birmingham and Liverpool; the "Royals" in Edinburgh, Bristol, Cardiff and Birmingham; and the Opera House, Manchester were all notable for their excellence, while the country's smaller theatres found no shortage of audiences if productions were up to standard.

It was not all plain sailing, however. Closing a theatre in order to prepare for the pantomime was sometimes necessary and managers were eager to keep this period as short as possible. Stage managers were often under pressure and occasionally, when their attention was elsewhere, gremlins were known to slip in through unguarded doors, especially when complicated special effects were scheduled to be used. The 1913 production of *Robinson Crusoe* in Exeter which featured a young Gillie Potter (1887-1975) as the villainous Will Atkins, was a prime example.

The most dramatic scene in the pantomime was a shipwreck caused by a huge tidal wave. At the back of the stage was a cyclorama on which a film depicting all the denizens of the sea could be projected whilst an aeroplane would be seen flying overhead. (Very innovative for the period) The local fire station had fixed up a hose pipe that would cause thousands of gallons of water to cascade onto the stage into troughs concealed by a groundrow of large "boulders", a boiler would provide steam for the storm-clouds, and a hundredweight of rice grains would shower the stage from above to represent the tidal wave.

The rice shower demanded perfect timing and after several failed attempts to get it right, the stage manager decided to give a vocal signal himself, telling the operator not to release one single grain until he heard the shout. The next problem arose when the Fire Chief refused to waste water by turning it on to test everything, and only reluctantly agreed to do it for the essential Dress Rehearsal on Boxing Day. At the crucial point, the hose was turned on and promptly split, sending hundreds of gallons of freezing water over the entire set. The rest of the day was spent trying to mop the scenery dry and the stage rehearsal was cancelled.

On opening night, everything appeared to be going well and the exhausted stage manager slipped out of the theatre and into the local bar for a much needed drink. Suddenly remembering the Shipwreck scene, he raced back to the theatre in time to see the water from the hosepipe exploding onto the stage, thundersheet shaking violently, steam from the boiler rising skywards, lights flickering wildly, but not a sign of the promised rice. Pushing aside the "panic stricken natives of the island" as they rushed off stage, he screamed to the operator overhead to "let go the rice". The startled man hastily did so, and a hundred and twelve pounds of it poured unerringly onto the head of the irate stage manager.

In a later scene, where four cannibals carried on a great pie for a feast, the gremlin struck again. The pie was placed over a star-trap, so that when it was opened, the comedian could spring out enabling a comic chase to end the scene. Having been unable to rehearse with the pie because of the previous day's flood, no-one realised its base was too small to allow the star-trap to open, and when the comedian was shot up from below stage, he knocked himself senseless on the underside of the trap, leaving the bewildered "natives" on stage to add-lib as best as they could to close the scene. It was the last time *Robinson Crusoe* was presented at that particular theatre.

By the nineteen thirties Music Hall had almost vanished, being replaced by Variety with its sketches, instrumentalists, stand-up comedians, adagio dancers, comedy acrobats, etc., and cinema was fast becoming a serious rival to live theatre. In almost every town and city, new "Picture Palaces" were being built while existing theatres were hastily converted to the silver screen, throwing hundreds of stage performers out of work. As the theatrical profession struggled to come to terms, World War Two broke out and pantomimes began to change again.

The Britannia Theatre, Hoxton was destroyed by German bombs in 1940, and the Surrey, which had passed out of the Conquest family's hands in 1904, (though they continued to perform in other theatres) had been demolished five years earlier. With no permanent home in central London, the Hippodrome, Casino, and Coliseum, etc. became temporary pantomime houses, but rationing and soaring costs forced managements to make reductions in almost every aspect. The huge companies of the past were no longer a viable proposition and a chorus of twenty four (plus juveniles), a cast of sixteen or so and a twelve piece orchestra was considered enough to sustain standards.

The Wireless, or radio as it later became, was by now an essential part of the British household and since its launch by the B.B.C. in 1922, was creating its own star performers. In the first few years of its introduction, and under the Directorship of John Reith, it had been a strange affair. The newspaper magnates objected to the broadcasting of news items – that, they felt, was their job – and many Variety managements hastily drew up contracts for their artistes forbidding them to participate in the new media. Reith himself, was indifferent to the ban. He was not overfond of popular entertainment and firmly believed that radio should be mainly used as a form of education. As George Nobbs remarks in his book *The Wireless Stars* (Wensum. 1972) "If audiences were often bored to tears, it mattered little because the B.B.C. enjoyed a monopoly of Broadcasting in Britain"

Light entertainment was, of course, part of the B.B.C.'s early output, with stars such as Helen Millais, Rob Wilton, G.H. Elliot, Jack Payne and Henry Hall playing prominent roles, though Reith's influence ensured that their contributions were kept to a bare minimum. In the 1930s, the British public were able to show their disapproval by tuning in to Radio Normandie and Radio Luxembourg, (which were now broadcasting English language programmes and popular record shows) and this forced the furious B.B.C. to increase its Light entertainment output in order to regain listeners. The Educational aspect, however, was still heavily plugged, even when Reith, who had been knighted in 1926, left office in 1938. By the time World War II began, scripted comedies such as *Bandwaggon*, and *I.T.M.A*, were turning performers like Arthur Askey, Richard Murdoch, Tommy Handley and Jack Train, into household names.

It was during this period that radio sets were introduced into pantomime. Cookery tips and "Health and Beauty" items were part and parcel of B.B.C. programmes, and many pantomimes of the thirties, forties and fifties, eventually contained a routine where the Dame attempted to make pastry by following a recipe read out by a radio cook. After leaving her kitchen momentarily, the programme was changed by the "Simple Simon" character to a "Keep Fit" or Football match before he exited again. On returning to continue her baking, the Dame followed the instructions on the new programme without realizing the alteration and the pastry was used as a prop for ridiculous antics that set the children shrieking with delight.

Another "radio" gag of the period was the burglary sequence in *Babes in the Wood* or *Dick Whittington*. The villains, faced with what appeared to be a large safe with a central combination dial, move the knob "five to the left, seven to the right and three to the left" ... only to discover they have turned on the new-fangled radio which blares out deafening music or a police message and panics them into flight. Both routines had vanished by the mid nineteen-sixties, but a variation of the former re-appeared in the early nineteen nineties at Swansea with a television set being substituted for the radio. It didn't work.

As the war rolled on, artistes who were already popular in Variety theatres were joined in programmes such as *Music Hall*, *Workers Playtime*, and *Variety Bandbox*, by virtual unknowns who suddenly caught the listener's interest and were transformed into overnight stars. Naturally, their enhanced reputations resulted in bookings for Variety and

Pantomime by the top theatre Circuits who even in those austere times could pay far larger wages than the B.B.C., and though everyone will have their own memories, my Golden Years of pantomime were undoubtedly the forties and early fifties.

Throughout that period, I saw many of the country's best Variety acts in pantomime, plus dozens who never topped the bills, but gave enormous pleasure in supporting roles. The "Dame", of course, was my favourite character and in addition to those great practitioners Norman Evans, Arthur Askey, Billy Whittaker, Nat Jackley, George Lacy (who claimed to have introduced the practice of wearing a different outfit for every entrance) and Jimmy James (in what I believe was his only excursion into skirts) one other deserves at least a mention – the wonderful Nat Mills.

Despite the deserved praise lavished on others, for me, Nat Mills and Bobbie (who was Nat's wife and partner), were the funniest performers I ever saw in pantomime. I saw their *Jack and the Beanstalk* several times during its enormous run at the Grand Theatre, Leeds, and from their very first entrance the theatre remained in an uproar for almost three hours. Apart from their hilarious version of "There's a hole in my bucket", which I've never seen bettered, and a scene in the giant's kitchen that provoked several "accidents" among the ladies in the audience (my Grandmother included), Bobbie's determined attempt to "rehearse" a solo entertainment as the approaching giant's footsteps shake the cottage and a panic stricken Nat attempted to speed her up, is as clear in my memory as it was fifty odd years ago. Again, a routine I've never seen since, yet I only have to think about it and the giggles start.

Her Larry-the-lamb bleat and his exasperated catch-phrase "Well let's get on with it" sent audiences into paroxysms of laughter as did the stupidity of their dialogue. A typical example from the pantomime follows. Nat was "Dame Trot" and Bobbie his maid-of-all-work.

| Nat | : (Curiously) What's the matter with you? Why are you looking like that? |
| Bobbie | : I'm thinking. |

Nat	: Thinking? (Looks incredulous) What about?
Bobbie	: Well....is it true that God made heaven and earth ?
Nat	: (Looking at her strangely) Well, of course he did. Everybody knows that. It's in the bible, isn't it? God made heaven and earth.
Bobbie	: And did he make all the stars and the clouds and the mountains – and all the nice little animals and everything else as well?
Nat	: (Another odd look) Of course he did. He made everything. All of it.
Bobbie	: In six days?
Nat	: (Nodding) Six days.
Bobbie	: And did he do it thousands and thousands of years ago?
Nat	: (Exasperatedly) Well of course he did it thousands and thousands of years ago. When else would he do it?
Bobbie	: Ohhhh. (A thoughtful look on her face) I wonder what he's been doing lately ?

To this day I can never understood why their names are all but forgotten by the general public. A magical pair. Bobbie died in 1955 and Nat in 1993.

Another curious pair were a speciality act known as "The Two Pirates". (Alfred "Jock" Cochrane and Reg Mankin). Though I saw them several times on Variety bills, I don't remember ever seeing them in pantomime. One of their routines, however, did find a place in the genre. A re-creation of the much earlier Laveen & Cross success, they performed ridiculous balancing feats, with the smaller of the pair being suspended on a wire. It was perfectly obvious to the audience what was happening, which is why the routine was met with indifference ... at first. The gag, of course, was not the balancing at all. The laugh came when the smaller one was positioned directly above his partner, supposedly being supported by a single fingertip, and the larger one remarked to the audience "There's no wire, you know" only to receive a scornful laugh in return. Indignantly leaving his partner dangling, he would march downstage, insisting "Oh, no there isn't", to which the entire audience would call back delightedly "Oh, yes there is". This could go on for several minutes while the smaller one wriggled and twisted on the end of the wire like a hooked fish. I don't know what happened to the

"Pirates", but the "Oh no there isn't" catch-phrase is used in 99% of all pantomimes today and audiences still love it.

As radio continued to create dozens of new stars, such as Peter Brough (with Archie Andrews), Max Bygraves, Jon Pertwee, Charlie Chester, Ted Ray, Brian Reece, Frankie Howerd, Alfred Marks, Hattie Jacques, Tony Hancock, Beryl Reid, Kenneth Horne, Harry Secombe, Ken Platt, Arthur English, Kenneth Connor, etc., yet another rival to live theatre began to stir.   Anticipation of the Coronation in 1953 resulted in gigantic sales of television sets and though managements and artistes alike felt they had nothing to fear from the new medium, they were soon to find otherwise.

Programmes such as *The Grove Family, The Larkins, Whacko, The Army Game, Take your Pick, Double your Money, I Love Lucy,* and *I Married Joan* attracted enormous audiences, and when *Sunday Night at the London Palladium* made its first appearance in 1955, millions of viewers switched on to watch top name Variety artistes from the comfort of their own armchairs. The effect was dramatic. Over the next few years, with frightening regularity, long established theatres and cinemas, faced with dwindling audiences, closed down and were demolished or converted into supermarkets and Bingo halls.

In the world of pantomime, soaring costs had further reduced cast and chorus numbers. By the mid fifties, second Principal Boys and Girls had become a rarity in all but the largest theatres. Kings, Queens and Barons, were losing their other halves, and the twenty something strong choruses were only a memory. Transformation scenes, (or the shadows of them that remained), were eradicated, the flying ballets became few and far between, and to me, the most regrettable change of all took place. The male Principal Boy made a come-back

*S*ince 1948, The Palladium Theatre in Argyll Street had been London's premier pantomime house. Opening with *Cinderella*, it had gone on to present such famous names as Jimmy Jewel and Ben Warriss in *Babes in the Wood*, Norman Evans, Terry Thomas and Betty Jumel in *Humpty Dumpty*, Frankie Howerd in *Dick Whittington*, Adele Dixon, Julie Andrews, Max Bygraves and Jon Pertwee in *Cinderella*, and Richard Hearne and Peter Sellers in *Mother Goose*. In subsequent years, the productions (with cast changes) would be presented all over Britain in rota.

For the *Aladdin* of 1956-7, impresario Val Parnell engaged comedian Norman Wisdom to top the bill, but instead of playing "Wishee Washee" as everyone expected, he appeared in the title role. A tremendous draw at the Box Office, he re-started a trend that later introduced Edmund Hockridge, Frankie Vaughan, Englebert Humperdinck, Frank Ifield, Cliff Richard, Edward Woodward and Jimmy Tarbuck, etc. to the hero's role. All were highly successful and delighted thousands, but though I've worked with several male "Boys", and found most of them great company, I have always disliked the practice as much as I dislike female "Dames". With either in the production, I feel that the "topsy-turvey fairytale element" has been removed and we have entered the realm of the Musical. I am also unimpressed by comical Principal Boys of either sex, no matter how many laughs they can raise. With so many opportunities for zany characters in pantomime, to make the romantic hero a comedian too, seems totally pointless.

In the latter part of the 1950s a determined effort was made to push pantomime into another shape. In 1956 America's C.B.S. Television company had commissioned Richard Rogers and Oscar Hammerstein to write a musical fairy tale for English star, Julie Andrews, who had recently created the role of Eliza Doolittle in the Broadway musical *My Fair Lady*. Eager to work with Julie, within six months they had devised a version of *Cinderella* which was transmitted live on March 31st, 1957. Songs such as "My own little corner", "A lovely night", "Ten minutes ago" and "Do I love you because you're beautiful" were instant hits, and together with the fairytale staging by C.B.S. attracted the interest of London impresario Harold Fielding who decided to stage it at the Coliseum as a pantomime. In 1958, with costumes and scenery designed by the brilliant Loudon Sainthill, it opened with Jimmy Edwards as the King, Yana as Cinderella, and Kenneth Williams and Ted Durante as the Ugly Sisters. There was no Buttons character in the original version, so the book was re-written and the role handed to Tommy Steele. It was beautiful to look at, delightful to listen to and packed the vast theatre, but despite the care lavished on it, after one revival in 1960 at the Adelphi Theatre, it vanished from the British scene and is now almost forgotten.

The following year's *Aladdin* shared the same fate. Sal Mineo and Cyril Richard had starred in C.B.S.'s production for which the ailing Cole Porter had provided music and lyrics, and in the English stage version, Bob Monkhouse took the title role with Doretta Morrow as the Princess, Ronald Shiner (one of my favourite comic actors) as Widow Twankey, and Ian Wallace the Emperor. Robert Helpmann directed and once again Loudon Sainthill designed the dazzling scenery and costumes. Though thousands flocked to see it and were duly impressed, it was not pantomime, and as far as I'm aware, has not been staged in Britain since. The opening chorus, however, "Come to the Supermarket in Old Pekin", has become not only a standard for "traditional" *Aladdin* productions, but has been known to pop up in *Ali Baba* and *Dick Whittington* with a word changed here and there.

As mentioned earlier, the music and songs used in pantomime were originally there for legal reasons. Until 1843, popular and traditional songs were used, some given new lyrics, others performed as written, but by the start of the twentieth century, music publishers such as Francis, Day & Hunter, Sheard & Co., Feldman & Co, Hopwood & Crew Ltd., and Bosworth & Co., were busy supplying theatres with the latest hits. As the 1930's approached, certain songs were being written expressly for pantomime use and if successful, the sheet music cover would depict the artiste in character with the words "As sung in the great pantomime success ..." in large lettering.

"You've got to Blow your own Trumpet" sung by Gwladys Stanley (the wife of Francis Laidler, who took over his business after he died) is a prime example of the type, but many others can be found in second-hand sheet music shops.

Though there had been experiments in the past, (notably the Oscar Barrett *Cinderella* of 1893) it was not until the Palladium pantomimes of the 1950's that complete musical scores were considered desirable. Though several songs with a true pantomime flavour emerged from these, when the shows moved out of London it soon became obvious that provincial audiences much preferred music they already knew and most of the original songs were replaced by popular "standards". Very little of those specially written Palladium scores remain in use today but the practice was successfully continued by writers such as Betty Astell, David Cregan & Brian Protheroe, John Crocker & Eric Gilder, and David Wood (though the latter's versions are more musical plays than pantomimes but use the same "traditional" storylines).

For my own part, I prefer a mixed bunch of show songs, "golden oldies", classical music and comedy numbers because

I'm absolutely convinced that no one composer can cover the vast range of musical items a pantomime demands. To begin with, not all musical interludes make sense. A bright and breezy opening chorus is all very well to start a pantomime, but what about songs for those principal artistes who have their own ideas of what audiences expect of them?

A.E.Wilson relates the story of a certain Demon King, who after capturing the Principal Girl and tossing her into a dungeon, advanced to the footlights and tenderly sang "When the Angelus is ringing", while in *Aladdin*, following a lusty chorus of "There'll always be an England" (sung by "Chinese peasants" in Dutch national costumes as the sails of a windmill turned merrily in the background), the evil magician Abanazar made his entrance to loud cheers and promptly greeted everyone with a military rendering of "Soldiers of the Queen".

Other sources tell of a Cannibal Chief in *Robinson Crusoe* warbling "I'm dreaming of a White Christmas", a 1990s Cinderella sweeping the kitchen floor while cheering herself up with "I don't know how to love him", and a male "Robin Hood" obliging the audience with "Memories". The mind boggles.

Not only singers livened up proceedings during the period when speciality acts were heavily featured in pantomimes. Music Hall star Gertie Gitana (singer of the song "Nellie Dean") also played the saxophone. During one production of *Cinderella*, in which she played the title role, she was discovered in a state of depression after everyone else had gone to the Ball. Letting out a sigh, she exclaimed "Here I am – all alone. I think I'll play my saxophone". Swiftly reaching up the chimney, she produced the instrument and went into her famous act.

Historian Leopold Wagner tells of a production of *The Yellow Dwarf* in the 1880s (which is set in Austria's Black Forest), when Tyler's Silver Band could be seen dressed in oriental costumes, playing "Come Back to Erin" on the terrace of King Rombo's Palace on the banks of the Ganges. Even more startling was the performer playing the Goose role in *Mother Goose*. As his act in Variety was saxophone playing (according to the late George Lacy), half way through the pantomime he waddled on-stage in a front-cloth scene, lifted off his

Goose-skin, and delivered a selection of "hot sax tunes" before re-donning the skin and waddling off again. Could any composer forsee *that*?

In 1960, the enormous success of a new pantomime made managements all over Britain sit up and take notice. *A Wish for Jamie* opened at the Alhambra Theatre, Glasgow on Dec. 9th, of that year. Starring Kenneth McKellar as Jamie, Rikki Fulton as Dame, Fay Lenore as Principal Boy, Donald, Reg Varney as Percy the farmhand and Russell Hunter as the King of the Frogs, it showed a profit of £16,000 in just eleven weeks. *A Love for Jamie* and *The World of Jamie* were to follow with equal success.

The three *Jamie* pantomimes did not spring from nowhere, of course. Since the early part of the century, Scottish managements had followed the example of The Brittania, Hoxton, and not restricted themselves to the same few titles as the rest of Britain. *Goosey Gander* had delighted audiences at the Royal Princess's Theatre in Glasgow as far back as 1904. Written by the popular Fred Locke, and with Daisy Dormer, Lily Morris, John E. Coyle and Dawson Dewick in leading roles, it was a typical example of Scottish ingenuity.

Set almost entirely in the village of Ganderdubbs, it told the story of Baron Gander's attempts to marry off his simple-minded son, Goosey, to the beautiful and orphaned Rosey Posey, who unknown to everyone but Baron Gander, is actually the daughter of his elder brother and heir to the Family estates and fortune. Rosey, of course, only has eyes for Fearless Fred, who is actually Prince Charming in disguise. Extremely topical in construction, it contained barbed references to the doings of local councillors and politicians that in todays politically correct times would probably provoke law suits, not to mention several jokes concerning Japan's attack on Imperial Russia's Baltic Fleet. The ten scenes included a realistic representation of *The Racecourse at Ayr* and the spectacular *Gardens of the Cafe Chantant*, but the highlight of the production was undoubtably a routine where the Baron and Goosey let the single bed of their Seaside lodging house to almost every comedian in the company who discover to their cost it is haunted by the Demon Discord. Even today it makes amusing reading.

Another famous Royal Princess's pantomime was *Tammy Trotter*. Produced by Harry McKelvie, it opened on Thursday 17th December, 1936, with a cast including George West as Tammy; Jose Donelli as Principal Boy, Colin; Ann Doel as Principal Girl, Cherry; and that great "feed" Jerry Desmond with his wife Peggy as the speciality dancers Willie and Tillie. Its sixteen scenes ranged from the Demon's swamp to a Red Indian camp in the Far West, taking in the Court of King Neptune at the bottom of the sea, a trip in a diving Bell and a visit to a palace on the planet Mars. The convoluted storyline makes an entertaining read and it is interesting to see that "Big Heads" were still being used even at that late date.

The interest shown in the *Jamie* productions may well have triggered off the revival of an almost forgotten pantomime subject that briefly re-entered the English cannon soon afterwards; *The Pied Piper*. If memory serves me correctly, it featured Freddy (Parrot-face) Davis as the principal comic, but after only a few airings, it was shelved again and rarely re-appears. Another casualty was the Palladium's *The Man in the Moon* of 1963. Not really a pantomime, but more of a space age musical with pantomimic elements and featuring knockabout comedian Charlie Drake, it failed to survive the end of the season.

As the demolition of provincial theatres continued, the boom in teenage music enabled artistes such as Billy Fury, Freddie and the Dreamers, Cliff Richard and the Shadows, Cilla Black and Dusty Springfield, etc., to join the dwindling number of Variety performers in pantomime. Though some made the adjustment from pop singer to pantomime star and were well received, others did not, the need to promote their latest record, no matter how unsuitable to the role they were playing, outweighing any other consideration. I shall never forget one *Dick Whittington* where the male Principal Boy made his first entrance carrying an electric guitar and trailing a cable, to immediately inform the audience that he had just arrived in London, and though having no job, no money and nowhere to live, he *did* have a record in the top twenty which was on sale in the theatre foyer. Anyone buying a copy was invited to go backstage after the show and have it autographed. In the meanwhile, he was going to play them both sides so they could hear how good it was. It was possibly a production such as this that prompted one critic to write a scathing review on what pantomime had descended to.

> "Even by standards of television as an entertainment, pantomime is generally abysmal. The plots are ludicrous. Even the most incompetent performers are in ruthless competition with each other. None of the dancers match, and few can dance, anyway. The orchestras are ham fisted, over-loud, blubber-mouthed, and almost as stoned as the stage-hands who have to shift mountains of battered scenery that has seen better days and better pantomimes".

In spite of this, and other similar critical carping, there was still much to be enjoyed in a 1960's pantomime. If some of the newer "stars" failed to please older audiences, many of the supporting casts had been in show-business for years and their polished acts brought applause the higher paid could only dream of.

Eccentric dancers "The Lyntons" had only to appear on stage and the place was in an uproar. I worked with Bill and Brian in several long running pantomimes and stood in the wings virtually every performance to watch their zany act. It was almost impossible to look at them and not laugh. Brian's innocent "dopey" expression and the painfully thin, rubbery legs of Bill (which had a life of their own) convulsed audiences, especially when, with Bill as a haggard prima ballerina in droopy tutu, oranges stuffed down his wrinkled tights for calves and wearing outsized pointe shoes, the pair performed a dreamy *pas de deux* whilst manipulating a huge balloon. Their slow motion "silent movie" routine was another absolutely fascinating and unique piece of theatre. They always had time for a laugh and it was Bill who talked me through the "sausages gag" and many of the "front-cloth" routines I've put to good use over the last thirty-odd years. As theatre work grew scarcer, Bill Lynton became a familiar member of the original *Candid Camera* team on television, while Brian Massie retired to a more normal life.

211

Another great speciality act was Ken Wilson. I saw him several times in Variety where he was billed as "The man with the deck-chair", and though not the first to use the idea, it's difficult to imagine anyone ever bettering his routine. The simple job of erecting a deck-chair led to several minutes of absolute hysteria, and the only other performer I can compare him with is George Carl whose "coat and microphone" routine produces the same kind of audience reaction today.

Ken's "slosh" scenes with Lauri Lupino Lane (another great "support") brought the place down at every performance and for a very good reason. The special mix, devised by the Lupino family, was freshly prepared for each performance and unlike modern "slosh" only went where it was intended to go. In addition, each "mishap" appeared to happen by accident; there was none of the "your turn, my turn" about this act; the timing was perfect. By the time the scene finished, the pair were almost invisible beneath the quaking and glistening multi-coloured foam while the audience were helpless with laughter. The most recent version I've seen of a "slosh routine" was so badly done I almost burst into tears. It was "Painting by numbers" instead of Rembrandt, and the apathetic audience obviously felt the same judging by the reaction.

Another memory of that period was supplied by Audrey Jeans who died so tragically in a road accident a few months after our season ended. A superb Principal Boy in her younger days and a warm and generous person, she was then playing Dame. As I mentioned earlier, I don't like female Dames, but Audrey could have converted me. Part of her act in the production involved inviting a group of youngsters to join her on stage (a "traditional" pantomime innovation that began only in the 1950s) and have their photo taken on a polaroid camera.

At one performance, a little boy stood apart from the rest and began looking at her with some apprehension. Aware of her somewhat bizarre costume and make-up, and thinking he may burst into tears at any moment, she tried to make him laugh by asking him if he was married. "No" he whispered. "Oh", said Audrey and moved in closer. "But I bet you're engaged, aren't you?" "No" he replied edging away. "Haven't you got a girlfriend, then?" she asked, crouching down beside him and extending her hand mic. "No" he said "I haven't". At this, she gave him a beaming smile and suggested he might like to have her as a girlfriend. "No" he answered in panic stricken tones "I wouldn't. I wouldn't" "Why not?" she asked in surprise, holding the hand-mic a little closer to him. "Cos you're an ugly old cow" he burst out. As Audrey rocked on her heels, the entire theatre exploded into hysterical laughter and the child made a hurried escape.

It was in the same production, just a few days later, that comedian Jack Douglas and his stage partner, George Truzzi almost had seizures in a scene that involved me. As everyone in the company knew, without my spectacles I was unable to see more than blurry outlines, and not only had I to remember my lines, but also how many steps I needed to take to get to a certain point. In the "Babes Nursery" I was dressed as a ghost and attempting to scare away the two robbers. As I moved into position with the audience screaming out its warning, Jack and George twisted and turned but appeared unable to see me. As the screams grew louder, a small child raced up the steps by the proscenium arch and onto the stage, shrieking at the top of her voice. Before anyone knew what was happening, she gave me an agonising kick on the shin that brought tears to my eyes. Not realizing what had struck me, I spun round, gasping in pain, just in time to collect another blow from her flailing feet. Like a wildcat, she launched an all-out attack on me while I staggered around, unable to see anything, kicks and punches coming from all directions. As I blundered into the wings, Jack and George were on the floor screaming with laughter and the audience were hysterical. For several minutes the show came to a halt and the audience cheered themselves hoarse. The next day we made the front page in almost every national paper in England and shortly afterwards, Jack presented the little "rescuer" with a bicycle for saving them from the "ghost". It was some days before I could walk without limping and, even after medical attention, the bruises took weeks to vanish. I'm still convinced she had steel toe-caps on her shoes.

By the 1970s, top-line entertainers were either concentrating on film and television or finding better paid employment in the huge variety Clubs which had replaced the vanishing theatres. Disillusioned by lack of opportunity, many established, but lesser "names" gave up the struggle and retired, or left Britain to find work in other countries. For example, those two unique comedians Joe Baker and Freddie Sales found their greatest fame in the USA. What a pity we had to lose them.

Television favourites, (with a few exceptions), were reluctant to accept pantomime engagements which would tie them up for weeks unless they were guaranteed salaries on a par with their television payments, and with depressing regularity, pantomime casts shrank further in order to accommodate the new financial demands. In my first professional pantomime, fourteen girls and eight boys had made up the chorus, with eleven principal performers being engaged. Less than ten years later, there were eight girls, four boys and eight principals.

Another casualty of the times were the stage traps. Almost overnight they began to vanish due to fears for the safety of the highly paid artistes, and yet another part of pantomime's evolution became history.

In 1979 I directed one of my own pantomimes in America which sparked off a small revival in the mid West and Northern States. The *Des Moines Register* reported (*Sing a Song of Sixpence*) "is possibly the first successful British pantomime to be seen this century" and by the mid 1980's, it had been re-staged several times and finally televised. In addition, my *Cinderella* had been seen in Ames and New York, and productions of my *Aladdin*, *Mother Goose* and other subjects were taking place all over America and Canada. With scripts also popular in Australia, Germany, Holland, Sweden and New Zealand I was tempted to rest on my laurels, but my first pantomime engagement on returning to England gave me a shock. In my short absence, another change had taken place. Performers from television Soaps and situation comedies had begun to replace the defecting variety performers and while several of these had already worked successfully in live theatre, many had only become popular through television exposure and hadn't a clue when it came to pantomime and its "traditions".

For one production, in which I was playing Dame, a popular actress from a long running sit-com was engaged as Principal Girl. Unfortunately, the management had not checked on her singing ability and after she discovered the role included several songs, fearfully revealed she was tone deaf. After initial disbelief and an excruciating "audition", the horrified producer was forced to supply an off-stage singer for all her vocals and the unhappy "star" mimed her lyrics for the entire run.

In contrast, another young television actress making her stage debut as Cinderella, terrified of letting everyone down, bewildered by the ad-libs and comic routines that were not in her carefully marked script and convinced that the Ugly Sisters (I was one of them) disliked her because of the way they sneered whilst delivering lines, spent the first few days of rehearsals in floods of tears. When the cause of her misery was finally discovered, a break was called and the whole company gently talked her through it over coffee and sandwiches. On opening night, she gave a dazzling performance. In almost sixty years, I can't recall a better "Cinders", but at the end of the season she showered the entire company with gifts and, as far as I know, has never performed in pantomime again.

By the early 1980s, the once booming Clubs were collapsing and pantomimes were awash with television names. Soap stars, announcers, quiz show hosts, etc., were all heavily featured at Major theatres whilst the few remaining variety artistes were swept aside. As one disgruntled comedian told me. "You can spend thirty years in the business and not get a look in at Christmas, but do a walk on in "Neighbours", and you can headline the Palladium". It was not entirely true, of course, but I could see his point. In most of those productions, there was no place for "unknowns". The public wanted television faces, not just in leading roles, but in supporting ones too, and managements were forced to oblige. That many pantomimes of the period were without charm and deadly dull as letters to the press regularly showed) was a direct result of public demand, though fortunately there were still enough "real" stars around for audiences who preferred the older style of presentation.

Jack Tripp, whose innocent face hid a devastating ability to puncture pomposity. The amazing Billy Dainty, whose cheeky grin, twinkling feet and wonderful personality made him the darling of millions, could have been one of pantomime's all-time "greats" but for his untimely death in 1986. His loss to the world of entertainment is incalculable. Anita Harris; in my opinion the best Principal Boy since Dorothy Ward and nice with it; Welsh comedian Wyn Calvin, the "butchest" of all Dames whose voice could (and still can) shatter a concrete mixer at half a mile, yet reduce an audience to helpless giggles with a simper that would un-nerve a mad gorilla. Ken Dodd, the funniest comedian I ever appeared with; gurning Les Dawson, and the inimitable Roy Hudd – last true King of pantomime performers, whose obvious love of the genre lifted them bodily to Command Performance stature, are just a few examples.

Another lifeline came in the form of the small scale pantomimes that had begun to emerge during the sixties and which by the 1980s were in full flower. With a maximum of eight (usually experienced) principals, a chorus of six teenage girls and six "babes" from a local dancing school plus a trio for accompaniment, an entertaining, though not very spectacular, production could be mounted. With seat prices far lower than the major theatres, families were happy to attend and many claimed they enjoyed them far better than the storyless, "star" overloaded and sometimes tasteless productions elsewhere. Using well written scripts, colourful costumes, attractive scenery and directors who knew the ropes, these compact productions retained almost everything that the major theatres had discarded and even created their own stars.

Two particular favourites of mine (and audiences) were Ronnie Collis, a "Simple Simon" par excellence who often worked with his pet goat, Sheena, and Welsh children's entertainer, Kevin Johns.

Sheena had a passion for toast and flowers, and Ronnie had worked out a lovely routine in which he arrived on stage with a bunch of flowers for the Principal Girl, and hid them behind his back to surprise her. As he bashfully chatted her up, Sheena would rush on behind him, munch her way through the bouquet, then exit in pursuit of the toast awaiting her in the wings, leaving Ronnie to present the stalks to his beloved. It was a gag that never failed, and the audience loved it. He was absolute magic to work with and when he retired from showbusiness, opened "Chaplin's", the famous theatre school in Northampton, continuing to teach there until a few days before his death in the year 2000.

Kevin Johns was the roundest person I ever came across. Like a giant beachball, he would bounce onto the stage and within seconds his exuberant personality had the audience eating out of his hand. I worked with him several times and have never seen him anything less than devastating. A cross between Harry Secombe and Lou Costello, he should have topped major productions around the country, and why he never became better known is a mystery. The last I heard of him, he was a disc jockey for Swansea Sound. What a loss to pantomime.

As we approached the end of the century, Variety became a dirty word and summer season shows which had been traditional training grounds for pantomime performers practically vanished. Though soap stars still dominated the pantomime scene in major theatres and several of the minor ones, they were gradually joined by Cricketers, Boxers, television Chefs, "Gladiators", and even the ubiquitous Mr. Blobby, all receiving higher billing and better pay than the usually experienced support artistes whom the magic wand of Television had studiously avoided.

To accommodate this influx, (and provide salaries for these new "stars"), familiar characters were written out of productions. By the end of the 1990s there were pantomimes without a "Dame" or "Simple Simon"; an *Aladdin* with "Wishee Washee" doubling up as "Genie of the Lamp" and "The Emperor of China"; a *Puss in Boots* and *Jack and the Beanstalk* without a "Giant"; and a *Dick Whittington* minus its "Alderman Fitzwarren" or "Idle Jack". As this trend has not yet been halted, and, more surprisingly, has drawn little response from critics or public, it's possible we shall eventually see *Cinderella's* "Dandini", or *Robinson Crusoe's* "Man Friday" suffer the same fate. Only time will tell.

217

Whilst some of todays pantomimes still fill the theatres – albeit for only a few weeks, as we move into a new millenium I often wonder if audiences extract as much pleasure from them as I have done for most of *my* life. Much of what made them what they were has been removed by accountants, political correctness, and whiz-kid directors whose talents would be of far more use to the alternative comedy circuit. It must be admitted, however, that for many Britons, a Christmas without a pantomime is not a Christmas at all, and, after almost three centuries, productions of them are still to be numbered in thousands. Clear evidence that the misbegotten offspring of Harlequin and Co. show little sign of relinquishing their hold on the theatregoing public in the foreseeable future.

One final question remains, for my rummaging in pantomimic history has turned up a curious fact. With official honours being handed out regularly to actors, singers, dancers, musicians, etc., and when one considers that more people have attended them in Britain than any other form of theatrical entertainment since the beginning of the eighteenth century, why is it that no performer, scenic designer, writer, manager or director has ever received an award for services to pantomime? The omission appears to smack of pure snobbery and utter disregard for a section of show-business that has given, and is still giving, pleasure to millions.

*O*ver the last twenty years of giving talks on the subject, some of the most asked questions are where the stories came from and when they were first presented. In this final chapter I'll attempt to fill in the backgrounds of most of those we can still see today. Four, at least, are based on true stories, and claims exist for two others. Readers can judge for themselves.

Aladdin, takes second place in the British most popular pantomimes list and its history has already been related in Chapter Nine. Another "Thousand Nights and One Night" tale, it is so well known that to find something new to say about it would seem an impossibility. There is, however, one interesting and long forgotten part of the story that has never made it to the stage. In the original manuscript, following the death of the evil Moorish magician, Aladdin and his Princess, the lovely Badr-al-budur, are plunged into misery at their failure to have a child. The Princess seeks the aid of an old prophetess, Fatmah, who tells her to ask Aladdin to find a Roc's egg and hang it from the crystal dome of their palace as this will soon solve the problem. On hearing this, Aladdin quickly calls up the Genie of the Lamp, but far from obliging, the enraged Genie vows to kill him.

To Aladdin's horror, he discovers that the Roc is a sacred bird to the Genie and his kind, and as he cowers in fright, explains the request came from Fatmah, the prophetess, and not from him. The Genie at once relents and reveals that Fatmah is not a woman at all but the equally evil brother of the dead magician, who, having divined his brother's fate, was now intent on revenge. Aladdin lures the false prophetess to his palace and cuts off her head, thus breaking the spell which had been cast to cause the Princess's barrenness and ensuring that the happy couple will soon be blessed with countless children.

******

Ali Baba and the Forty Thieves was first presented as a melodrama at Drury Lane in 1806, and was written by George Colman the younger. Gilbert A'Beckett provided another version at the Lyceum in 1844, but it entered the pantomime cannon in 1846 as an equestrian entertainment at Astley's Ampitheatre. Written by Nelson Lee, and entitled *The Forty Thieves; or Harlequin Ali Baba and the Robber's Cave* the Robber Band were introduced riding tiny ponies. H. J. Byron wrote a burlesque version entitled *Ali Baba and the Thirty Nine Thieves* for The Strand Theatre in 1863, but there was no reduction in numbers for Augustus Harris's production of *The Forty Thieves* in 1866 at Drury Lane, for he gave each of his thieves a dozen "slaves" to make things more interesting and crowded the Magic Cave with over 400 "supers".

For many years, the Eastern settings alone attracted audiences who revelled in the sensuous splendour of colourful silks and gauzes. Oscar Asche and Frederick Norton's spectacular musical *Chu Chin Chow* (presented at Her Majesty's Theatre, London in 1916), is the Ali Baba story in a different guise, and its memorable songs and dances were used in pantomime productions of *Ali Baba* and *Aladdin* for many years after. By the end of the 1940's, however, *The Forty Thieves* or *Ali Baba* appeared on posters less frequently, and today it survives only in the amateur field where large casts can be used without the horrendous expense that unfortunately prevent a professional production. It is still, however, a wonderful pantomime.

******

The Babes in the Wood is based on a true story, and was first referred to in an old ballad entitled *The Children in the Wood; or, The Norfolk Gentleman's Last Will and Testament* in 1595. The subject received operatic treatment at the hands of Dr. Samuel Arnold the versatile composer of not only operas and oratorios, but *burlettas* and the 1771 pantomime *Mother Shipton*, when he used it for his production at the Haymarket Theatre in 1793. In 1812 it became the subject of a burletta at The Surrey Theatre under R.W.Elliston as *The Children in the Wood*.   The pantomime version arrived 15 years later in 1827.

The story tells of two small Norfolk children who are placed in their venal uncle's care following the death of their wealthy father. Discovering they have inherited their father's fortune, their uncle hired two footpads to kidnap the babes, murder them, and hide their bodies in what is known today as Wayland Wood. The first part of the plan was carried out, but for some reason, the two footpads came to blows and one killed the other. Leaving the children deep inside the woods, the killer fled, only to be arrested some time later on another charge, and eventually confessing to the crime. The children, long dead from exposure and starvation, were only located after a prolonged search. Their uncle went bankrupt after a series of misfortunes and died in gaol.

In Arnold's opera the children were rescued, but in the pantomime version *Harlequin Cock Robin; or the Babes in the Wood*, they were covered with leaves by the forest birds and left to die. Another version had them carried off to Heaven by angels, who reunited them with their dead parents, but in a 1894 Welsh version, following the disappearance of the Babes, everything goes wrong for Baron Ystrad Rhondda (who has political aspirations) and he quickly repents his crime. Fortunately, Robin Hood finds the Babes, and the delighted

Baron takes everyone to Ilfracombe to celebrate. Later on, the bungling Robbers are captured and are condemned to sit on Cardiff City Council for the rest of their lives. A fate, as kind Maid Marion says, that is far worse than death.

Quite what Robin Hood was doing in the middle of *Babes in the Wood* is not certain, for since 1795's *Merry Sherwood; or Harlequin Forester* he had had his own pantomime and was doing very nicely. In 1867, however, he turned up in the Covent Garden version and with few exceptions has remained the hero of it ever since. Historically speaking, as Robin supposedly lived two hundred years before the Babes were born, to have been involved in their story he must qualify for the most ancient Principal Boy ever. Like the world of politics, however, pantomime has never hesitated to fabricate its own version of truth, so as both make us laugh, who really cares?

Extraordinary additions were made to the simple storyline in the early part of last century. The Drury Lane version of 1907, had the robbers handing the Babes over to The Old Woman Who Lived in a Shoe, who planned to feed them on poisoned mushrooms. Managing to escape, they were frightened by an encounter with a family of Giants and took refuge in a large rabbit hole. There they were captured by angry rabbits and imprisoned in cages, but the timely arrival of friendly ferrets enabled them to escape to Lollipop Land, where they became King and Queen. The Baron, Baroness, and the Babes' French Governess were arrested and brought to them for punishment, but the Old Woman turned up again and transformed Lollipop Land into Nightmare Land, cackling:

> "With aches and pains these children I will harrow,
> Dispepsia shall rack them to the marrow.
> Syrup of squills shall be their morning manna,
> With Epsom Salts and Ipecacuanha"

Fortunately the Fairy and Robin Hood arrived in time to rescue them, and the unexpected return of King Richard the Lionheart enabled the villains to be punished and everything to end happily.

A 1916 version had a decidedly more modern approach. Following their abandonment by the robbers, the Babes found their way out of the wood and opened their very own Music

Hall where, many years later, their uncle's villainy is revealed to all. In the meantime, the impoverished Baron and Baroness were forced to sink their pride and open a hairdressing saloon, where due to their lack of knowledge and general incompetence, most of the customers lose their hair or have terrible accidents. This scene has often been "lifted" into *Cinderella* as a routine for Buttons and the Ugly Sisters, and I last saw it in Liverpool in the 1980s. Another interesting point is that the character of Nurse Glucose, (or some other health connected name) the Babes' governess is an invention of the 20th century. Prior to this, the Baroness, a character rarely seen today, was the Dame role.

******

Beauty and The Beast originated as a story by Mme. le Prince de Beaumont, and was introduced to the stage in 1841, when a *burletta* of that title was written for Madam Vestris by J.R.Planché and presented at Covent Garden. In 1852, it emerged at the same venue as a pantomime *Harlequin Beauty and The Beast* and was repeated in 1862. In 1890, it was the Drury Lane pantomime, written by Harris and Wilton Jones, and as mentioned in Chapter Twelve, was joined to *The Sleeping Beauty* by Arthur Collins and J, Hickory Wood in 1900 as a vehicle for Dan Leno and Herbert Campbell. As *Beauty and the Beast* it remained popular until the second Word War, but was rarely done afterwards. Fortunately the Disney animated cartoon and subsequent stage musical have thrust it back into the limelight, and once again audiences have been reminded what an attractive pantomime this can be.

******

Bluebeard is based on the life of mass murderer Gilles de Retz, Marshall of France, who supposedly killed several of his wives and was executed in 1440. In order to make it into a pantomime, the story was sprinkled with situations from "The tale of the Third Kalendar Prince" in The Thousand Nights and One Night, the location was changed to an Oriental one to provide more spectacle, the characters became comical ones and the murdered wives turned out to be not as dead as Bluebeard would have wished.

It was first presented in 1791 at Covent Garden and though often revived until the beginning of the 20th century when Dan Leno turned it in to a huge success, is seldom seen today and regarded as "unlucky" by superstitious managements. The inexhaustible Jaques Offenbach, however, was not slow to pen his sparkling operetta version of *Bluebeard* which was presented at the Olympic in 1866 as *Blue Beard Re-paired*. Its brilliant overture is still a favourite concert item and well worth hearing for its infectious melodies.

******

Cinderella really needs no explanation. It is by far the most popular of British pantomimes, and the story has provided a basis for Operas, musicals, films, etc for almost two centuries. (See Chapters Nine and Fourteen). For something slightly different, however, both Nicholas Stuart Gray's play *The Other Cinderella* (Oxford University Press 1958), and Aurand Harris's *A Toby Show* (Anchorage Press Inc. 1978) make interesting reading. During my time in the USA, I was introduced to a remarkable lady by the name of Caroline Schaffner who with her late husband, Neil, had toured the mid-West during the first half of last century presenting "Toby" shows. These were played in circus-like tents and were the closest thing America had to British pantomime, with Toby, a "Buttons" type character speaking directly to audiences and encouraging participation. Like pantomimes, they could draw audiences of a thousand customers a night for three nights in a township of less than four hundred. Caroline and Neil are remembered by the foundation of The Museum of Repertoire Americana, Mount Pleasant, Iowa, where much of their memorabilia can be seen.

******

Dick Whittington is based on the life of Richard Whittington who was born around 1358, the third son of Sir William Whittington of Pauntly, Gloucestershire. According to one authority, he left home aged 14 and travelled to London where he found employment at the hospital of St John's, Clerkenwell, as a general servant, remaining there until the Prior introduced him to wealthy merchant John Fitzwarryn who trained him as a mercer. By 1379 Whittington was a wealthy man and his name was included on the roll of the Mercer's Company as a supplier of fine silks, velvets, gold cloth and damasks to the nobility, including the future Henry IV and his daughters.

Around 1382, shortly after the peasant's revolt and the murder of Wat Tyler, Richard Whittington married Alice Fitzwarryn, daughter of Sir Ivo Fitzwarryn, a relation of the mercer who had trained Richard so well. Sarah, eventually portrayed as a pantomime Dame, was the Fitzwarryn family cook. In 1387, Whittington was a member of the Court of Common Council, and in June, 1397, following the sudden death of the Mayor half way though his term of office, was appointed by King Richard II to complete the term. An extremely popular and generous man, he was elected Mayor again in 1398, 1406 and 1419, and became Member of Parliament for the City of London in 1416.

During his lifetime, he provided the money to re-build Newgate jail and improve its facilities, erected London's first public drinking fountains, repaired the fabric of St Bartholomew's Hospital, built the Library at Greyfriars, founded a college of priests, and gave extensively to the poor. Shortly before his sixtieth birthday, Alice Whittington died of a lingering illness (possibly tuberculosis) and Richard followed in 1423 leaving his entire estate to various charities who continue to benefit even today – almost six hundred years later. He was buried in the grounds of St. Michael Paternoster Royal, which he himself had founded, but legend has it that during the reign of Edward VI, the tomb was plundered by the venal rector of the parish who was convinced that further riches had been sealed inside the lead coffin. Being disappointed in his search, the broken coffin was discarded, Whittington's remains were re-buried, and the shattered monument was left where it lay. During the reign of Queen Mary, indignant and caring parishioners had the bones disinterred, re-cased, and buried again before a new monument was erected over them which existed until the Great Fire of 1666 irreparably damaged it.

A new tomb, designed and constructed by Sir Christopher Wren was destroyed by German bombs during the Blitz and a mummified cat, (which was later disposed of by the priest-in-charge) was discovered in the rubble. It was not, unfortunately, the famous cat of legend, for where that particular addition to Whittington's life came from, no-one is certain. Until the beginning of the seventeenth century there is not even a reference to a feline companion, though several theories have been propounded since. One is that the "cat" was in fact a light barge designed and named by Whittington for carrying coal from Newcastle to London, hence his sudden rise to riches, but it is difficult to understand why a mercer, of all people, would be involved in such an enterprise. Another is that the old English word "acate", meaning "purchase" had been abased over the years to "cat", but the most probable origin is that the cat was simply a fanciful addition to the myriads of stories concerning Whittington's generosity of two hundred years earlier and derived from a Persian (now Iranian) legend which tells of a poor boy who arrives in India with only a cat for company. Discovering the King's palace is over-run with rats and mice, he sets his cat free which quickly dispatches them. The delighted King buys the cat for a huge sum, enabling the boy to return home and live the rest of his life in comfort.

The tale would certainly have been known to frequenters of fairs in the sixteenth century where story-tellers and puppeteers from all over Europe would ply their trades, for like *Cinderella*, there are versions of it in almost every country and a "rags to riches" explanation of Whittington's fabled wealth would have greatly appealed to the lower classes of the day who probably dreamed of finding fame and fortune themselves.

The first reference to Whittington's cat appeared in a 1605 comedy play, which indicates that the legend was fairly well known at that time, and by 1668, Samuel Pepys was able to write in his famous diary that he had been to Southwark Fair where he had seen the puppet show of Whittington, which "was pretty to see". In 1731, according to A.E.Wilson in his book Pantomime Pageant (Stanley Paul & Co.), *Dick*

Whittington and His Cat was performed at Southwark Fair with an actor by the name of Harper playing Sarah the Cook but despite several years of research, I can find no reference to this production, and have no idea if it was a play, *burlesque* or pantomime or where the information came from in the first place. "Tommy the Cat" however, was firmly entrenched by this time as an inseparable part of the Whittington story.

The great Grimaldi was the star attraction of *Harlequin Whittington* when Covent Garden used the legend as a pantomime subject in 1814, (see Chapter Five) and even Offenbach was to use it for his Operetta *Whittington* which was presented at the Alhambra Theatre, London in 1874 and later reworked as *Le Chat du Diable* for Paris in 1893. As a modern day pantomime, the story of Dick Whittington continues to delight millions.

******

The story of **Goldilocks and the Three Bears** is another taken from the collection by Countess d'Aulnois and as far as I can ascertain, its first appearance as a pantomime subject was the Haymarket Theatre production of *Harlequin and The Three Bears; or Little Silver Hair and the Fairies* in 1853. The Three Bears were principal characters in W.S.Gilbert's pantomime *Harlequin Cock Robin* of 1867, though there was no sign of Goldilocks (or Silver Hair), and this time they were the villains. R.C.Olham's 1923 version for John Hart at the Opera House, Manchester, treated them more kindly. The Bears were in reality, the Royal Family of Rococo who have been transformed into bears by the evil robber magician, Red Dirk. Goldilocks and her lover, Victor, the son of Widow Tippet vow to release them from the spell, but Red Dirk plans to kill the bears and take over the country. Goldilocks searches for their cottage to warn them, but when she finally finds it, the bears are absent. Hungry and tired, she tries the porridge they have left to cool and falls asleep in Baby Bear's bed. The bears return home and discover her, but as they prepare to frighten her away, she wakes and urges them to hide from Red Dirk who will soon be arriving with his brigands. The bears hurry off, but are captured and sentenced to death.

The timely arrival of Victor and Goldilocks with the fairy's "Talisman of Love" breaks the spell and Red Dirk is punished. The restored Royal Family bestow their blessings on Goldilocks and Victor and all ends in the traditional wedding.

A different storyline by John Morley in the 1960s set the action in the world of Circus, but like so many of the less popular subjects, when *Goldilocks and the Three Bears* is staged today, it appears to be mainly performed by amateur societies.

******

Goody Two Shoes is based on a nursery story written by Oliver Goldsmith in 1765, and concerns the gift of a pair of magic shoes to Goody. It was first turned into a pantomime by the reliable Blanchard in 1862 for Drury Lane under the title *Little Goody Two Shoes; or Harlequin and Cock Robin*, and featured Lydia Thompson as Principal Boy. In 1899 it could be seen at George Conquest's The Surrey Theatre, and in 1912, the Theatre Royal, Birmingham was attracting audiences in a Philip Rodway presentation. Emile Littler presented it at the London Coliseum in 1944, and I saw two productions of it in the 1950s, one in the Midlands – which featured comedienne Beryl Reid as Marlene, and the other at the Empire Theatre, Leeds, in 1959 with Ken Platt as Lord Gorgeous of Glamour, Henry Lytton as "Bluebell", The Old Woman who Lived in a Shoe, Charlie Cairoli as Lord Gorgeous's son, Charlie, and Bill Pertwee & Roy Hudd as the Town Councillors, Late and Early.

The last two were also Emile Littler productions, but despite excellent casts, I was unimpressed by the weak storyline, and am not too surprised that the past forty years have seen a sharp decline in its popularity.

******

Humpty Dumpty is my favourite pantomime, though like *Red Riding Hood* it is seldom seen today. Everyone knows the nursery rhyme, but where the term originated remains a mystery. It was suggested some years ago that the original Humpty was Richard III (1452-1485) because of his humped back, but as most people are now aware, Richard was no

Quasimodo and his disability was not as obvious as legend would have it. In any case, the nursery rhyme of Humpty Dumpty was unknown until around 1803, so a satire on him at this late date would have had little or no purpose.

Another popular piece of wishful thinking is the claim that Humpty Dumpty was a large cannon used during the English Civil War and when the ramparts supporting it were destroyed, it fell to the ground below and was smashed to pieces. Not very likely, I'm afraid, and why wait almost two hundred years to poke fun at the destruction of a solitary cannon?

In the Oxford English Dictionary, a humpty-dumpty is described as a boiled ale and brandy drink enjoyed during the latter part of the seventeenth century, while the Collins English Dictionary states the term indicates a short and clumsy person of either sex. The truth of the matter is that no-one really knows. Since 1803, Humpty Dumpty has been portrayed as a huge egg perched on top of a wall, and according to Iona and Peter Opie in the Oxford Dictionary of Nursery Rhymes, the rhyme is as famous in other countries as it is in England, indicating its ancestry may be far older than anyone imagines.

1850 seems to have marked its first appearance as a pantomime subject in a script by Edward Fitzball, and it reappeared in the Lyceum's production of *Harlequin Humpty Dumpty and Dame Trot and Her Cat* of 1868 which introduced the fearsome Vokes Family. The story we know today, however, is based on the Drury Lane version of 1903, written by J. Hickory Wood and Arthur Collins, and which featured Dan Leno and Herbert Campbell for the last time.

In 1943, Emile Littler staged a brilliant production at the Coliseum with Pat Kirkwood as Principal Boy that attracted an audience of 122,000, in the first month alone, and Francis Laidler's version at the Grand Theatre, Leeds, (with Norman Evans as Dame and Betty Jumel as Humpty) ran from Boxing Day 1944 to May 26th, 1945. I saw this several times and still remember their hilarious "Pipes of Pan" routine. Pure magic.

Harry Secombe was Humpty in the Palladium's 1959 version, and Wyn Calvin also shone in the role in the early sixties. In 1965, Ken Dodd played the title role at Birmingham

Hippodrome for eighteen weeks with a supporting cast that included Joy Jackley and Seth Gee, (King and Queen of Hearts) Ken Roberts, (Simple Simon) Judy Collins and Barbara Helliwell, (Tommy Tucker and Mary Quite Contrary) Iris Sadler and Claude Zola (Mother Goose and Goose) and Andrew Cregeen as Grimm. Any one of these artistes could have topped a pantomime bill today and I regard this as the best one I ever appeared in. Why the subject has fallen out of favour with managements is a mystery. I can only surmise that like *Mother Goose*, it needs to be perfectly cast to get the best out of it, and too few of our present performers have the ability to tackle such a demanding role.

******

Jack and the Beanstalk made its first appearance in 1819 at Drury Lane with the aforementioned Eliza Povey in the title role. E.L. Blanchard also wrote a version in 1859, entitled *Jack and the Beanstalk; or Harlequin Leap Year and the Merry Pranks of the Good Little People*, which was set in the improbable location of Devon. As usual in a Blanchard pantomime, the "Dark Opening" employs an ingenious device for leading the audience into the story proper, and for *Jack*, it begins in "The Atmosphere, 45 miles above the Earth's Surface", where Old Moore (of Almanack fame) and his companions are surprised by the visit of Weather who confesses she is "unsettled". After begging her to provide them with a Christmas pantomime, she introduces them to all the famous Jacks of history, nursery rhyme and story; Jack Frost, Jack Cade, Jack Straw, Jack in the Box, Jack the Giant Killer, Jack Horner, Jack Sprat and Jack of *Jack and Jill* fame, etc. so that one can be the hero of it. Jack of *Jack and the Beanstalk* is selected and Weather commands the first six Months of the Year to assist him and help the magic beanstalk grow, while the remaining Months remain close by and eventually depict the fun of the "Harlequinade". The pantomime proper then begins in January where Devon villagers are engaged in snowballing, skating, etc., and moves on through the months to its conclusion in the "Merry Halls of Happy Old Christmas".

230

By 1935 when Marriot Edgar (who wrote the famous monologue "The Lion and Albert") wrote Drury Lane's final *Jack*, which featured Binnie Hale as Principal Boy and Shaun Glenville as Dame, it was firmly fixed into the storyline we recognise today and though not seen as often as it used to be, remains a popular subject. Like *Cinderella*, and *Beauty and the Beast* it has attracted the attention of Hollywood on at least two occasions. Walt Disney's animated cartoon *Mickey and the Beanstalk* is still delighting millions worldwide, and zany duo Bud Abbott and Lou Costello also managed to find themselves involved with the famous Beanstalk towards the end of their career, though in spite of several funny episodes, it can hardly be considered one of their classics.

******

Jack and Jill was first presented by the Drury Lane Company at the Lyceum Theatre in 1812, as *Jack and Jill; or The Clown's Disasters*, whilst the present Drury Lane theatre was being rebuilt following Sheridan's disastrous fire. Blanchard's more polished version *Jack and Jill; or Harlequin King Mustard and Four and Twenty Blackbirds Baked in a Pie* was staged at Drury Lane in 1854. *Jack and Jill; or Mother Goose at Home Once More* arrived at the Adelphi Theatre, the following year, while Frank Green used the same subject for the Surrey's 1876 *Jack and Jill; or Harlequin Sing a Song of Sixpence* using some excruciating puns to delight the audiences.

In 1898, George Conquest and Henry Spry devised another version for the Surrey which had George Jnr. appearing as a larger than life Fairy, but the version written by Emile Littler in the 1940s is perhaps the best known.

Set in the village of Fairywell, Jill is the daughter of the landlord of the "Pail o' Water" inn, and in love with Jack Horner. Unfortunately, the Crooked Man (a collector of crooked sixpences) wants Jack to marry his niece, Mary Quite Contrary, and is furious when Jill claims Jack for herself. Following a meeting with an evil Witch who promises to make him a rich man providing he obtains for her the crooked coin on a chain around the neck of Jack's mother, Dame Horner, he agrees and asks how this miracle will occur. She tells him to wash his crooked sixpences in water from the magic well on top of the hill, and they will straighten out again, but being lame and unable to climb it himself, he sends Jack to fetch some. After Jack departs, the Crooked Man proposes marriage to Dame Horner who confesses she is so poor her only dowry is the crooked coin she wears around her neck and shows it to him.

News suddenly arrives of a huge reward for whoever finds the King's long lost son, stolen from his nursery twenty years ago. In the excitement that follows, Dame Horner leaves the coin and chain on her table and when Jill arrives seeking Jack, she is told by the Fairy to take it to him, as he is the long lost Prince. After dropping the coin into the well, they fish it out again to discover it has been restored to its original shape and the words "John, Prince of Sylvania" can clearly be read.

Jack hurries off to claim the throne, but the Witch manages to substitute it for a crooked sixpence, and pins the Royal coin on Simple Simon for revenge. Jack is turned away in despair by the mocking crowd as Simon is hailed the true Prince. Jack and Jill return to the well for more of the magic water, but fall down and Jack is carted off to have his head patched with vinegar and brown paper. As the Witch and the Crooked Man celebrate their triumph, the Fairy reappears and points out to the King that a few drops of magic water remain in the little pail and if he gazes upon them, the truth will be revealed. He does so and quickly discovers the deception. The two villains are punished, the King is reunited with his real son, Prince Jack marries his sweetheart, Jill, and as usual, all ends happily.

All the above versions make interesting reading, but have very complex storylines by today's standards. To restore "Jack and Jill" to its former popularity may now be too late, but a modern version could still attract interest. Though professional managements generally stick to productions of *Cinderella*, *Aladdin*, etc., I find amateur companies are much more adventurous and with productions of my own "unusual subject" pantos continuing to increase, it may be well worth a try.

******

The story of **Puss in Boots** comes from Italy and first appeared in a 1534 collection published as *Nights of Straporola*. Charles Perrault included it in his famous collection of fairy stories, *Tales of Mother Goose* which arrived in England in 1729 and in 1817 it was first presented as a pantomime at Covent Garden. In 1832, it re-appeared as *Puss in Boots; or Harlequin and the Millers Sons* with Elizabeth Poole as Josselin, the youngest son, and J.R. Planché turned it into a one act burletta for Madame Vestris at the Olympic in 1837.

It was this version that inspired Blanchard when he penned his Drury Lane "annual" in 1868, *Grimalkin the Great; or Harlequin Puss in Boots and the Miller's Son*, and he was to produced two more versions of the story before his death; one for the Crystal Palace in 1873, the other for Drury Lane in 1887. George Conquest and Henry Spry devised *Puss in Boots, the Ogre, the Miller, and King of the Rats; or The Pretty Princess and the Queen of the Cats* for the Surrey Theatre in 1882, a version which proved to be a more unusual interpretation of the now familiar story, and J. Hickory Wood produced yet another version of the old story for the Garrick Theatre shortly before taking up residence at Drury Lane.

Puss continued to be a popular subject throughout the first half of the 20th century, (Frankie Vaughan and Joan Regan headed the cast at the London Palladium in 1962) but appears to be losing ground as we enter the 21st. Let's hope it is only a temporary situation.

******

Red Riding Hood is another Perrault story, and adapted by Charles Dibdin, made its first appearance as a pantomime at Sadler's Wells in 1803 under the title of *Red Riding Hood; or The Wolf Robber*. As mentioned in Chapter Nine, it re-opened the new Opera House in Covent Garden in 1858 under the title of *Little Red Riding Hood; or Harlequin and the Wolf in Grannie's Clothing* and remained fairly popular throughout the nineteenth century. By the start of the twentieth century, however, productions of it were rapidly diminishing, and Francis Laidler's 1938 version has the doubtful honour of being the last pantomime ever to be seen at Covent Garden.

Since 1938 I have seen seen more than two hundred pantomimes, but apart from amateur productions, can count on one hand the unfortunate *Red Riding Hood's*. A revival of it is well overdue.

******

Robinson Crusoe, as mentioned in Chapter Four, is based on the book of the same title by Daniel Defoe. When Sheridan wrote the first pantomime version in 1781 there was no Dame, Will Atkins, Polly Perkins, etc; these were all added in the 19th century to bring the story into line with "traditional" pantomime. Offenbach wrote a funny and very tuneful operetta version in 1867 and an English language recording of this may still be available on C.D. The villainous Will Atkins appears to make his debut in H.J.Byron's 1860 *burlesque*/pantomime *Robinson Crusoe* which was presented at the Princess's Theatre, London.

The Opening scene is set in Hull where ship's Captain Atkins is Crusoe's jealous rival for the hand of pretty Jenny Pigtail, a tobacconist's daughter. In an attempt to rid himself of Crusoe, who is an apprentice at The Golden Teapot, a grocer's shop, Atkins arranges for him to be press-ganged and carried off to sea. The ship is wrecked and Robinson arrives on the island as the only survivor. Two years later, helped by a dog, a parrot and a goat, he rescues Friday from cannibal Indians. Shortly afterwards, Atkins and Jenny arrive on the island having also been shipwrecked and both are captured by the cannibals.

Following their rescue by Robinson and Friday, Atkins attempts to kill his rival but is defeated by the three animals. The arrival of the cannibals and the rest of Atkins's crew seems to signal defeat for Robinson, but Fairy Liberty appears and transforms Robinson into Harlequin, Jenny into Columbine, Atkins to Pantaloon and the Cannibal King to Clown. Then followed four comic scenes of a Harlequinade.

In the 1870s, Robinson was married to a widow before his adventures began, but Blanchard's 1881 Drury Lane version saw him in love with Polly Perkins, a neighbour's daughter, and living in London where his mother owned the Primrose

Farm Dairy on the banks of the River Thames. He had also gained a brother by the name of Timothy.

By the 1920s Robinson had returned to live in Hull, and apart from a name change for his zany brother, now known as Billy Crusoe, all the familiar characters were in place. During the latter part of the century, Will Atkins (who was generally a smuggler, a pirate, or a disgruntled crew member) was often replaced for unknown reasons by Blackbeard the Pirate and even *Treasure Island* managed to involve itself in what had been up to then a straightforward story. Political correctness and accusations of racial bias over the character of Man Friday have practically removed the pantomime from today's cannon and the last time I saw a major production it was very badly presented with much of the "humour" being distinctly lavatorial. Hopefully common sense will eventually prevail and *Crusoe* will regain its one time popularity.

******

Sindbad the Sailor is based on the stories of The Seven Voyages of Sindbad, in "The Thousand Nights and One Night", which were simply a collection of folk tales dating back several centuries, supposedly related by Sheherazade as a ruse to save her from execution. It has been suggested that Sindbad was a real person who lived sometime during the 12th century, though like Robin Hood and King Arthur, no actual proof exists of this. If, however, he *did* exist, and one takes the stories of his adventures with a pinch of salt, certain events might well have a basis of truth.

For centuries, sailors had returned home carrying tales of sea serpents, mermaids, and monsters, but on the island of Madagascar, which would have been well known to Eastern mariners, one of the most incredible creatures ever to co-exist with man was still alive; Aepyornis Maximus, or the Elephant Bird.

Until they became extinct around the year 1700, they were the largest birds ever to walk the earth. Ten feet (300cm) tall, and weighing in at around 78 stone (504 kilos), this monstrous relative of the ostrich laid eggs over three feet (91cm) in circumference, containing almost two imperial gallons (9ltrs) of liquid. Fearless and ferocious, these flightless creatures could have disembowelled a Rhinoceros with a single kick, and if we can accept an exaggerated description of the gigantic Roc that supposedly carried Sindbad off, then the Elephant Bird would easily fit the bill. Similarly, his "Old Man of the Sea" is a perfect description of the Orang-utan, and if Sindbad enthralled his listeners (who may never have left the city in their life), with tales of the incredible creatures he had encountered in distant lands, the stories would have been re-told in a thousand versions and pass into folk-lore.

Whatever the truth behind the matter, *Sindbad* was first performed as a pantomime at Drury Lane in 1814 as *Harlequin Sindbad; or The Valley of the Diamonds* and remained a popular subject until early last century. If performed today, it is mainly by amateur companies and versions have been written by Paul Reakes, John Crocker and Eric Gilder, John Morley, and Pauline Stuart.

******

Sleeping Beauty is a reluctant pantomime. Based on the story by Charles Perrault (who had taken it from a Persian folk story), it was first turned into a melodrama in 1806, but emerged as a pantomime at Covent Garden in 1822, entitled *Harlequin and the Ogress; or The Sleeping Beauty*. Though highly successful, (it is reported that the principal performers were allowed one pint of wine each for every night it was played) its biggest stumbling block has always been the hundred year lapse between the pricking of the heroine's finger on the spindle of the Wicked Fairy's spinning wheel, and the arrival of the Prince to wake her from enchanted sleep. A pantomime where the lovers only meet in the final scene is not an ideal situation, so several methods were used to obviate this.

One had the story of the curse and its fulfillment related in the first scene, which enabled the Prince to start his search for Beauty "one hundred years later" in scene two. The drawback to this was after finding her in scene four or five and breaking the spell, another plot was needed to fill up the rest of the evening.

For the Drury Lane presentation of 1900, the story of *Beauty and the Beast* was tagged onto it, (see Chapter Twelve), while the Lyceum's 1932 version had the Prince visiting his beloved's Castle when the calamity occurred and was sent to sleep with the rest of the Court. When the fairy revived them "a hundred years later", he had only to locate the still comatose Beauty before bestowing the famous kiss that awoke her. It didn't really make sense, but remained a popular option for many years. For the 1958 London Palladium version, Carabosse reappeared in Act Two and turned the newly awakened Princess into a white dove that was shot and injured by the Prince whilst hunting. An appeal by the fairy to an ancient and powerful Wizard restored Beauty to normality and had Carabosse punished by divesting her of her magic powers. My own version solved the problem by having the Princess dream of meeting the yet-to-be-born Prince, thus allowing him to join her in Act One where they could meet and fall in love. In Act Two, one hundred years later, the Prince, who has dreamed of meeting the legendary Sleeping Beauty, comes in search of her and the usual story continues.

******

Snow White and the Seven Dwarfs is a relative newcomer to the pantomime rosta. Until the 1980s it was not regarded as a pantomime at all, and even today, is still wavering between pantomime and a children's play. While many productions have added a Dame and loads of comedy to the proceedings, others still favour the original storyline and perform it accordingly. It was possibly the release of Walt Disney's famous animated cartoon version on Home Video that sparked off the upsurge in stage productions, but though several scripts are now available for amateurs, it should be remembered that the seven dwarfs were never named in the Grimm Brothers' story, and those used in the Disney version are copyrighted by the Disney Organization ... as are the songs.

******

The above are just a few of the pantomimes that have entertained audiences for the past two centuries. There were, of course, hundreds more, and with a little care and attention many could provide a cheerful alternative to the "Baker's Dozen" regularly staged today. In the meantime, pantomime continues to evolve. New "stars", new forms of lighting, new special effects, and new (pre-recorded) music may have hurled it into the 21st century, but still hanging in there are two apparently insignificant reminders of its fascinating past. The **Slap-stick** for the Schoolroom scene, and the animated string of dog-meat **Sausages**.

Acknowledgements

Though much of my life has been occupied in the writing, directing, acting in and watching of pantomime, a book like this would have been impossible to write without the assistance of others. I am indebted to Martin Phillips for access to his amazing collection of pantomime "books of words". John and Karen Watkins for the loan of innumerable volumes from their incredible "library". Professor Frank Brandt (New Mexico) for Americana. The late Caroline Schaffner of Mount Pleasant, Iowa for tea and "Toby". The Staff of the Performing Arts Dept. of Exeter Library for long out of print volumes. The Victoria and Albert Museum. The Trustees of the Theatre Museum, Covent Garden. The Birmingham Hippodrome. The Theatre Royal, Nottingham. Max Tyler of the British Music Hall Society. Jim Lawes, for information on lighting. Samuel French Ltd, for information and encouragement. My wife, Ailsa, for chauffeuring me around the country as I did research, then advising on the results, re-typing, editing, cover designing and at the same time holding down her own job without going insane. My heartfelt thanks to you all.

Pictorial acknowledgements.

The illustrations in this book have been reproduced by kind permission of The Theatre Royal, Nottingham, the Hippodrome Theatre, Birmingham, The Victoria and Albert Museum, London, The Theatre Museum, London, The Illustrated London News, or taken from the author's own collection.

Bibliography

Title	Author(s)	Published
A Book of Burlesque	W.D.Adams	Henry and Co., 1891
A History of Pantomime	R.J. Broadbent	1901
A Register of Theatrical Documents	Milhouse and Hume	Southern Illinois University Press, 1991
Annals of Covent Garden	Henry Saxe Wyndham	Chatto & Windus, 1906
Birmingham Repertory Theatre	J.C.Trewin	Barrie & Rockliff, 1963
Bon Mots	Ed) Walter Jerrold	J.M.Dent and Co, 1894
Book of Heroic Failures (The)	Stephen Pile	Book Club Ass., 1979
Bring on the Clowns	Beryl Hugill	David & Charles, 1980
British Music Hall	R. Manders & J. Michenson	Studio Vista, 1965
British Music Hall "Who's Who"	Roy Busby	Paul Elek, 1976
British Theatre (The)	Alec Clunes	Cassell, 1964
Burlesque tradition in the English Theatre after 1660	V.C.Clinton-Baddeley	Methuen, 1952
Can you hear me, mother?	S. Powell and H. Stanley	Jupiter, 1975
Cavalcade by Candlelight	E.R. Delderfield	Raleigh Press, Exeter, 1950
Christmas Pantomime	A.E.Wilson	George Allen & Unwin, 1934
Clowns of the Hopi	Barton Wright	Northland Publishing (U.S.A.),1994
Clowns and Pantomimes	M. Willson Disher	Constable, 1925
Conquest	Frances Fleetwood	W.H. Allen, 1953
Dan Leno	J. Hickory Wood	(Not Known), 1905
Development of Theatre (The)	Alladyce Nicoll	Harrap and Co., 1927
Dunciad	Alexander Pope	1728
Entertainers (The)	(Ed) Clive Unger	HamiltonPitman House 1980
Funniest Man in the World (The)	Gyles Brandreth	Hamish Hamilton, 1977

Title	Author(s)	Published
Garrick's Folly	Johanne M. Stochholm	Methuen, 1964
Great Chicago Theatre Disaster (The)	Marshal Everett	(Not Known), 1904
Gilbert and Sullivan Book (The)	Leslie Bailie	Cassell & Co., 1952
Haymarket	W. Macqueen Pope	W.H.Allan, 1948
Here Comes the Circus	Peter Verney	Paddington Press, 1930
History of the London Stage-famous players	H. Barton Baker	1904
Jacques Offenbach	Alexander Farris	Faber and Faber, 1980
Life of Sheridan (The)	L. Sanders	Walter Scott, 18 ?
Life and Enterprises of Robert William Elliston	George Raymond	Routledge, 1857
Life and Reminiscences of E.L.Blanchard (The)	Blanchard	1891
Life of Dick Whittington	Milner and Co.	c1900
London's lost theatres of the 19th century	Erroll Sherson	Bodley Head, 1925
Lyceum (The)	A.E. Wilson	Dennis Yates, 1952
Madame Vestris	Clifford John Williams	Sidgwick & Jackson, 1973
Marie Lloyd and Music Hall	Daniel Farson	Tom Stacey, 1972
Memoirs of Grimaldi	C. Dickens	Richard Bentley, 1838
New Theatre in Lincoln's Inn Fields(The)	Paul Sawyer	Soc. For Theatre Research, 1979
Northern Music Hall (The)	G.J.Mellor	Frank Graham, 1970
Oh, yes it is	Gerald Frow	B.B.C., 1985
Pageant of English Actors	Donald Brook	Rockliff, 1950
Pantomimes and all about them	Leopold Wagner	1881
Pantomime Pageant	A.E.Wilson	Stanley Paul, 1946
Pantomime	R. Mander and J. Michenson	Peter Davis, 1973
Peg Woffington and her world	Janet Dunbar	Heinemann, 1968
Recollections and Reflections of J. R. Planché	J.R.Planché	1872
Story of Sadler's Wells (The)	Dennis Arundell	Hamish Hamilton, 1965
Theatrical Anecdotes	Jacob Larwood	Chatto & Windus, 1882
Theatre Royal, Drury Lane	W. Maqueen Pope	W.H.Allen, 1945
Theatre Royal, Bristol (The)	Kathleen Barker	Soc. For Theatre Research 1974
Theatre through the Ages	Cesare Molinari	Cassell, 1975
Theatre U.S.A.	Barnard Hewitt	McGraw-Hill, 1955
Thousand Nights and One Night	Mardrus & Mathers	Routledge & Kegen Paul, 1964
Wireless Stars(The)	George Nobbs	Wensum Books (Norwich) Ltd., 1972

INDEX
Names of Plays and Pantomimes in Italics

INDEX

Names of Plays and Pantomimes in Italics

INDEX

Names of Plays and Pantomimes in Italics

INDEX

Names of Plays and Pantomimes in Italics

INDEX

Names of Plays and Pantomimes in Italics

INDEX
Names of Plays and Pantomimes in Italics

INDEX

Names of Plays and Pantomimes in Italics

INDEX

Names of Plays and Pantomimes in Italics

INDEX

Names of Plays and Pantomimes in Italics

INDEX

Names of Plays and Pantomimes in Italics